An Introduction to the American Legal System, Government, and Constitution

Aspen College Series

An Introduction to the American Legal System, Government, and Constitution

Diane S. Kaplan

Wolters Kluwer

Published by Wolters Kluwer in New York.

Wolters Kluwer serves customers worldwide with CCH, Aspen Publishers, and Kluwer Law International products. (www.wolterskluwerlb.com)

To contact Customer Service, e-mail customer.service@wolterskluwer.com, call 1-800-234-1660, fax 1-800-901-9075, or mail correspondence to:

Wolters Kluwer
Attn: Order Department
PO Box 990
Frederick, MD 21705

Printed in the United States of America.

1 2 3 4 5 6 7 8 9 0

ISBN 978-1-4548-5733-4

Library of Congress Cataloging-in-Publication Data

Kaplan, Diane S., author.
    An introduction to the American legal system, government, and Constitution / Diane S. Kaplan, the John Marshall Law School.
        pages cm.—(Aspen college series)
        ISBN 978-1-4548-5733-4
    1. Constitutional law—United States. 2. Federal government—United States. 3. Separation of powers—United States. 4. Civil rights—United States. 5. United States. Constitution. 1st Amendment. 6. Justice, Administration of—United States. 7. Courts—United States. 8. Criminal justice, Administration of—United States. 9. Law—United States. I. Title.

    KF4550.K35 2015
    342.73—dc23

                                                                2015020806

About Wolters Kluwer Law & Business

Wolters Kluwer Law & Business is a leading global provider of intelligent information and digital solutions for legal and business professionals in key specialty areas, and respected educational resources for professors and law students. Wolters Kluwer Law & Business connects legal and business professionals as well as those in the education market with timely, specialized authoritative content and information-enabled solutions to support success through productivity, accuracy and mobility.

Serving customers worldwide, Wolters Kluwer Law & Business products include those under the Aspen Publishers, CCH, Kluwer Law International, Loislaw, ftwilliam.com and MediRegs family of products.

CCH products have been a trusted resource since 1913, and are highly regarded resources for legal, securities, antitrust and trade regulation, government contracting, banking, pension, payroll, employment and labor, and healthcare reimbursement and compliance professionals.

Aspen Publishers products provide essential information to attorneys, business professionals and law students. Written by preeminent authorities, the product line offers analytical and practical information in a range of specialty practice areas from securities law and intellectual property to mergers and acquisitions and pension/ benefits. Aspen's trusted legal education resources provide professors and students with high-quality, up-to-date and effective resources for successful instruction and study in all areas of the law.

Kluwer Law International products provide the global business community with reliable international legal information in English. Legal practitioners, corporate counsel and business executives around the world rely on Kluwer Law journals, looseleafs, books, and electronic products for comprehensive information in many areas of international legal practice.

Loislaw is a comprehensive online legal research product providing legal content to law firm practitioners of various specializations. Loislaw provides attorneys with the ability to quickly and efficiently find the necessary legal information they need, when and where they need it, by facilitating access to primary law as well as state-specific law, records, forms and treatises.

ftwilliam.com offers employee benefits professionals the highest quality plan documents (retirement, welfare and non-qualified) and government forms (5500/ PBGC, 1099 and IRS) software at highly competitive prices.

MediRegs products provide integrated health care compliance content and software solutions for professionals in healthcare, higher education and life sciences, including professionals in accounting, law and consulting.

Wolters Kluwer Law & Business, a division of Wolters Kluwer, is headquartered in New York. Wolters Kluwer is a market-leading global information services company focused on professionals.

Summary of Contents

Table of Contents

Chapter 3 ★ Article II: The Executive Branch

Chapter 4 ★ Article III: The Judicial Branch

Chapter 5 ★ *The Constitutional Doctrines of Separation of Powers, Checks and Balances, and Federalism*

Chapter 6 ★ *First Amendment Constitutional Rights*

Chapter 7 ★ The American Litigation System

Chapter 8 ★ The Criminal Litigation Process

Appendices

An Introduction to the American Legal System, Government, and Constitution introduces the reader to the basic structures of government that inform the everyday thinking of lawyers in America. It presents historical and contemporary events that demonstrate how the American government has accommodated social progress while maintaining the rule of law in an ever-changing and highly diverse nation.

Chapter 1 presents a brief history of the Constitution of the United States. It explains the historical events and philosophical doctrines that influenced the colonists' efforts to seek independence from England and, as thirteen colonies, unite as one nation under the Constitution. Chapters 2, 3, and 4 examine the distribution of powers among the three branches of the federal government. Chapter 2 describes the organizational structure, powers, and limitations on the powers of the legislative branch. Chapter 3 examines the executive branch and the nature of presidential authority. Chapter 4 explains the organization of the judicial branch, its jurisdictional authority, and its role in developing national policy.

Chapter 5 presents the constitutional principles of separation of powers, checks and balances, and federalism by examining how these doctrines have influenced the relationships among the three branches of government. Chapter 6 presents First Amendment principles that affect the relationships between the rights and responsibilities of American citizens, and the powers, and restraints on the powers, of the government.

Chapter 7 explains how the federal and state judicial systems operate, and the relationships between the two systems. Chapter 8 examines the criminal law system and the due process protections the government must provide to criminal defendants.

Acknowledgments

The author wishes to express her gratitude to the numerous people whose valuable contributions made this book possible: Editors and proofreaders Matthew A. Rooney, Eileen Clabby, Susan Hilkevitch, and Terrence Flynn; anonymous reviewers and Anne Abramson, Barry Kozak, and Arthur Acevedo, who, on behalf of Wolters Kluwer offered commentaries and critiques to improve the subject matter and organization of the book; Cindy Uh, Developmental Editor at The Froebe Group; Carianne King, Production Editor at The Froebe Group, and Carol McGeehan, Publisher of Wolters Kluwer Legal Education.

The author is grateful for permission to reprint material from the following sources:

"Daniel Ellsberg," photograph. Hulton Archive / Stringer / Getty Images. Reprinted by permission of Getty Images.

"Gideon at 50," photograph. Associated Press / Wide World Photos. Reprinted by permission of AP Images.

"Remembering 9-11 – The World Trade Center Tragedy," photograph. Debra L Rothenberg / FilmMagic / Getty Images. Reprinted by permission of Getty Images.

"US Flag and Constitution," photograph. John-Mark Odero / Alamy. Reprinted by permission of Alamy.

"Wallace Integration," photograph. AP Photo. Reprinted by permission of AP Images.

"West Face of the United States Supreme Court Building in Washington, D.C.," photograph. CC-BY-SA-3.0/Matt H. Wade at Wikipedia; http://en.wikipedia.org/wiki/User:UpstateNYer; http://creativecommons.org/licenses/by-sa/3.0. Reprinted by permission of Matt H. Wade.

"World Trade Center Attacked," photograph. Robert Giroux / Getty Images. Reprinted by permission of Getty Images.

An Introduction to the American Legal System, Government, and Constitution

A Brief History of the Constitution of the United States

The *Constitution*[1] establishes the structure of the federal government, distributes power among the *legislative, executive,* and *judicial branches* of the government, defines the *rights* and *liberties* of the American people, and specifies the *sovereign powers* retained by the 50 states. Any law passed by either the federal government or any of the state governments that conflicts with the Constitution is unconstitutional and void.

Constitutional History

America's story began in the early 1600s when English Pilgrims traveled across the Atlantic Ocean to develop *colonies* (settlements) along the eastern coast of the North American continent. During the first 100 years, England and the colonies had mutually beneficial and compatible relations with each other. While the colonies remained loyal to England and operated with self-sufficiency, England provided them with military protection, a financial system, and a market for trade. However, in 1760, when George III became the King of England and began imposing oppressive laws, taxes, and trade restraints on the colonies, many colonists' attitudes toward England shifted from mutual co-operation to resentment and opposition. The slogan "No Taxation Without Representation" reflected their concerns about the new King and his new regime of regulations and taxes, which they believed were being imposed on them without the opportunity to be represented in the British Parliament. An example of the colonists'

---

[1] Appendix A contains a copy of the Constitution. Italicized words are defined in the Glossary.

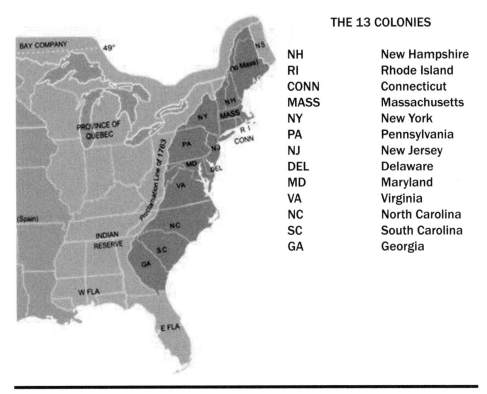

THE 13 COLONIES

NH	New Hampshire
RI	Rhode Island
CONN	Connecticut
MASS	Massachusetts
NY	New York
PA	Pennsylvania
NJ	New Jersey
DEL	Delaware
MD	Maryland
VA	Virginia
NC	North Carolina
SC	South Carolina
GA	Georgia

The 13 Colonies.

concern is a famous incident called "The Boston Tea Party," during which a band of colonists protested against a British tax on imported tea by dressing like Native Indians, boarding the British ships that brought the tea to the colonies, and dumping the tea into the Boston Harbor. In retaliation, the British Parliament passed a series of laws that the colonists referred to as "The Intolerable Acts of 1774." One such law barred ships from entering or leaving the Boston Harbor until the colonies repaid England for the destroyed tea. Another law required the colonists to open their homes to the soldiers England had sent to quash their rebellion.

The Declaration of Independence

The more England demanded obedience and loyalty from the colonists, the more the colonists demanded freedom and independence from England. Military skirmishes between England and colonists began in 1775. By 1776, the colonies declared their independence from England in a document entitled *The Declaration of Independence.*[2] The Declaration stated:

---

[2] Appendix B contains The Declaration of Independence.

We hold these truths to be self-evident, that all Men are created equal, that they are endowed by their Creator with certain unalienable Rights, that among these are Life, Liberty, and the Pursuit of Happiness.—That to secure these Rights, Governments are instituted among Men, deriving their just Powers from the Consent of the Governed, that whenever any Form of Government becomes destructive of these Ends, it is the Right of the People to alter or to abolish it, and to institute new Government, laying its Foundation on such Principles, and organizing its Powers in such Form, as to them shall seem most likely to effect their Safety and Happiness.

The Declaration of Independence expressed the philosophy of John Locke, an Englishman who believed that people are born with natural and *"unalienable Rights"* to *"Life, Liberty, and the Pursuit of Happiness"* that the government must protect, and cannot deny. According to John Locke, the primary purpose of government is to protect such natural rights, and if a government fails to do so, the people are justified in rebelling against and replacing the government. Notwithstanding their commitment to this philosophy, the colonists understood that rebelling against King George III would be treasonous, and the price of losing would not be just their liberty but their lives. Benjamin Franklin, one of the leaders of the rebellion, humorously characterized this dilemma by stating, "We must all hang together, or assuredly we shall all hang separately."

The Revolutionary War

The *Revolutionary War* between England and the colonies lasted from 1775 to 1783. Initially, King George believed that the colonists' rebellion would be easily defeated. England had the world's largest navy, a highly capable army, and the loyalty of 50,000 *Tories* who comprised one-third of the colonists and opposed the insurgents' rebellion against England. England also developed strong alliances with colonial black slaves who were promised freedom if they joined the British forces, and numerous Native Indian tribes that sought protection from the colonists. In contrast, the first colonial fighting forces lacked organization, equipment, food, weapons, and, most importantly, leadership. To unite these disorganized soldiers, General George Washington created America's first military force, called the *Continental Army.*

The Continental Army did not fight according to the formal rules of military engagement used by the British. Unlike British soldiers, who were highly visible as they stood in well-organized rows in open fields wearing red jackets, Continental soldiers fought based on their familiarity with local areas by jumping out of trees, blocking roads, and raiding British camps and ships. When the British won a battle and moved on, the colonists would reclaim the battleground. The Continental Army also benefited from the substantial financial and military support it received from France, Spain, and Holland. As the war progressed,

General George Washington

the colonists began referring to themselves as "Americans" and to the colonies as "states." After eight years of transporting soldiers and supplies across the Atlantic, King George concluded that the value of the colonies was not worth the cost of the war. Britain and America signed the Treaty of Paris in 1783, and the Revolutionary War came to a formal end in 1784.

The Articles of Confederation

As the Revolutionary War progressed, the Americans began to understand that if they won their new country would be a nation without a government. In 1776, the states sent *delegates* (representatives) to Philadelphia, Pennsylvania, to create a plan for a *federal* (national) government. The plan they created, called the *Articles of Confederation,* was *ratified* (enacted into law) by the 13 states. The Articles of Confederation preserved the sovereign authority of the individual states but granted no authority to the federal government to unite the states into one nation. Consequently, each state continued to operate as if it were independent of the other states. For example, because the federal government lacked the power to create a national currency, many states created their own currencies, most of which were treated as worthless by the other states. Because the federal government lacked the power to regulate commerce among the

Illustration of British Soldiers at the Battle of Bunker Hill, by Howard Pyle.

states, the states taxed each other's goods and products, thereby discouraging interstate trade. Because the federal government lacked the power to tax the states, the states refused to contribute to the national treasury. Because the federal government lacked money, it was unable to repay the nation's war debts. As the nation's debts increased and its ability to raise money decreased, prices rose and anarchy soared. Within six years, it became clear that the federal government created under the Articles of Confederation was failing.

The Constitutional Convention

During a very hot summer in 1787, delegates from 12 of the 13 states[3] met again in Philadelphia, Pennsylvania to develop a plan for another federal government. The delegates unanimously elected General George Washington as the *Constitutional Convention's* president. Benjamin Franklin, one of the signers

---

[3] The state of Rhode Island refused to participate in the Constitutional Convention because it opposed the idea of a centralized national government.

Benjamin Franklin
Portrait, by
Joseph-Siffrein Duplessis

Alexander Hamilton
Portrait, by
John Trumbull

James Madison
Portrait, by
John Vanderlyn

of the Treaty of Paris, represented Pennsylvania. Alexander Hamilton, a military officer and financier, represented New York. James Madison, who later became the fourth President of the United States, represented Virginia. These men, along with 52 other delegates, became known as the *Founding Fathers* of the United States.

The goal of the Constitutional Convention was to create a national government that was powerful enough to unite the 13 states into one nation but not powerful enough to destroy the sovereignty of the states or the inalienable rights of the people. Although the delegates agreed with this basic idea, they had many disagreements about how to balance the competing powers, and the limitations on the powers, of the new government. Almost all of these disputes were resolved with compromises. For example, one compromise involved the question of how many persons could represent each state in the federal *legislature* (law-making unit of government). Delegates from largely populated states wanted the number of representatives to be based on each state's population, whereas delegates from less populated states wanted all states to have the same number of representatives. The dispute was settled by a compromise that divided the federal legislature, called *Congress*, into two *chambers*, the *Senate* and the *House of Representatives*. According to the compromise, each state would be represented by two Senators, but representation in the House of Representatives would be based on population.

The debate over whether the states would be represented in Congress equally or in proportion to their populations raised the first of many disagreements about the legality and morality of slavery. The agricultural economy of the southern states was based primarily on cotton and tobacco farming. The economic success of these *plantations* (farms) depended on slave labor. The economy of the northern states, however, was primarily industrial and did not require slave labor to succeed. More importantly, most northern states opposed slavery. When the southern states wanted slaves to be included in their population totals to increase their representation in the House of Representatives in order to increase their political power to continue slavery, they were opposed by the northern states. This dispute was resolved by another compromise by which the delegates agreed that state population totals would include all "free persons" plus *"three-fifths of all other persons."*[4] The phrase *"three-fifths of all other persons"* referred to slaves.

The three-fifths compromise, however, did not end the dispute over slavery. The delegates also debated whether the federal government or the individual state governments should have the authority to decide if slavery was legal. Knowing that the federal government would severely limit slavery, the northern states wanted the legality of slavery to be determined by Congress. Fearing for their economic survival, the southern states wanted each state to retain the authority to determine the legality of slavery within its borders. This dispute was resolved by another compromise by which every state was granted the authority to determine the legality of slavery within its borders until 1808; after which, the power to determine the legality of slavery throughout the nation would shift to Congress.

The Founding Fathers also debated the issue of how power should be distributed between the federal and state governments. In yet another compromise, the delegates agreed that the states would retain authority over domestic matters arising within their geographic borders such as education, family relations, and crime control, while the federal government would have authority over matters that affected the entire nation such as currency, interstate commerce, and military defense. And, in yet another major compromise, the delegates agreed that if a state law conflicted with a federal law, the federal law, as the supreme law of the land, would prevail.

Despite their many disagreements, the Founding Fathers shared a profound distrust in both government and people. They agreed that the first goal of the federal government would be to control the American people, and the second goal of the federal government would be to control itself. More specifically, they believed that most people were by nature selfish and concerned primarily with their own well-being rather than that of others. Consequently, they believed that wealth inequality would become a major source of conflict throughout the nation since most Americans were poor, and few were wealthy. If the federal government could not control the conflicts between the "haves" and "have nots," then each *faction* (self-interested group) would try to control the government for its own benefit, at the expense of the other: the wealthy minority would exploit the government to increase its wealth, while the poor majority would exploit the government to redistribute the wealth among themselves. As a result, if the federal government was exclusively controlled by either faction, it would become despotic and the people would become violent. As Founding Father James Madison said, "If men were angels, no government would be necessary."

---

[4] Quoted provisions of the Constitution are printed in bold italics.

"Scene at the Signing of the Constitution of the United States," by Howard Chandler Christy.

By the end of the summer, the delegates had written the Constitution of the United States.[5] Unlike the Articles of Confederation, the Constitution created a strong federal government with significant authority over the states while also preserving many of the powers of the individual states. In order for the Constitution to be enacted into law, it had to be ratified by at least nine of the 13 states. At the end of the Convention, the delegates returned to their home states to gain support for the new plan of government.

The Constitutional Plan of Government

The Constitution divides the powers of the federal government into three branches: the executive branch, the legislative branch, and the judicial branch. It establishes the powers of each branch and explains how government powers are to be distributed among the federal government, the state governments, and the people.

Article I creates the legislative branch, which it divides into the Senate and the House of Representatives. It lists 27 powers of Congress such as the powers to

---

[5] The original copy of the Constitution is preserved in the National Archives Building in Washington, D.C.

create national laws, determine the distribution of federal funds, and develop the federal *judicial* (court) *system*. In addition to the *enumerated powers*, Article I also grants Congress the authority to exercise *implied powers*–powers that are not expressly listed but are *necessary and proper* to carry out its 27 enumerated powers.

Article II establishes the executive branch and creates the offices of the *President* (chief executive officer of the federal government) and *Vice President* (presidential successor). It lists the President's qualifications, term of office, duties, and powers. Specifically, Article II authorizes the President to preside over the executive branch, enforce federal laws, command the military, and develop foreign policy for the nation.

Article III establishes the judicial branch. It creates the United States *Supreme Court* (the highest federal court) and specifies the powers of the federal judicial system to interpret and apply laws to individual cases.

The constitutional distribution of power among the three branches of government is based on the *separation of powers doctrine*. The separation of powers doctrine prevents any one branch of government from becoming too powerful. Consequently, each branch has the constitutional power to *check* (counteract or restrain) the improper assertion of power by the other two branches. For example, Congress has the power to pass a *bill* (a proposed law), but the President has the power to *veto* (reject) the bill from being enacted into law; however, if a bill is signed by a President and becomes a law, the Supreme Court has the power to declare that the law is unconstitutional. As a result, the three branches must cooperate with each other to accomplish their legislative, executive, and judicial functions.

Ratifying the Constitution

At the end of the Convention, the delegates returned to their home states to gain support for the new plan of government. Two of the most influential states, New York and Virginia, fiercely debated the merits of ratification. The *Anti Federalists* believed that "government is best which governs least," and argued that the Constitution gave too much power to the federal government while denying too much power to the individual states and the people. They opposed ratification unless the Constitution included a *Bill of Rights*—a list of the rights and liberties of the people that the federal government had the duty to protect, but had limited authority to control.

By contrast, due to the government's failure under the Articles of Confederation, the *Federalists* believed that the new nation needed to have a strong federal government. They supported the Constitution because it allowed the federal government to unite the states into one nation but did not allow it to weaken the rights of the people. The Federalists also believed that a Bill of Rights would be less, rather than more, protective of the people because if a specific right was not expressly listed it could be considered excluded and, therefore, subject to government restraint.

In yet another very hard fought compromise, the Federalists and Anti Federalists resolved their dispute by agreeing that after the Constitution was ratified, Congress would amend it to include a Bill of Rights. The Constitution was ratified in 1788. A few months later, in 1789, the nation elected George Washington as its first President, and one month later commenced the first session of Congress during which the Bill of Rights was passed.

The Bill of Rights

The Bill of Rights (1) creates the legal framework for the political and civil rights of the American people; (2) imposes constitutional duties on the federal government to protect those rights; (3) preserves powers of the individual state governments; and (4) denies the federal government the authority to diminish or destroy those rights and powers.

Amendment I

> *Congress shall make no law respecting an establishment of religion, or prohibiting the free exercise thereof; or abridging the freedom of speech, or of the press; or the right of the people peaceably to assemble, and to petition the Government for a redress of grievances.*

The *First Amendment* limits the federal government's authority to restrict the rights of the people to freedom of speech, religion, press, peaceful assembly, and petitioning of the government to resolve grievances.

Amendment II

> *A well regulated Militia, being necessary to the security of a free State, the right of the people to keep and bear Arms, shall not be infringed.*

The *Second Amendment* protects the right of the people to *"bear arms,"* such as guns and other firearms.

Amendment III

> *No Soldier shall, in time of peace be quartered in any house, without the consent of the Owner, nor in time of war, but in a manner to be prescribed by law.*

The *Third Amendment* prohibits the federal government from seizing private homes for military use without the owner's consent.

Amendment IV

The right of the people to be secure in their persons, houses, papers, and effects, against unreasonable searches and seizures, shall not be violated, and no Warrants shall issue, but upon probable cause, supported by Oath or affirmation, and particularly describing the place to be searched, and the persons or things to be seized.

The *Fourth Amendment* requires the federal government to obtain valid *"Warrants"* (court orders) based on *"probable cause"* (good reason) before conducting *"searches and seizures"* (investigations) of suspected criminals.

Amendment V

No Person shall be held to answer for a capital, or otherwise infamous crime, unless on a presentment or indictment of a Grand Jury, except in cases arising in the land or naval forces, or in the Militia, when in actual service in time of War or public danger; nor shall any person be subject for the same offence to be twice put in jeopardy of life or limb; nor shall be compelled in any criminal case to be a witness against himself, nor be deprived of life, liberty, or property, without due process of law; nor shall private property be taken for public use, without just compensation.

The *Fifth Amendment* prohibits the federal government from taking any action against a person's *"life, liberty, or property"* without *"due process of law."* Due process refers to the legal protections the government must provide in order for a person to have a full and fair opportunity to protect himself from coercive government action. More specifically, the Fifth Amendment requires the federal government to obtain a *grand jury indictment* (determination of criminal conduct by a panel of independent citizens) before prosecuting a person for a crime; forbids the federal government from subjecting a person to *double jeopardy* (prosecution of a person more than once for the same crime); protects persons accused of crimes from *self-incrimination* (testifying against oneself in a court proceeding), and loss of private property without *"just compensation"* (financial reimbursement).

Amendment VI

In all criminal prosecutions, the accused shall enjoy the right to a speedy and public trial, by an impartial jury of the State and district wherein the crime shall have been committed; which district shall have been previously ascertained by law, and to be informed of the nature and cause of the accusation; to be confronted with the witnesses against him; to have compulsory process for obtaining witnesses in his favor, and to have the Assistance of Counsel for his defence.

The *Sixth Amendment* guarantees *criminal defendants* (persons accused of crimes) the rights to the *"Assistance of Counsel"* (a lawyer who is licensed to represent people in legal proceedings); a *"speedy and public trial"* (a court proceeding in which evidence and legal arguments are presented to determine the guilt or innocence of an accused person); *confrontation* (challenging by questioning) of adverse witnesses during a criminal trial by the defendant's lawyer; and a *verdict* (judgment) rendered by an *"impartial jury"* (a panel of local citizens who observe the presentation of evidence during a trial and determine the guilt or innocence of the defendant.)

Amendment VII

In Suits at common law, where the value in controversy shall exceed twenty dollars, the right of trial by jury shall be preserved, and no fact tried by a jury, shall be otherwise reexamined in any Court of the United States, than according to the rules of the common law.

The *Seventh Amendment* guarantees a *"trial by jury"* to the parties in most federal *"common law"* cases (civil lawsuits brought by and against private persons, entities, or the government).

Amendment VIII

Excessive bail shall not be required, nor excessive fines imposed, nor cruel and unusual punishments inflicted.

The *Eighth Amendment* forbids the federal government from imposing *"cruel and unusual punishments"* (penalties that are of disproportionate severity to the convicted offense), *"excessive fines"* (financial penalties), and unreasonable *"bail"* (financial guarantees to appear at trial) in criminal cases.

Amendment IX

The enumeration in the Constitution of certain rights, shall not be construed to deny or disparage others retained by the people.

The *Ninth Amendment* provides that the people have *"certain rights"* in addition to those expressly listed in the Bill of Rights that the federal government cannot violate.

Amendment X

The powers not delegated to the United States by the Constitution, nor prohibited by it to the States, are reserved to the States respectively, or to the people.

The *Tenth Amendment* provides that the states and the people retain any *"powers"* that the Constitution has *"not delegated"* expressly to the federal government.

Since 1788, over 11,000 constitutional amendments have been proposed, but only 27 have been enacted. Some of these amendments have been more successful than others. For example, the *Fourteenth Amendment,* passed in 1868, granted former male slaves full rights of citizenship, including the right to vote. Women, however, were not granted the right to vote until the *Nineteenth Amendment,* which was passed in 1920. In 1971, the *Twenty-Sixth Amendment* again expanded the right to vote by lowering the voting age from 21 years of age to 18 years of age. The *Eighteenth Amendment,* passed in 1919, and generally known as "Prohibition," banned the manufacture, sale, and transportation of "intoxicating liquors" everywhere within the United States. Thirteen years later, in 1933, the *Twenty-First Amendment* repealed the Eighteenth Amendment after it proved to be the most disobeyed law in American history.

CHAPTER 1 QUESTIONS

1. **a.** What is a constitution?
   b. What purposes does a constitution serve?
   c. How would a government operate without a constitution?

2. **a.** What is a constitutional power?
   b. What is a constitutional right?

3. What is the difference between an inalienable right and a right given to the people by a government?

4. Why did the Articles of Confederation fail?

5. Why were the Federalists concerned that including a Bill of Rights in the Constitution would limit rather than protect individual freedoms? Do you agree or disagree? Explain your answer.

6. Do you agree or disagree with the Anti Federalist belief that "government is best which governs least"? Explain your answer.

7. Do you agree or disagree with the concern of the Founding Fathers that people need government to control their greed and self-interest in order to promote the well-being of the entire nation? Explain your answer.

8. Do you agree or disagree with the proposition that people always distrust their governments and that governments always distrust their people? Explain your answer.

Article I: The Legislative Branch

The Capitol Building where both chambers of Congress are located.

Article I Section 1: Congress

All legislative Powers herein granted shall be vested in a Congress of the United States, which shall consist of a Senate and House of Representatives.

Article I Section 1 establishes the federal legislature, called *"Congress"*, which it divides into two chambers, the *"Senate"* and the *"House of Representatives"* ("House"). Together, both chambers make federal laws that apply to the entire nation. This power-sharing arrangement requires the two chambers to cooperate and compromise with each other throughout the *legislative process* (lawmaking process). Under the *doctrine of checks and balances*, this power-sharing arrangement also authorizes each chamber to *check* (counter) the actions of the other chamber so that neither can control the entire legislative process. As a result, the legislative process by which Congress develops laws can be time-consuming because it places a higher value on cooperation and compromise than on efficiency. An interesting story tells of two Founding Fathers, George Washington and Thomas Jefferson, who were drinking coffee together while debating the merits of dividing the powers of Congress into two chambers. While arguing against a divided Congress, Jefferson said that he would pour his coffee into a saucer "to cool it." "So," responded Washington, who favored a divided Congress, "we will pour our legislation into the Senatorial saucer, to cool it."

Article I Section 2: The House of Representatives

The House of Representatives shall be composed of Members chosen every second Year by the People of the several states, and the Electors in each State shall have the Qualifications requisite for Electors of the most numerous Branch of the State Legislature.

Each member of the House of Representatives is referred to as a Congressman, Congresswoman, or Representative and is elected by the voters of his or her state for a two-year term of office. The entire membership of the House is elected every two years.

Representative Terms of Office

No Person shall be a Representative who shall not have attained to the Age of twenty five Years, and been seven Years a Citizen of the United States, and who shall not, when elected, be an Inhabitant of that State in which he[1] shall be chosen.

A House member must be at least 25 years of age, a resident of the state that he or she represents, and a citizen of the United States for at least seven years.

Representative Qualifications

~~Representatives and direct Taxes shall be apportioned among the several states~~ ~~which may be included within this Union, according to their respective~~

---

[1] The constitutional use of the word "he" also refers to "she."

Map of each state's total number of Representatives as of 2010.

~~Numbers, which shall be determined by adding to the whole Number of free Persons, including those bound to Service for a Term of Years, and excluding Indians not taxed, three fifths of all other Persons.~~[2] *The actual Enumeration shall be made within three Years after the first Meeting of the Congress of the United States, and within every subsequent Term of ten Years, in such Manner as they shall by Law direct. The number of Representatives shall not exceed one for every thirty Thousand, but each State shall have at Least one Representative; and until such enumeration shall be made, the State of New Hampshire shall be entitled to chuse three, Massachusetts eight, Rhode Island and Providence Plantations one, Connecticut five, New York six, New Jersey four, Pennsylvania eight, Delaware one, Maryland six, Virginia ten, North Carolina five, South Carolina five, and Georgia three.*

The number of Representatives per state is based on each state's population. As a result, states with small populations have fewer Representatives than states with large populations. Representatives are elected by the citizens of their *congressional districts* (geographic sections of states) for a two-year term. The states

---

[2] Crossed-out words show constitutional provisions that have been modified or repealed. The crossed-out apportionment provision in Article I Section 2 was modified in 1868 by the Fourteenth Amendment, which allowed African Americans who previously were former slaves and counted as *"three-fifths of all other persons"* to be fully counted as citizens of each state.

create their congressional districts by a system called *apportionment,* which subdivides states into geographic sections where comparable numbers of people reside. Consequently, densely populated areas are subdivided into numerous small congressional districts, resulting in many Representatives, while low population areas are subdivided into fewer congressional districts, resulting in fewer Representatives. For example, California has 53 congressional districts and 53 Representatives whereas Alaska, South Dakota, and Vermont each have only one Representative. As of 2014, the average congressional district consisted of approximately 710,767 people.

To maintain each state's representation in proportion to its population, the United States takes a nationwide *census* every ten years to count the total number of people living within each state. If, after the census, a state's population has increased or decreased, the composition of its congressional districts and the number of its Representatives will also increase or decrease.

The following maps show the congressional districts of Arizona, Illinois, and Wyoming. Notice how the size and shape of the congressional districts reflect the more and less densely populated areas of each state. For example, the state of Illinois has a total of 18 congressional districts, 11 of which are located within the Chicago area, its most densely populated city.

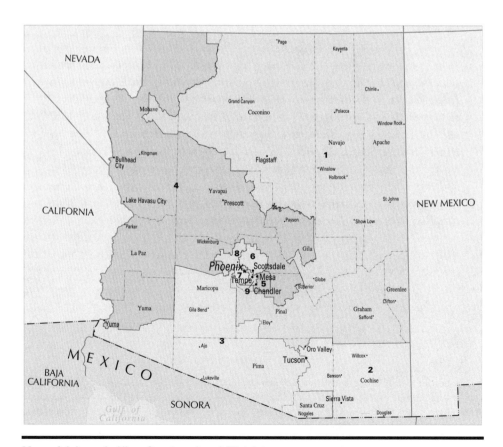

Map of Arizona's Nine Congressional Districts

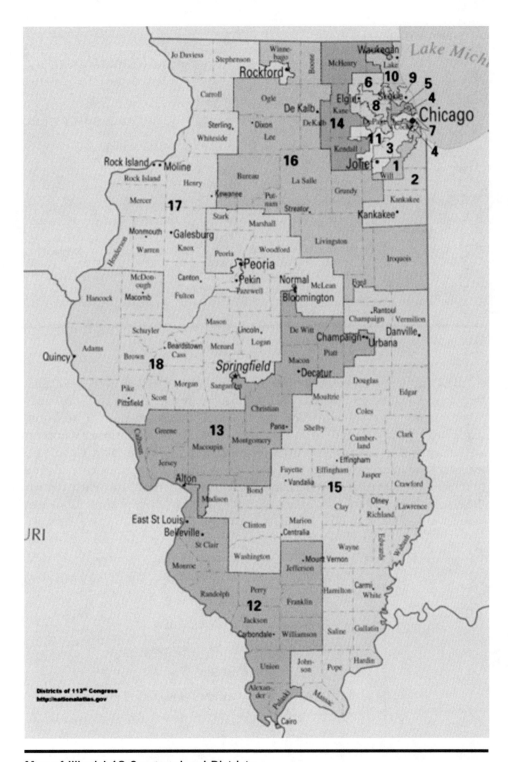

Map of Illinois' 18 Congressional Districts

Congressional District: At large

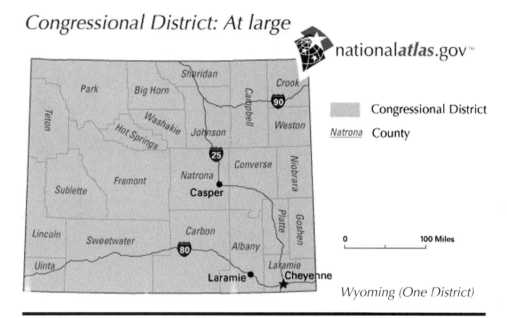

Map of Wyoming's One Congressional District

Because Representatives run for election and re-election every two years, they must become very familiar with the people in their districts. Most candidates campaign throughout their districts by making presentations, distributing pamphlets, posting signs outside the homes of residents, and printing campaign advertisements in newspapers, on the Internet, radio, and television. Candidates frequently invite voters to their homes to discuss matters of public concern and, in return, voters frequently invite candidates to their homes to introduce them to their neighbors and friends. Below is in invitation from an Illinois Congresswoman for a dinner and discussion at her home:

Please join Congresswoman

Jan Schakowsky for her Annual BBQ

benefiting Schakowsky for Congress

Sunday, August 8th

3:00 PM — 5:00 PM at Jan's House

$50 per individual

House Vacancies

When vacancies happen in the Representation from any State, the Executive Authority thereof shall issue Writs of Election to fill such Vacancies.

If a House vacancy occurs due to the death, resignation, or removal of a Representative from office, the state's *Governor* (executive leader) is required to hold an election to fill the vacancy.

House Leadership

The House of Representatives shall chuse their Speaker and other Officers

The leader of the *"House of Representatives"* is called the *Speaker of the House*. The *"Speaker"* is elected by the political party that has the most Representatives. The Speaker interprets and applies the House procedural rules, assigns Representatives to committees, determines which bills each House committee will develop, schedules when bills will be voted on, and officially signs the bills passed by the House. The Speaker is not required to vote on a bill except to break a *tie*, an evenly divided number of votes that renders the bill one vote short of passage or rejection. The Speaker also determines when and if a Representative may make a formal presentation in the House. Most importantly, pursuant to the Presidential Succession Act,[3] the Speaker is second in the line of presidential successors after the Vice President.

House Impeachment Power

and shall have the sole Power of Impeachment.

The House has the exclusive power to *impeach* (accuse) federal officials of conduct constituting **"treason, bribery and other high crimes or misdemeanors."**[4] *"Impeachment"* is the first of two stages of the process by which a President, Vice President, federal judge, Supreme Court Justice, or other federal official is removed from office. A *Bill of Impeachment* lists accusations of wrongdoing that must be approved by a majority of Representatives. In the second stage, the Senate conducts the impeachment *trial*, a judicial proceeding in which evidence and legal arguments are presented to determine if the impeached party should be removed from office.

---

[3] The Presidential Succession Act, 3 U.S. Code §19, was passed by Congress in 1947. *"§"* refers to a section of a statute.

[4] Article II Section 4.

Article I Section 3: The Senate

The Senate of the United States shall be composed of two Senators from each state, ~~chosen by the legislature thereof~~, for six Years; and each Senator shall have one Vote.

Immediately after they shall be assembled in Consequence of the first Election, they shall be divided as equally as may be into three Classes. The Seats of the Senators of the first Class shall be vacated at the Expiration of the second Year, of the second Class at the Expiration of the fourth Year, and of the third Class at the Expiration of the sixth Year, so that one third may be chosen every second Year; ~~and if Vacancies happen by Resignation, or otherwise, during the Recess of the Legislature of any State, the Executive thereof may make temporary Appointments until the next Meeting of the Legislature, which shall then fill such Vacancies.~~ [5]

Each state elects *"two Senators."* Consequently, Alaska, with 736,399 residents, and California, with 37,253,956 residents, each has two Senators. Senators are elected to serve a six-year term of office, unlike House members who are elected to serve two-year terms. Also, unlike House members who are concerned primarily with the interests of their individual congressional districts, Senators are expected to be concerned with the interests of the entire nation.

Senatorial Qualifications

No Person shall be a Senator who shall not have attained to the Age of thirty Years, and been nine Years a Citizen of the United States, and who shall not, when elected, be an Inhabitant of that State for which he shall be chosen.

A Senator must be at least 30 years old, a citizen of the United States for *"nine years,"* and a resident of the state from which he or she is elected.

Senatorial Leadership

The Vice President of the United States shall be President of the Senate, but shall have no Vote, unless they be equally divided.

---

[5] These two provisions were modified in 1913 by the *Seventeenth Amendment* which grants citizens, rather than state legislatures, the right to elect Senators. Initially, citizens were not allowed to elect Senators because the Founding Fathers believed they were too ill-informed and self-interested.

The Senate shall chuse their other Officers, and also a President pro tempore, in the Absence of the Vice President, or when he shall exercise the Office of President of the United States.

Although Section 3 states that the Vice President is the presiding officer of the Senate who is allowed to vote to break a tie, today the Vice President is actually the ceremonial leader of the Senate. In early American history, the Vice President presided over daily Senate sessions, but a *"President pro tempore"* (President for the day) was appointed when the Vice President was unavailable. Today, the real leader of the Senate is the President Pro Tempore, who is chosen by the political party with a majority of Senators. Unlike the Speaker of the House, the President Pro Tempore does not control Senatorial proceedings. Instead, the President Pro Tempore makes procedural rulings, signs bills passed by the Senate, and represents the Senate on formal occasions. More importantly, the President Pro Tempore is third in the line of presidential successors after the Vice President and the Speaker of the House.

Senatorial Impeachment Power

The Senate shall have the sole Power to try all Impeachments. When sitting for that Purpose, they shall be on Oath or Affirmation. When the President of the United States is tried, the Chief Justice shall preside: And no Person shall be convicted without the Concurrence of two thirds of the Members present.

Judgment in Cases of Impeachment shall not extend further than to removal from Office, and disqualification to hold and enjoy any Office of honor, Trust, or Profit under the United States: but the Party convicted shall nevertheless be liable and subject to Indictment, Trial, Judgment and Punishment according to Law.

The Senate conducts the trial of any official impeached by the House. Conviction requires the approval of *"two thirds"* of the Senators who were present during the trial. If convicted of treason, bribery, or other high crimes and misdemeanors the official is removed from office and may not hold another federal office. The Senate has no power to impose additional punishments, although the former official can be tried, convicted, and punished in a court of law for any crime involved in the impeachment case.

To date, 18 federal officials have been impeached by the House, but only seven have been convicted by the Senate. Fourteen of the impeached officials were federal judges, four of whom were impeached by the House but *acquitted* (found not guilty) by the Senate; two other federal judges were impeached by the House but resigned before the Senate conducted their trials. Presidents Andrew Johnson, in 1868, and Bill Clinton, in 1999, were both impeached by the House but acquitted by the Senate. In 1974, the House began impeachment proceedings against President Richard Nixon, who resigned in order to avoid conviction and removal by the Senate.

Article I Section 4: Elections and Annual Meetings

The Times, Places and Manner of holding Elections for Senators and Representatives shall be prescribed in each State by the Legislature thereof; but the Congress may at any time by Law make or alter such Regulations, except as to the Places of chusing Senators.

The Congress shall assemble at least once in every Year, and such Meeting shall be ~~on the first Monday in December~~, unless they shall by Law appoint a different Day.

Section 4 authorizes *"each State"* to establish its own method for electing members of Congress and requires Congress to meet at least once every year. In 1933, the *Twentieth Amendment* changed the opening date of Congress from the first Monday in December to January 3.

Article I Section 5: Internal Congressional Governance

Each House[6] shall be the Judge of the Elections, Returns, and Qualifications of its own Members, and a Majority of each shall constitute a Quorum to do Business; but a smaller Number may adjourn from day to day, and may be authorized to compel the Attendance of absent Members, in such Manner, and under such Penalties as each House may provide.

Each House may determine the Rules of its Proceedings, punish its Members for disorderly Behavior, and, with the Concurrence of two thirds, expel a Member.

Section 5 authorizes the Senate and the House to develop and enforce their own rules of procedure and discipline. Both chambers have the authority to compel their members to attend meetings, impose *"Penalties"* for nonattendance, and *"expel"* disobedient members. In practice, however, the chambers rarely enforce their disciplinary rules.

The Senate and the House may conduct official business only at a meeting attended by a *"Quorum"* (the minimum number of persons required to attend) of

---

[6] As used in Article I Section 5, and Articles 2 and 5, the term "House" refers to both chambers of Congress, not just the House of Representatives.

members. Once a quorum is present, a meeting can legally be held and proceed even if some members leave before the meeting *adjourns* (ends). In practice, both chambers often proceed without a quorum, and such proceedings are valid unless challenged.

Congressional Records

Each House shall keep a Journal of its Proceedings, and from time to time publish the same, excepting such Parts as may in their Judgment require Secrecy; and the Yeas and Nays[7] of the Members of either House on any question shall, at the Desire of one fifth of those Present, be entered on the Journal.

Each chamber creates a written, public *"Journal of its Proceedings"*, called the *Congressional Record.* However, highly sensitive information, such as national security matters, may be excluded from the journal.

Congressional Adjournment

Neither House, during the Session of Congress, shall, without the Consent of the other, adjourn for more than three days, nor to any other Place than that in which the two Houses shall be sitting.

A *congressional term* lasts for two years and is divided into two *sessions* lasting one year each. Neither chamber may *"adjourn"* (end) a one-year session *"for more than three days without the Consent of the other"* chamber.

Article I Section 6: Compensation and Immunity from Arrest

The Senators and Representatives shall receive a Compensation for their Services, to be ascertained by Law, and paid out of the Treasury of the United States.

Each chamber determines its members' *"Compensation"* (salary), which is paid from the United States Treasury.

---

[7] "Yea" means yes. "Nay" means no.

Congressional Immunity

They shall in all Cases, except Treason, Felony and Breach of the Peace, be privileged from Arrest during their Attendance at the Session of their respective Houses, and in going to and returning from the same; and for any Speech or Debate in either House, they shall not be questioned in any other Place.

Members of Congress receive *legislative immunity* (protection) from arrest and prosecution while going to and from a congressional session. Similarly, the *"Speech or Debate"* clause protects congressional members from arrest and prosecution while performing legislative functions, such as making statements during formal debates or presentations.

Prohibitions Against Non Congressional Appointments

No Senator or Representative shall, during the Time for which he was elected, be appointed to any civil Office under the Authority of the United States, which shall have been created, or the Emoluments whereof shall have been increased during such time and no Person holding any Office under the United States, shall be a Member of either House during his Continuance in Office.

To avoid divided loyalties and conflicts of interest, members of Congress may not hold other government positions during their congressional terms of office. They may, however, continue to pursue private occupational and professional interests.

Article I Section 7: Revenue Bills, the Legislative Process, and the Presidential Veto

All Bills for raising Revenue shall originate in the House of Representatives; but the Senate may propose or concur with Amendments as on other Bills.

A *bill* is a proposed law developed by Congress. All *revenue bills* (proposed laws to raise money for the government) must originate in the House of Representatives, although the Senate has the authority to modify such bills. All other bills may start in either chamber.

Legislative Committees

The *legislative process* is the system by which bills are developed and passed by both chambers of Congress. The legislative process involves four types of committees: *Standing Committees, Conference Committees, Joint Committees,* and *Select Committees*. Standing Committees are permanent committees in each chamber that specialize in specific topics such as national security, agriculture, and veterans affairs. Conference Committees are composed of members of both chambers who work together to *reconcile* (resolve) disagreements about a bill and *draft* (write) a compromise bill that both chambers will agree to pass. Joint Committees also consist of members of both chambers who work together to research matters of continuing national concern such as financial and economic matters. Select Committees are separate committees within each chamber that are temporarily *convened* (assembled) to investigate matters that are beyond the authority of other committees. Two famous Select Committees were the Watergate Senate Select Committee and the Iran Contra Select Committee. During the 1970s, the Watergate Select Committee investigated whether the Nixon administration had been involved in the burglary of the Democratic Party's National Campaign Headquarters during a presidential campaign. During the 1980s, the Iran Contra Select Committee investigated whether the Reagan administration had engaged in illegal funding of Nicaraguan rebels by selling United States military equipment to Iran. More recently, Select Committees have investigated the failure of United States intelligence agencies to predict the September 11, 2001 al-Qaeda terrorist attacks that took place in New York, Pennsylvania, and Washington D.C.; accusations of mistreatment of Iraqi and Afghani combatants imprisoned in Guantanamo Bay, Cuba; and the causes and effects of climate change.

After a bill is introduced into a chamber, it is assigned to a Standing Committee, which then assigns it to a specialized Subcommittee. The Subcommittee studies the reasons for the bill, prepares a draft of the bill, and holds an open public hearing during which people can present opinions favoring or opposing the bill. Once the hearing is over, the Subcommittee votes on the bill. If the Subcommittee rejects the bill, it goes no further. If the Subcommittee approves the bill, it is sent back to the Standing Committee.

The Standing Committee must then approve or reject the bill. If the Standing Committee approves the bill, it is sent to the chamber's *floor* (central meeting area) to be debated. The floor debate is open to the public and the press. After the debate, chamber members vote to approve the bill, reject the bill, send the bill back to its Subcommittee for more work, or *table* the bill, which means to ignore the bill and results in its defeat. If the bill is approved, it is signed by the chamber leader. If a bill is not approved, it can be reintroduced in the future. Once a bill is approved in one chamber, it is sent to the other chamber to undergo the same process. If the bill is modified in the second chamber, it will be sent to a Conference Committee to resolve the differences because both chambers must pass the identical bill.

How a Bill Is Enacted into Law

> *Every Bill which shall have passed the House of Representatives and the Senate, shall, before it become a Law, be presented to the President of the*

President Barack Obama signs the American Recovery and Reinvestment Act of 2009, an economic stimulus program to create jobs and improve the economy, as Vice President Joe Biden stands behind him. February 17, 2009.

United States; If he approve he shall sign it, but if not he shall return it, with his Objections to the House in which it shall have originated, who shall enter the Objections at large on their Journal, and proceed to reconsider it. If after such Reconsideration two thirds of that House shall agree to pass the Bill, it shall be sent, together with the Objections, to the other House, by which it shall likewise be reconsidered, and if approved by two thirds of that House, it shall become a Law. But in all such Cases the Votes of both Houses shall be determined by Yeas and Nays, and the Names of the Persons voting for and against the Bill shall be entered on the Journal of each House respectively. If any Bill shall not be returned by the President within ten Days (Sundays excepted) after it shall have been presented to him, the Same shall be a Law, in like Manner as if he had signed it, unless the Congress by their Adjournment prevent its Return, in which Case it shall not be a Law.

Every Order, Resolution, or Vote, to which the Concurrence of the Senate and House of Representatives may be necessary (except on a question of Adjournment) shall be presented to the President of the United States; and before the Same shall take Effect, shall be approved by him, or being disapproved by him, shall be repassed by two thirds of the Senate and House of Representatives, according to the Rules and Limitations prescribed in the Case of a Bill.

Once a bill is passed by both chambers there are several ways it can be enacted into law. Most commonly, a bill is enacted into law when it is presented

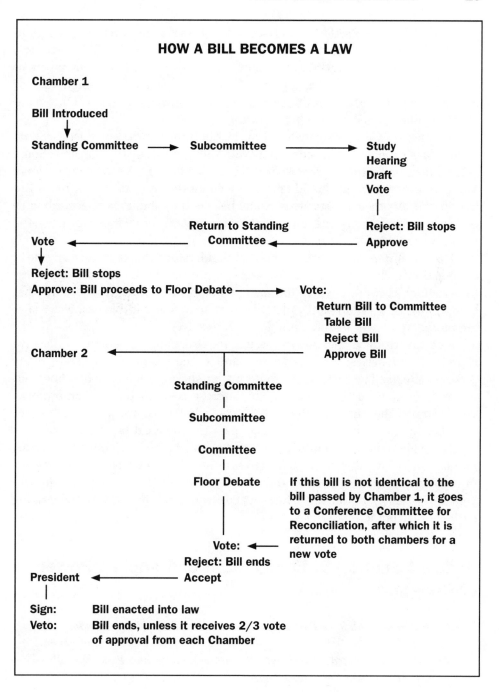

HOW A BILL BECOMES A LAW

Chamber 1

Bill Introduced

Standing Committee ⟶ Subcommittee ⟶ Study
                                       Hearing
                                       Draft
                                       Vote

Return to Standing Committee   Reject: Bill stops
Vote ⟵   Approve

Reject: Bill stops
Approve: Bill proceeds to Floor Debate ⟶ Vote:
                                          Return Bill to Committee
                                          Table Bill
                                          Reject Bill
Chamber 2 ⟵   Approve Bill

Standing Committee

Subcommittee

Committee

Floor Debate   If this bill is not identical to the
                    bill passed by Chamber 1, it goes
                    to a Conference Committee for
                    Reconciliation, after which it is
                    returned to both chambers for a
Vote: ⟵   new vote
Reject: Bill ends

President ⟵ Accept

Sign: Bill enacted into law
Veto: Bill ends, unless it receives 2/3 vote
         of approval from each Chamber

to and signed by the President. If the President *vetoes* a bill by refusing to sign it, the bill will not be enacted into law. If Congress still wants the bill to become a law, it can *override* (defeat) the President's veto if two-thirds of the members of each chamber vote to approve it. Alternatively, if a President fails to sign, veto, or return a bill to Congress within ten days, it will be enacted into law. Once a bill becomes a law, it is called an *act* or *statute*.

Members of Congress vote for or against bills for a variety of reasons. Some believe they should vote in accordance with their political party's agenda. Some believe their votes should represent the interests of their *constituents* (voters). Some believe their votes should take into account the best interests of the entire nation, not just their constituents. Some believe they should vote according to their best judgment, notwithstanding the current views of their constituents, the public, or their political party.

Historically, members of Congress have understood that they must engage in cooperation, collegiality, negotiation and compromise for the legislative process to function. However, when too many members of Congress believe that compromise and negotiation violate their principles and ideologies, fewer laws are passed and fewer national problems are resolved.

Not surprisingly, the power-sharing requirements of the two legislative chambers and between the legislative and executive branches create many power conflicts. The purpose of these power-sharing requirements, however, is not to promote conflict. Rather, the purpose is to encourage compromise. For example, the chamber that introduces a bill must work with the other chamber to ensure that both chambers pass the identical bill. Since Congress wants the bill to be signed into law, it must persuade the President of its merits. Similarly, a President who wants Congress to pass a bill must persuade Congress of its merits. Consequently, the only way one branch of government can successfully assert its power to perform its constitutional duties is by cooperating with another branch.

Article I Section 8: Enumerated and Implied Powers of Congress

The Congress shall have Power To lay and collect Taxes, Duties, Imposts and Excises, to pay the Debts and provide for the common Defence and general Welfare of the United States; but all Duties, Imposts and Excises shall be uniform throughout the United States;

To borrow money on the credit of the United States;

To regulate Commerce with foreign Nations, and among the several States, and with Indian Tribes;

To establish an uniform Rule of Naturalization, and uniform Laws on the subject of Bankruptcies throughout the United States;

To coin Money, regulate the Value thereof, and of foreign Coin, and fix the Standard of Weights and Measures;

To provide for the Punishment of counterfeiting the Securities and current Coin of the United States;

To Establish Post Offices and Post Roads;

To promote the Progress of Science and useful Arts, by securing for limited Times to Authors and Inventors the exclusive Right to their respective Writings and Discoveries;

To constitute Tribunals inferior to the supreme Court;

To define and punish Piracies and Felonies committed on the high Seas, and Offences against the Law of Nations;

To declare War, grant Letters of Marque and Reprisal, and make Rules concerning Captures on Land and Water;

To raise and support Armies, but no Appropriation of Money to that Use shall be for a longer Term than two Years;

To provide and maintain a Navy;

To make Rules for the Government and Regulation of the land and naval Forces;

To provide for calling forth the Militia to execute the Laws of the Union, suppress Insurrections and repel Invasions;

To provide for organizing, arming, and disciplining, the Militia, and for governing such Part of them as may be employed in the Service of the United States, reserving to the States respectively, the Appointment of the Officers, and the Authority of training the Militia according to the discipline prescribed by Congress;

To exercise exclusive Legislation in all cases whatsoever, over such District (not exceeding ten Miles square) as may, by Cession of particular States, and the Acceptance of Congress, become the Seat of the Government of the United States, and to exercise like Authority over all Places purchased by the Consent of Legislature of the State in which the Same shall be, for the Erection of Forts, Magazines, Arsenals, dock-Yards, and other needful Buildings;–And

To make all Laws which shall be necessary and proper for carrying into Execution the foregoing Powers, and all other Powers vested by this Constitution in the Government of the United States, or in any Department or Officer thereof.

Section 8 enumerates 27 powers that the Constitution expressly grants to Congress, many of which are shared by the House and the Senate. For example, the powers to declare war, raise armies and navies, borrow and print money, regulate interstate and foreign commerce, and create the federal court system must be agreed to by both chambers. Below are some of the most important of these enumerated powers.

The Power to Tax

Congress's *"power to lay and collect taxes . . . to pay the debts, and provide for the common defence and general welfare of the United States"* dates back to the Constitutional Convention, during which the Founding Fathers decided that the federal government would repay each state's Revolutionary War debts in exchange for each state's agreement to financially support the federal treasury. As a result of this decision, each state was subject to political pressure from every other state to contribute to the federal treasury by paying its taxes. As the federal treasury's wealth increased, so did Congress's power over the nation.

The Power to Regulate Commerce

Congress has the power *"to regulate Commerce . . . among the several States."* The *commerce clause* authorizes Congress to regulate *interstate commerce* activities that cross state boundaries and affect commerce in more than one state. For example, the commerce clause allows Congress to promote, protect, and prohibit airline and railroad transportation, interstate use of national currency, financial investment transactions, and the operations of television, radio, and the Internet.

In 1824, *Gibbons v. Ogden* was the first commerce clause case to be decided by the United States Supreme Court. *Gibbons* involved a dispute between the State of New York and the federal government over the use of steamboats on interstate waterways. The New York State legislature had granted Robert Fulton, the steamboat inventor, exclusive authority to operate his steamboats along New York waterways. Fulton then granted part of his authority to Aaron Ogden to operate steamboats along the waterways between New York and the neighboring state of New Jersey. The federal government, however, had already granted Thomas Gibbons the authority to operate steamboats along the waterways between New York and New Jersey. Gibbons and Ogden soon found their steamboat operations to be in conflict. Ogden sued Gibbons to prevent him from interfering with his exclusive New York authority. The Supreme Court, however, ruled in Gibbons' favor, finding that New York's grant of exclusive authority to Fulton conflicted with Congress's grant of authority to Gibbons, which was superior under Congress's commerce clause power.

The immediate consequence of the *Gibbons* ruling was an end to state-sponsored grants of exclusive authority to operate steamboats. The more important consequence, however, was the recognition of Congress's broad commerce clause authority, which greatly increased its power to regulate commercial activities in one state that affected other states. One hundred and forty years after the *Gibbons v. Ogden* ruling, Congress used its commerce clause power to pass the *Civil Rights Act of 1964* that made it unlawful for businesses engaged in interstate commerce to deny people the use of their facilities because of their race, color, religion, or national origin.

In *Heart of Atlanta Motel v. United States*, a motel sued the United States based on the argument that the commerce clause did not give Congress the authority to apply the Civil Rights Act to an intrastate motel that operated solely within one state. The Court disagreed. It found, instead, that because 75 percent of the motel's clientele came from other states, its policy of refusing to rent rooms to black people violated their right to interstate travel. Excerpts of the opinion follow:

Heart of Atlanta Motel v. United States
379 U.S. 241 (1964)[8]

Mr. Justice Clark delivered the opinion of the Court.

Appellant[9] [Heart of Atlanta Motel][10] owns and operates the Heart of Atlanta Motel which has 216 rooms available to transient [traveling] guests.... It is readily accessible to interstate highways 75 and 85 and state highways 23 and 41. Appellant solicits patronage from outside the State of Georgia through various national advertising media, including magazines of national circulation.... [I]t accepts convention trade from outside Georgia and approximately 75% of its registered guests are from out of State. Prior to passage of the [Civil Rights] Act the motel had followed a practice of refusing to rent rooms to Negroes, and it alleged that it intended to continue to do so. In an effort to perpetuate that policy this suit was filed.

The appellant contends that Congress in passing this Act exceeded its power to regulate commerce under Art. I, 8, cl. 3, of the Constitution of the United States.... The appellees [the United States Department of Justice] counter that the unavailability to Negroes of adequate accommodations interferes significantly with interstate travel, and that Congress, under the Commerce Clause, has power to remove such obstructions and restraints....

The sole question posed is ... the constitutionality of the Civil Rights Act of 1964 as applied to these facts. The legislative history of the Act indicates that Congress based the Act on ... its power to regulate interstate commerce under Art. I, 8, cl. 3, of the Constitution as applied to these facts....

---

[8] 379 U.S. 241 (1964) is the official citation of the case.

[9] The *appellant* is the party who lost the lawsuit in the lower court and has filed an *appeal* (a higher court proceeding that evaluates the accuracy of a lower court's decision) against the *appellee* (the party who won the lawsuit) seeking reversal of the lower court's decision.

[10] A [ ] within an opinion provides a definition or explanation.

The power of Congress to deal with [discrimination by hotels and motels that racially discriminate against interstate travelers] . . . depends on the meaning of the Commerce Clause. Its meaning was first enunciated 140 years ago by the great Chief Justice John Marshall in <u>Gibbons v. Ogden</u>, 9 Wheat. 1 (1824), in these words:

> "What is this [Commerce Clause] power? It is the power to regulate; that is, to prescribe the rule by which commerce is to be governed. This power, like all others vested in Congress, is complete in itself, may be exercised to its utmost extent, and acknowledges no limitations, other than are prescribed in the constitution. . . ."

In short, the determinative test of the exercise of power by the Congress under the Commerce Clause is simply whether the activity sought to be regulated is "commerce which concerns more States than one" and has a real and substantial relation to the national interest.

The same interest in protecting interstate commerce which led Congress to deal with segregation in interstate carriers and the white-slave traffic has prompted it to extend the exercise of its power to gambling, to criminal enterprises, to deceptive practices in the sale of products, to fraudulent security transactions, to misbranding of drugs, to wages and hours, to members of labor unions, to crop control, to discrimination against shippers, to the protection of small business from injurious price cutting, to resale price maintenance, to professional football, and to racial discrimination by owners and managers of terminal restaurants.

That Congress was legislating against moral wrongs in many of these areas rendered its enactments no less valid. In framing Title II of this Act Congress was also dealing with what it considered a moral problem. But that fact does not detract from the overwhelming evidence of the disruptive effect that racial discrimination has had on commercial intercourse. It was this burden which empowered Congress to enact appropriate legislation, and, given this basis for the exercise of its power, Congress was not restricted by the fact that the particular obstruction to interstate commerce with which it was dealing was also deemed a moral and social wrong.

It is said that the operation of the motel here is of a purely local character. . . . As Chief Justice Stone put it in <u>United States v. Darby</u>:

> "The power of Congress over interstate commerce is not confined to the regulation of commerce among the states. It extends to those activities intrastate which so affect interstate commerce or the exercise of the power of Congress over it as to make regulation of them appropriate means to the attainment of a legitimate end, the exercise of the granted power of Congress to regulate interstate commerce."

Thus the power of Congress to promote interstate commerce also includes the power to regulate the local incidents thereof, including local activities in both the States of origin and destination, which might have a substantial and harmful effect upon that commerce. One need only examine the evidence which we have discussed above to see that Congress may—as it has—prohibit racial discrimination by motels serving travelers, however "local" their operations may appear.

We, therefore, conclude that the action of the Congress in the adoption of the Act as applied here to a motel which concededly serves interstate travelers is within the power granted it by the Commerce Clause of the Constitution, as interpreted by this Court for 140 years. It may be argued that Congress could have pursued other methods to eliminate the obstructions it found in interstate commerce caused by racial discrimination. But this is a matter of policy that rests entirely with the Congress not with the courts. How obstructions in commerce may be removed—what means are to be employed—is within the sound and exclusive discretion of the Congress. It is subject only to one caveat—that the means chosen by it must be reasonably adapted to the end permitted by the Constitution. We cannot say that its choice here was not so adapted. The Constitution requires no more.

Affirmed.[11]

Based on the Court's *rulings* (decisions) in <u>Gibbons</u> and <u>Heart of Atlanta Motel</u>, one might think that the commerce clause gives Congress unlimited authority to regulate local as well as interstate commercial activities. However, the more recent case of <u>U.S. v. Lopez</u> demonstrates that Congress's commerce clause authority is subject to limitations. In 1990, Congress passed the federal Gun-Free School Zones Act[12] that made it a crime to knowingly possess a gun at or near a school. Alfonso Lopez, Jr. was a twelfth-grade student who had brought a gun to a Texas high school and was charged with violating the new federal law. In his defense, Lopez argued that the Gun-Free School Zones Act exceeded Congress's commerce clause authority because mere possession of a gun was not a commercial activity. The federal government defended the law as a valid exercise of Congress's commerce clause authority because guns purchased and sold in interstate commerce were used to commit crimes near schools. Here is the Court's response to both arguments.

---

[11] *Affirmed* means that the higher court accepted the ruling of the lower court from which the case was appealed.
[12] 18 U.S.C. §921(a)(25).

United States v. Lopez
514 U.S. 549 (1995)

Chief Justice[13] Rehnquist delivered the opinion of the Court.

In the Gun-Free School Zones Act of 1990, Congress made it a federal offense "for any individual knowingly to possess a firearm at a place that the individual knows, or has reasonable cause to believe, is a school zone." 18 U.S.C. Section 922(q)(1)(A). The Act neither regulates a commercial activity nor contains a requirement that the possession be connected in any way to interstate commerce. We hold that the Act exceeds the authority of Congress "to regulate Commerce among the several States. . . ." U.S. Const., Art. I, 8, cl. 3.

On March 10, 1992, respondent[14] who was then a 12th-grade student, arrived at Edison High School in San Antonio, Texas, carrying a concealed .38 caliber handgun and five bullets. Acting upon an anonymous tip, school authorities confronted respondent, who admitted that he was carrying the weapon. . . . A federal grand jury indicted respondent on one count of knowing possession of a firearm at a school zone, in violation of 922(q). Respondent moved to dismiss[15] his federal indictment on the ground that 922(q) "is unconstitutional as it is beyond the power of Congress to legislate control over our public schools." . . .

The Government's essential contention . . . is that . . . 922(q) is valid because possession of a firearm in a local school zone does indeed substantially affect interstate commerce. The Government argues that possession of a firearm in a school zone may result in violent crime and that violent crime can be expected to affect the functioning of the national economy in two ways. First, the costs of violent crime are substantial, and . . . those costs are spread throughout the population. Second, violent crime reduces the willingness of individuals to travel to areas within the country that are perceived to be unsafe. The Government also argues that the presence of guns in schools poses a substantial threat to the educational process by threatening the learning environment. A handicapped educational process, in turn, will result in a less productive citizenry. That, in turn, would have an adverse affect on the Nation's economic well-being. As a result, the Government argues that Congress could rationally have concluded that 922(q) substantially affects interstate commerce. We pause to consider the implications of the Government's arguments. The Government admits, under its "costs of crime" reasoning, that Congress could regulate not only all

---

[13] The *Chief Justice* is the presiding Justice of the United States Supreme Court.

[14] A *respondent* is the party against whom a law suit or appeal is filed.

[15] A *Motion to Dismiss* is filed by a defendant or respondent and asks the court to terminate the case.

violent crime, but all activities that might lead to violent crime, regardless of how tenuously they relate to interstate commerce. Similarly, under the Government's "national productivity" reasoning, Congress could regulate any activity that it found was related to the economic productivity of individual citizens.... Under the theories that the Government presents in support of 922(q), it is difficult to perceive any limitation on federal power, even in areas such as criminal law enforcement or education where States historically have been sovereign. Thus, if we were to accept the Government's arguments, we are hard-pressed to posit any activity by an individual that Congress is without power to regulate.

The Government's essential contention...is that...922(q) is valid because possession of a firearm in a local school zone does indeed substantially affect interstate commerce. The possession of a gun in a local school zone is in no sense an economic activity that might, through repetition elsewhere, substantially affect any sort of interstate commerce. Respondent was a local student at a local school; there was no indication that he had recently moved in interstate commerce, and there is no requirement that his possession of the firearm have any concrete tie to interstate commerce....

To uphold the Government's contentions here, we would have to...convert Congressional authority under the Commerce Clause to a general police power of the sort retained by the States. Admittedly, some of our prior cases have taken long steps down that road, giving great deference to congressional action. The broad language in these opinions has suggested the possibility of additional expansion, but we decline here to proceed any further. To do so would require us to conclude that the Constitution's enumeration of powers does not presuppose something not enumerated and that there never will be a distinction between what is truly national and what is truly local. This we are unwilling to do.

Affirmed.

The *Lopez* Court held that Congress exceeded its constitutional authority under the commerce clause when it passed the Gun-Free School Zones Act because gun possession was not a commercial activity and did not affect interstate commerce. Consequently, if the American people wanted gun possession near schools to be criminalized, each state, individually, had to enact its own law. Some states did so; many did not.

The Power to Establish Naturalization Laws

Congress has the exclusive power to establish a *"uniform Rule of Naturalization." Naturalization* is the process by which a citizen of one country becomes a citizen of another country. Consequently, only the federal government can create *naturalization laws* because states do not have the sovereign authority to grant or deny American citizenship to citizens of foreign nations.

The Power to Establish Bankruptcy Laws

Congress has the exclusive power to establish *"uniform laws on the subject of bankruptcies throughout the United States."* A *bankrupt* is a person or business that cannot pay its debts. *Bankruptcy laws* provide the legal procedures by which the bankrupt's assets are distributed to its creditors. The bankruptcy procedures provide creditors with repayment of some of the debts owed to them, while also relieving the bankrupt of some of its debt obligations.

The Power to Coin Money and Develop Standards for Weights and Measures

Congress has the exclusive authority *"To coin Money . . . and fix the Standard of Weights and Measures"* that apply throughout the nation. The power to coin money refers to Congress's authority to create and regulate the national monetary system. The power *to fix the standard of weights and measures* refers to Congress's authority to establish uniform units of time, distance, weights, and measurement. The United States currency is based on the dollar; the entire nation is divided into nine time zones; distance is measured by miles; weight is measured by pounds.

The Power to Protect Intellectual Property

Congress has the power *"To promote the Progress of Science and useful Art, by securing for limited Times to authors and Inventors the exclusive Right to their respective Writings and Discoveries."* To exercise this power, Congress has enacted *patent, copyright,* and *trademark* laws. A patent grants to the patent holder the sole right to control the manufacture or sale of the patent holder's art, machinery, composition, or invention. A copyright grants an author the exclusive right to reproduce, publish, sell, or transfer his or her creative works such as books, magazines, newspapers, music, plays, paintings, sculptures, maps, motion pictures, and sound recordings. A trademark is a word, name, symbol, or phrase that identifies commercial products and professional services for the purpose of distinguishing them from other similar products and services.

The Power to Establish a Federal Court System

Congress has the authority *"To constitute Tribunals inferior to the supreme Court."* Although Article I grants Congress the authority develop the federal court system, Article III establishes the United States Supreme Court. Consequently, Congress has no authority to create or dissolve the Supreme Court.

Military Power

Congress has the powers *"To declare War ... raise and support Armies ... provide and maintain a Navy."* The nation's military power is shared by Congress and the President. Congress has the sole power to make a formal declaration of war and to authorize funding for the nation's military forces. The President, however, as *Commander in Chief* of the armed forces, has the sole power to command the military and send the nation's military forces into combat.

The Power to Command the Militia

Congress has the powers to authorize *"the Militia to execute the Laws of the Union, suppress Insurrection and repel Invasions ... reserving to the States respectively, the Appointment of the Officers, and the Authority of training the Militia according to the discipline prescribed by Congress."* Every state has a volunteer *militia* (military force), called the *National Guard*. National Guard units primarily assist states in maintaining order during weather-related emergencies, criminal disruptions, and civil disputes. Ordinarily, each state's National Guard is under the command of the state's Governor, but Article II also grants the President the power to *call-up* (order) a state's National Guard into federal service when necessary.

The Power to Make All Laws Necessary and Proper to Execute Congress's Enumerated Powers

The last clause of Section 8 grants Congress the power *"To make Laws which shall be necessary and proper for carrying into Execution the foregoing Powers, and all other Powers vested by this Constitution in the Government of the United States, or any Department or Officer thereof."* The *necessary and proper clause* is the basis for Congress's *implied powers*. Although not explicitly listed in the Constitution, implied powers are considered essential for Congress to perform its enumerated powers. For example, the enumerated power to borrow money implies the necessary power to establish a federal financial system to regulate monetary policies; similarly, the enumerated power to tax implies the necessary power to establish a regulatory system to collect taxes.

The first Supreme Court case to *construe* (interpret) the meaning of the necessary and proper clause was _McCulloch v. Maryland,_ decided in 1819. In

1816, Congress established the Second Bank of the United States to collect and distribute money among the states. Many states opposed the Second Bank for violating their sovereignty and being unnecessarily competitive with their own banks. The State of Maryland attempted to frustrate the Second Bank's success by taxing its operations within its borders. When the Second Bank's cashier, James McCulloch, refused to pay the Maryland tax, Maryland sued McCulloch in a Maryland state court. Maryland based its opposition to the Second Bank on the Tenth Amendment, which states, ***"The powers not delegated to the United States by the Constitution, nor prohibited by it to the States, are reserved to the States respectively, or to the people."*** Not surprisingly, the Maryland state court ruled in Maryland's favor, finding that the Tenth Amendment confined Congress's authority to powers specifically enumerated in the Constitution. The Supreme Court reversed, holding that the necessary and proper clause granted Congress the implied power to enact laws that were necessary to carry out its enumerated powers. Since the Constitution expressly granted Congress the power to impose taxes on the states, the Court reasoned that the Constitution also granted Congress the implied power to create a bank to carry out its taxing power. Excerpts from the opinion follow:

McCulloch v. Maryland
17 U.S. 316 (1819)

Chief Justice Marshall delivered the opinion of the Court.

The first question made in the cause is—has congress power to incorporate a bank?....

This government is acknowledged by all, to be one of enumerated powers.... Among the enumerated powers, we do not find that of establishing a bank.... But there is no phrase in the [Constitution] which... excludes incidental or implied powers; and which requires that [every power]... granted shall be expressly and minutely described....

Although, among the enumerated powers of government, we do not find the word "bank"... we find the great powers to lay and collect taxes; to borrow money; to regulate commerce; to declare and conduct a war; and to raise and support armies and navies. The sword and the purse... are entrusted to the government.... A government entrusted with such ample powers... must also be entrusted with ample means for their execution.... Throughout this vast republic... from the Atlantic to the Pacific, revenue is to be collected and expended, armies are to be marched and supported. The exigencies of the nation may require that the treasure raised in the north should be transported to the south, that raised in the east conveyed to the west....

To its enumeration of powers is added that of making "all laws which shall be necessary and proper for carrying into execution the foregoing powers and all other powers vested by the constitution in the government of the United States, or in any department thereof." . . .

Take, for example, the power "to establish post offices and post roads." . . . [F]rom this has been inferred the power and duty of carrying the mail along the post-road, from one post-office to another. And from this implied power, has again been inferred the right to punish those who steal letters from the post-office, or rob the mail. It may be said . . . that the right to carry the mail, and to punish those who rob it, is not indispensably necessary to the establishment of a post-office and post-road. This right is indeed essential to the beneficial exercise of the power, but not indispensably necessary to its existence. . . .

The [necessary and proper clause] is placed among the powers of congress, not among the limitations on those powers . . . Its terms purport to enlarge, not to diminish the powers vested in the government. It purports to be an additional power, not a restriction on those already granted. . . .

It being the opinion of the Court that the act incorporating the bank is constitutional, and that the power of establishing a branch in the State of Maryland might be properly exercised by the bank itself, we proceed to inquire: Whether the State of Maryland may, without violating the Constitution, tax that branch? . . .

On this ground, the counsel for the bank place its claim to be exempted from the power of a State to tax its operations. There is no express provision [in the Constitution] for the case, but the claim has been sustained on a principle which so entirely pervades the Constitution . . . as to be incapable of being separated from it without rending it into shreds.

This great principle is that the Constitution and the laws made in pursuance thereof are supreme; that they control the Constitution and laws of the respective States, and cannot be controlled by them. . . . That the power of taxing it [the Bank] by the States may be exercised so as to destroy it [the Bank] is too obvious to be denied. . . . [T]he power to tax involves the power to destroy. . . .

We admit . . . that the powers of the government are limited, and that its limitations are not to be transcended. But we think the sound construction of the constitution must allow to the national legislature that discretion . . . to perform the high duties assigned to it, in the manner most beneficial to the people. Let the end be legitimate, let it be within the scope of the constitution, and all means which are appropriate, which are plainly adopted to that end, which are not prohibited, but consistent with the letter and spirit of the constitution, are constitutional. . . .

[If the states may tax the Bank] they may tax the mail; they may tax the mint; they may tax patent-rights; they may tax the papers of the custom-house; they may tax judicial process; they may tax all the means employed by the government, to an excess which would defeat all the ends of government. This was not intended by the American people. They did not design to make their government dependent on the states.

The court has bestowed on this subject its most deliberate consideration. The result is a conviction that the states have no power, by taxation or otherwise, to retard, impede, burden, or in any manner control, the operations of the constitutional laws enacted by congress to carry into execution the powers vested in the general [federal] government. This is, we think, the unavoidable consequence of that supremacy which the constitution has declared. We are unanimously of opinion, that the law passed by the legislature of Maryland, imposing a tax on the Bank of the United States, is unconstitutional and void.

It is the opinion of this court, that the act of the legislature of Maryland is contrary to the constitution of the United States, and void.... It is, therefore ... reversed.[16]

McCulloch's ruling that Maryland's tax on the Second Bank, not the federal government's creation of the Bank, violated the Constitution was based on the Court's _construction_ (interpretation) of the necessary and proper clause as allowing Congress to exercise implied powers that the Constitution did not expressly enumerate. As a consequence, _McCulloch_ substantially expanded congressional power.

Article I Section 9: Limitations on Congressional Powers

The Migration or Importation of Such Persons as any of the States now existing shall think proper to admit, shall not be prohibited by the Congress prior to the Year one thousand eight hundred and eight, but a Tax or duty may be imposed on such Importation, not exceeding ten dollars for each person.

The privilege of the Writ of Habeas Corpus shall not be suspended, unless when in Cases of Rebellion or Invasion the public Safety may require it.

No Bill of Attainder or ex post facto Law shall be passed.

No Capitation, or other direct, Tax shall be laid, unless in Proportion to the Census or Enumeration herein before directed to be taken.

No Tax or Duty shall be laid on Articles exported from any State.

---

[16] _Reversed_ means that the higher court has rejected the opinion of the lower court.

No Preference shall be given by any Regulation of Commerce or Revenue to the Ports of one State over those of another: nor shall Vessels bound to, or from, one State be obliged to enter, clear, or pay Duties in another.

No money shall be drawn from the Treasury, but in Consequence of Appropriations made by Law; and a regular Statement and Account of the Receipts and Expenditures of all public Money shall be published from time to time.

No Title of Nobility shall be granted by the United States: And no Person holding any Office of Profit or Trust under them, shall, without the Consent of the Congress, accept of any present, Emolument, Office, or Title, of any kind whatever, from any King, Prince, or foreign State.

Section 9 sets forth specific limitations on congressional powers. For example, the provision that *"Importation of Such Persons as any of the States now existing shall think proper to admit, shall not be prohibited by the Congress prior to the Year one thousand eight hundred and eight"* granted states the authority to import slaves until 1807, after which it granted Congress the sole authority to prohibit further importations. Section 9 also grants prisoners *"the privilege of the Writ of Habeas Corpus"* by which they can challenge their imprisonment and be released if a court determines their custody to be unlawful. Under the *suspension clause,* Section 9 also prohibits Congress from cancelling the writ of habeas corpus privilege except in the extraordinary circumstances of rebellion or invasion. Notwithstanding the suspension clause's limitations on Congress's power, President Abraham Lincoln suspended the writ of habeas corpus at the beginning of the *Civil War,* which was fought between the northern and southern states over the legality of slavery. Despite the Supreme Court's objection, President Lincoln continued the suspension of habeas corpus writs to prevent captured southern soldiers from reuniting with their military forces to continue fighting against the northern forces.

By the President of the United States of America: A Proclamation

That the Writ of Habeas Corpus is suspended in respect to all persons arrested, or who are now, or hereafter during the rebellion shall be, imprisoned in any fort, camp, arsenal, military prison, or other place of confinement by any military authority or by the sentence of any Court Martial or Military Commission

Section 9 also prohibits Congress from passing a *"Bill of Attainder or ex post facto Law."* A *bill of attainder* is a law that punishes a person for a crime without a trial. An *ex post facto law* criminalizes conduct that was legal when committed, or increases the *sentence* (punishment) for a crime after it was committed. For example, in recent years the state and federal governments have passed criminal sex offender laws requiring that persons *convicted* (found guilty) of sexually molesting children undergo psychiatric evaluations before being released from prison. If the evaluation determines that the sex offender continues to suffer from the same mental disorder that caused him to offend in the past, the state can commit him to a mental institution until he is cured. Some offenders have challenged these statutes as ex post facto laws, arguing that they indefinitely extend their detentions beyond their criminal sentences. The Supreme Court has rejected this argument on the *grounds* (the legal basis for a criminal accusation) that post sentence detention of child molesters for medical treatment is not punishment as long as the person is still suffering from the same mental disorder that caused him to molest children in the past.

Other Section 9 limitations on Congressional powers include prohibitions against taxing states disproportionately, passing laws that favor one state over another, taxing goods exported between the states, spending money except as specified by legislation passed for that purpose, and granting titles of nobility, such as King or Prince.

Article I Section 10: Limitations on State Powers

> *No State shall enter into any Treaty, Alliance, or Confederation; grant Letter of Marque and Reprisal; coin Money; emit Bills of Credit; make any Thing but gold and silver Coin a Tender in Payment of Debts; pass any Bill of Attainder, ex post facto Law, or Law impairing the Obligations of Contracts, or grant any Title of Nobility.*
>
> *No State shall, without the Consent of the Congress, lay any Imposts or Duties on Imports or Exports, except what may be absolutely necessary for executing its inspection Laws: and the net Produce of all Duties and Imposts, laid by any State on Imports or Exports, shall be for the Use of the Treasury of the United States; and all such Laws shall be subject to the Revision and Control of the Congress.*
>
> *No State shall, without the Consent of Congress, lay any Duty of Tonnage, keep Troops, or Ships of War in time of Peace, enter into any Agreement or Compact with another State, or with a foreign Power, or engage in War, unless actually invaded, or in such imminent Danger as will not admit of delay.*

Section 10 specifies the sovereign powers that states relinquish to the federal government in order to join the nation. For example, states relinquish their sovereign powers to *"enter into any Treaty," "coin Money," "pass any Bill of Attainder, ex post facto Law,"* or *"grant any Title of Nobility."*

CHAPTER 2 QUESTIONS

1. **a.** Why did the United States Constitution divide the federal legislature into two chambers?
   b. What are the benefits of this government structure?
   c. What are the detriments of this government structure?

2. **a.** How are federal laws developed?
   b. Why must the identical bill be agreed to by both chambers of Congress?
   c. Why is compromise of greater value than efficiency in the development of American laws?
   d. What happens to a bill if it is vetoed by a President?

3. Why do you think members of Congress are immune from arrest and prosecution while participating in congressional matters?

4. A judicial *opinion* is a written explanation of a court's ruling that includes the court's analysis of the disputed facts, legal arguments, applicable law, and its decision. An opinion is formatted as follows: The title of the opinion is called the *caption*, which contains the names of the *parties* (participants in the lawsuit) to the lawsuit. The caption is followed by the *citation*, which sets forth the volume and page number of the *case reporter* (book) in which the opinion is published. The citation is followed by the name of the *judge* (presiding officer of a trial or legal proceeding) who wrote the opinion. The first section of the opinion contains the facts that caused the lawsuit. The second section of the opinion presents and analyzes the laws and *legal issues* (disputed versions of the law) that apply to the resolution of the lawsuit. At the end of the opinion, the court states its decision, called a *holding*. *Affirmed* means that the appellate court accepted the decision of the lower court. *Reversed* means that the appellate court rejected the decision of the lower court and ordered the case to be corrected based on its analysis.

   Based on this information, write a *case brief* (summary) of *Heart of Atlanta Motel v. United States* that answers the following questions:
   a. What is the case citation? What does it mean?
   b. Which party was the appellant? Which party was the appellee?
   c. What were the facts of the case?
   d. What was the legal issue the Supreme Court addressed?
   e. What laws did the Supreme Court apply to the legal issue?
   f. How did the Supreme Court analyze the laws it applied to the legal issue?
   g. What was the holding of *Heart of Atlanta*? Why did the Supreme Court reach that result?

    h. Which party won? Which party lost?

    i. How will the Supreme Court's holding affect similar issues in the future?

5. In *United States v. Lopez*, the Supreme Court held that Congress exceeded its commerce clause authority when it passed the Gun-Free School Zones Act.

    a. What was the respondent's argument?

    b. What was the Government's opposing argument?

    c. What were the Court's reasons for its holding?

6. **a.** How do you explain the different holdings in *Heart of Atlanta Motel* and *Lopez?*

    b. Based on these holdings, how does the commerce clause affect the relationship between intrastate and interstate commerce?

7. How does the necessary and proper clause affect congressional power?

8. In *McCulloch v. Maryland*, why did the Supreme Court hold that it was constitutional for Congress to create the Second Bank but unconstitutional for the State of Maryland to tax the Bank?

9. What limitations does Article I Section 9 place on congressional powers? Explain your answer.

10. What limitations does Article I Section 10 place on state powers? Explain your answer.

Article II: The Executive Branch

The White House, located in Washington, D.C.

Article II Section 1: The Office of the President and Vice President

The executive Power shall be vested in a President of the United States of America. He shall hold his Office during the Term of four years, and,

together with the Vice President, chosen for the same term, be elected, as
follows:

Article II Section 1 creates the office of the President and the Vice President,
who serve the same four-year term.[1] The President is primarily responsible for
managing domestic and foreign policies, the military, and the federal bureaucracy
that enforces federal laws and implements federal programs throughout the nation.

Despite the broad range of presidential powers, the President is only one leader
among many in the United States. Congressional members operate independently of
the President because most continue to be re-elected longer than any President's one
or two terms in office. Similarly, although the President nominates federal judges,
they too operate independently–once again because federal judges are appointed for
life and cannot be removed for ruling against a presidential policy. Consequently, in
dealing with the other branches of government, the real power of a President is to
persuade, not to command. Nonetheless, despite the limitations on presidential
authority, when a President speaks, the entire nation listens.

It is also important to understand that a President, like all other persons, is
not "above the law" when exercising presidential powers. Unlike monarchs and
dictators, a President must obey the same laws that everyone else must obey.
However, under the *doctrine of official immunity*, Presidents are protected from
private lawsuits and criminal prosecutions for official acts and policies no matter
how much criticism they receive. Official immunity, however, does not protect a
President from private suits related to private conduct. In 1994, Ms. Paula Jones
filed a private lawsuit against President Bill Clinton alleging that he had made
inappropriate sexual advances toward her while he was the Governor of Arkansas and she was an Arkansas state employee. In order to postpone the lawsuit,
President Clinton argued that the doctrine of official immunity prevented Jones
from suing him during his presidency. The Supreme Court disagreed. Here are
excerpts from the Supreme Court's opinion on that issue:

Clinton v. Jones
520 U.S. 681 (1997)

Justice Stevens delivered the opinion of the Court.

This case raises a constitutional . . . question concerning the Office
of the President of the United States. Respondent [Paula Jones], a private
citizen, seeks to recover damages from the current occupant of that office

---

[1] The Constitution originally did not limit the number of terms a President could serve. However,
after Franklin D. Roosevelt won his fourth presidential term in 1944, the nation passed the *Twenty-
Second Amendment* in 1950 to limit a President to two four-year terms in office.

based on actions allegedly taken before his term began. The President submits that in all but the most exceptional cases the Constitution requires federal courts to defer such litigation until his term ends and that, in any event, respect for the office warrants such a stay [postponement]. Despite the force of the arguments supporting the President's submissions, we conclude that they must be rejected.

Petitioner, William Jefferson Clinton, was elected to the Presidency in 1992, and re elected in 1996. His term of office expires on January 20, 2001. In 1991 he was the Governor of the State of Arkansas. Respondent, Paula Corbin Jones, is a resident of California. In 1991 she lived in Arkansas, and was an employee of the Arkansas Industrial Development Commission.

On May 6, 1994, she commenced this action in the United States District Court for the Eastern District of Arkansas by filing a complaint [the document that initiates a lawsuit] naming petitioner and Danny Ferguson, a former Arkansas State Police officer, as defendants [the accused party against whom the lawsuit is brought].... [The] allegations principally describe events that are said to have occurred on the afternoon of May 8, 1991, during an official conference held at the Excelsior Hotel in Little Rock, Arkansas. The Governor delivered a speech at the conference; respondent—working as a state employee—staffed the registration desk. She alleges that Ferguson persuaded her to leave her desk and to visit the Governor in a business suite at the hotel, where he made "abhorrent" sexual advances that she vehemently rejected. She further claims that her superiors at work subsequently dealt with her in a hostile and rude manner, and changed her duties to punish her for rejecting those advances. Finally, she alleges that after petitioner was elected President, Ferguson defamed her by making a statement to a reporter that implied she had accepted petitioner's alleged overtures, and that various persons authorized to speak for the President publicly branded her a liar by denying that the incident had occurred....

[It] is perfectly clear that the alleged misconduct of petitioner was unrelated to any of his official duties as President of the United States and, indeed, occurred before he was elected to that office.

In response to the complaint, petitioner promptly advised the District Court [the lowest level federal court] that he intended to file a motion to dismiss on grounds of Presidential immunity, and requested the court to defer all other pleadings [the first stage of a lawsuit in which the parties set forth their allegations and defenses] and motions [court processes] until after the immunity issue was resolved.... The District Judge denied [rejected] the motion to dismiss on immunity grounds and ruled that discovery [factual investigation] in the case could go forward, but ordered any trial stayed until the end of petitioner's Presidency.... Both parties appealed....

Petitioner's principal submission—that "in all but the most exceptional cases," the Constitution affords the President temporary immunity from civil damages litigation arising out of events that occurred before he took office–cannot be sustained on the basis of precedent [prior cases].

Only three sitting Presidents have been defendants in civil litigation involving their actions prior to taking office. Complaints against Theodore Roosevelt[2] and Harry Truman[3] had been dismissed before they took office.... Two companion cases arising out of an automobile accident were filed against John F. Kennedy[4] in 1960 during the Presidential campaign...and the matter was settled [resolved] out of court. Thus, none of those cases sheds any light on the constitutional issue before us.

The principal rationale for affording certain public servants immunity from suits for money damages [compensation] arising out of their official acts is inapplicable to unofficial conduct. In cases involving prosecutors, legislators, and judges we have repeatedly explained that the immunity serves the public interest in enabling such officials to perform their designated functions effectively without fear that a particular decision may give rise to personal liability. We explained in Ferri v. Ackerman, 444 U.S. 193 (1979):

> "As public servants, the prosecutor and the judge represent the interest of society as a whole. The conduct of their official duties may adversely affect a wide variety of different individuals, each of whom may be a potential source of future controversy. The societal interest in providing such public officials with the maximum ability to deal fearlessly and impartially with the public at large has long been recognized as an acceptable justification for official immunity. The point of immunity for such officials is to forestall an atmosphere of intimidation that would conflict with their resolve to perform their designated functions in a principled fashion."

This reasoning provides no support for immunity for unofficial conduct.... As our opinions have made clear, immunities are grounded in "the nature of the function performed, not the identity of the actor who performed it." Forrester v. White, 484 U.S. 219, 229 (1988)....

Petitioner's strongest argument supporting his immunity claim is based on the text and structure of the Constitution. He does not contend that the occupant of the Office of the President is "above the law," in the sense that his conduct is entirely immune from judicial scrutiny. The President argues

---

[2] Theodore Roosevelt was the 26th President, from 1901-1909.
[3] Harry Truman was the 33rd President, from 1945-1953.
[4] John F. Kennedy was the 35th President, from 1961-1963.

merely for a postponement of the judicial proceedings that will determine whether he violated any law....

As a starting premise, petitioner contends that he occupies a unique office with powers and responsibilities so vast and important that the public interest demands that he devote his undivided time and attention to his public duties. He submits that—given the nature of the office—the doctrine of separation of powers places limits on the authority of the Federal Judiciary to interfere with the Executive Branch that would be transgressed by allowing this action to proceed.

We have no dispute with the initial premise of the argument. Former presidents, from George Washington to George Bush, have consistently endorsed petitioner's characterization of the office. After serving his term, Lyndon Johnson observed: "Of all the 1,886 nights I was President, there were not many when I got to sleep before 1 or 2 a.m., and there were few mornings when I didn't wake up by 6 or 6:30."... As Justice Jackson has pointed out, the Presidency concentrates executive authority "in a single head in whose choice the whole Nation has a part, making him the focus of public hopes and expectations. In drama, magnitude and finality his decisions so far overshadow any others that almost alone he fills the public eye and ear." Youngstown Sheet & Tube Co. v. Sawyer, 343 U.S. 579, 653 (1952). We have, in short, long recognized the "unique position in the constitutional scheme" that this office occupies....

As a factual matter, petitioner contends that this particular case ... may impose an unacceptable burden on the President's time and energy, and thereby impair the effective performance of his office....

First, we have long held that when the President takes official action, the Court has the authority to determine whether he has acted within the law. Perhaps the most dramatic example of such a case is our holding that President Truman exceeded his constitutional authority when he issued an order directing the Secretary of Commerce to take possession of and operate most of the Nation's steel mills in order to avert a national catastrophe. Youngstown Sheet & Tube Co. v. Sawyer, 343 U.S. 579 (1952)....

Second, it is also settled that the President is subject to judicial process in appropriate circumstances.... Chief Justice Marshall, when presiding in the treason trial of Aaron Burr, ruled that a subpoena duces tecum [a court order commanding a person to produce documents] could be directed to the President. United States v. Burr, 25 F. Cas. 30 (No. 14,692d) (CC Va. 1807). We unequivocally and emphatically endorsed Marshall's position when we held that President Nixon was obligated to comply with a subpoena commanding him to produce certain tape recordings of his conversations with his aides. United States v. Nixon, 418 U.S. 683 (1974)....

Sitting [current] Presidents have responded to court orders to provide testimony and other information with sufficient frequency that such interactions between the Judicial and Executive Branches can scarcely be thought a novelty. President Monroe[5] responded to written interrogatories [lawsuit questions], President Nixon[6]—as noted above—produced tapes in response to a subpoena duces tecum, President Ford[7] complied with an order to give a deposition [oral questioning] in a criminal trial, <u>United States v. Fromme</u>, 405 F. Supp. 578 (ED Cal. 1975), and President Clinton[8] has twice given videotaped testimony in criminal proceedings, see <u>United States v. McDougal</u>, 934 F. Supp. 296 (ED Ark. 1996); <u>United States v. Branscum</u>, No. LRP-CR-96-49 (ED Ark., June 7, 1996). Moreover, sitting Presidents have also voluntarily complied with judicial requests for testimony [answers to questions made under oath in a judicial proceeding]. President Grant[9] gave a lengthy deposition in a criminal case under such circumstances and President Carter[10] similarly gave videotaped testimony for use at a criminal trial. . . .

We add a final comment on two matters that are discussed at length in the briefs: the risk that our decision will generate a large volume of politically motivated harassing and frivolous litigation, and the danger that national security concerns might prevent the President from explaining a legitimate need for a continuance.

We are not persuaded that either of these risks is serious. Most frivolous and vexatious litigation is terminated at the pleading stage or on summary judgment [before trial], with little if any personal involvement by the defendant. Moreover, the availability of sanctions [penalties] provides a significant deterrent to litigation [lawsuits] directed at the President in his unofficial capacity for purposes of political gain or harassment. History indicates that the likelihood that a significant number of such cases will be filed is remote. Although scheduling problems may arise, there is no reason to assume that the District Courts will be either unable to accommodate the President's needs or unfaithful to the tradition—especially in matters involving national security–of giving "the utmost deference to Presidential responsibilities." . . .

The Federal District Court has jurisdiction [authority] to decide this case. Like every other citizen who properly invokes that jurisdiction, respondent has a right to an orderly disposition of her claims. Accordingly, the judgment of the Court of Appeals is affirmed.

---

[5] President Monroe was the 5th President, from 1817-1825.
[6] President Nixon was the 37th President, from 1969-1974.
[7] President Ford was the 38th President, from 1974-1977.
[8] President Clinton was the 42nd President, from 1993 -2001.
[9] President Grant was the 18th President, from 1869-1877.
[10] President Carter was the 39th President, from 1977-1981.

As a result of this ruling, President Clinton was required to defend against Ms. Jones's lawsuit. He eventually prevailed after the court found that Jones lacked sufficient evidence to prove her accusations and dismissed the case. In the course of the proceedings, however, Clinton had given testimony that was later found to be false and which eventually led to his impeachment.

Many Presidents have expressed highly conflicting feelings about their presidencies. While they appreciate their extraordinary power and authority, they soon became aware of the limitations and burdens imposed on them by their opponents. Thomas Jefferson[11] described his presidency as "a place of splendid misery." John Quincy Adams[12] described his presidency as "the four most miserable years of my life." Woodrow Wilson[13] stated that during his presidency he "never knew such loneliness and desolation of heart was possible." John F. Kennedy[14] stated, "When I ran for the presidency . . . I knew the country faced serious challenges, but I did not realize—nor could any man who does not bear the burden of this office—how heavy and constant would be those burdens." Similarly, Lyndon B. Johnson[15] stated, "No one can experience with the President of the United States the glory and the agony of his office." And Bill Clinton[16] satirically characterized the White House as "the crown jewel of the federal penal system."

Despite presidential concerns about opposition to and frustration of their powers, many Presidents have used their powers very successfully. Thomas Jefferson doubled the size of the nation by acquiring the "Louisiana Purchase" from France for $15 million. After the northern and southern states commenced the Civil War, Abraham Lincoln[17] ended slavery throughout the nation by issuing the Emancipation Proclamation, which stated, "I do order and declare that all persons held as slaves . . . are, and henceforward shall be free." Theodore Roosevelt[18] fought against high levels of corruption in the railroad and oil industries and created federal preservation sites for over 125 million acres of national forests. Woodrow Wilson ended American isolationism from foreign nations and led the country through World War I. Franklin Roosevelt[19] led the nation through World War II and ended the Great Depression during the 1930s by creating numerous federal programs that increased jobs and improved the economy. George W. Bush[20] developed the Department of Homeland Security

---

[11] Thomas Jefferson was the 3rd President from 1801-1809.

[12] John Quincy Adams was the 6th President from 1825-1829.

[13] Woodrow Wilson was the 28th President from 1913-1921.

[14] John F. Kennedy was the 35th President from 1961 to 1963.

[15] Lyndon B. Johnson was the 36th President from 1963-1969.

[16] Bill Clinton was the 42nd President from 1993-2001.

[17] Abraham Lincoln was the 16th President, from 1861-1865.

[18] Theodore Roosevelt was the 26th President, from 1901-1909.

[19] Franklin Roosevelt was the 32nd President, from 1933-1945.

[20] George W. Bush was the 43rd President, from 2001-2009.

Five Presidents of the United States: George H.W. Bush, Barack Obama, George W. Bush, Bill Clinton, and Jimmy Carter in the Oval Office of the White House on January 7, 2009

to protect America from terrorism. And Barack Obama[21] successfully prevailed over constant opposition to enact the Affordable Care Act that provides medical insurance for people throughout the nation.

The Electoral College

Each State shall appoint, in such Manner as the Legislature thereof may direct, a Number of Electors, equal to the whole Number of Senators and Representatives to which the State may be entitled in the Congress: but no Senator or Representative, or Person holding an Office of Trust or Profit under the United States, shall be appointed an Elector.

~~The Electors shall meet in their respective States, and vote by Ballot for two Persons, of whom one at least shall not be an Inhabitant with the same State with themselves. And they shall make a List of all the Persons voted for, and of the Number of Votes for each; which List they shall sign and certify,~~

---

[21] Barack Obama was the 44th President, from 2009-2017.

~~and transmit sealed to the Seat of the Government of the United States,~~
~~directed to the President of the Senate. The President of the Senate shall, in~~
~~the Presence of the Senate and the House of Representatives, open all the~~
~~Certificates, and the Votes shall then be counted. The Person having the~~
~~greatest Number of Votes shall be the President, if such Number be a Majority~~
~~of the whole Number of Electors appointed; and if there be more than one who~~
~~have such Majority, and have an equal number of Votes, then the~~

~~House of Representatives shall immediately choose by Ballot one of~~
~~them for President; and if no Person have a majority, then from the five~~
~~highest on the List the said House shall in like Manner chuse the President.~~
~~But in choosing the President, the Votes shall be taken by States—the~~
~~Representation from each State having one Vote; A quorum for this Purpose~~
~~shall consist of a Member or Members from two thirds of the States, and a~~
~~Majority of all the States shall be necessary to a Choice. In every Case, after~~
~~the Choice of the President, the Person having the greatest Number of Votes of~~
~~the Electors shall be the Vice President. But if there should remain two or~~
~~more who have equal Votes the Senate shall chuse from them by Ballot the~~
~~Vice President.~~[22]

The Congress may determine the Time of chusing the Electors, and the
Day on which they shall give their Votes; which Day shall be the same
throughout the United States.

The method of electing the President is unique to the American political system. The Founding Fathers believed that the people who lived throughout the 13 states would not have access to sufficient information to make informed choices about presidential candidates. They also believed that allowing the people to directly elect a President could result in mob rule. To avoid these problems the Founding Fathers developed the *Electoral College* system by which the President and Vice President were elected directly by *"Electors"* (members of the Electoral College) and only indirectly by the people.

The total number of electors throughout the nation and the total number of electoral votes is currently 538. Each state has the same number of electors as it has Senators and Representatives in Congress.[23] In November of every fourth

---

[22] Originally, Article II Section 1 provided that electors could vote only for a presidential, but not a vice presidential, candidate. Consequently, the presidential candidate who received the most electoral votes became the President, and the candidate who received the second highest number of electoral votes became the Vice President. In 1800, because candidates Thomas Jefferson and Aaron Burr received the same number of electoral votes, the House of Representatives was required to choose the next President. To avoid the reoccurrence of another presidential voting tie, in 1804, the *Twelfth Amendment* was passed requiring each elector to cast separate votes for the presidential and vice presidential candidates. The *Twentieth Amendment*, passed in 1933, changed the starting dates for presidential and vice presidential terms of office from March 4th to January 20th.

[23] The total of 538 electors is based on the 435 members of the House of Representatives, 100 Senators, and 3 electors from the District of Columbia.

year, when citizens cast their votes for a presidential candidate, they are actually casting their votes for the elector who is required to vote for that specific candidate. In December, the electors who win the majority of popular votes meet in their state capitols and cast their votes for the specified presidential candidate. In January, both chambers of Congress meet to count the electoral votes, after which the winner of the presidential election is officially announced. However, since most electors are pledged to vote for a specific candidate, the country actually knows who won the presidency the day after the November election.

In order to win a presidential election, a candidate must receive more than half (270) of the 538 electoral votes. Most states use a "winner-take-all" electoral system by which the candidate who receives the most popular votes wins *all* of that state's electoral votes. For example, assume that in New York 49 percent of the popular votes are cast for Candidate X and 51 percent are cast for Candidate Y. Because New York has 33 electoral votes, Candidate Y will take *all* of New York's 33 electoral votes, not just the 51 percent that Candidate Y won. In 1992, Bill Clinton received *all* of New York's 33 electoral votes, although he won just 49.7 percent of that state's popular votes.

The winner-take-all system means that, sometimes, the candidate who wins the most popular votes does not also win the presidency. This has happened four times, most recently in 2000 when presidential candidate Al Gore won 500,000 more popular votes than candidate George W. Bush, but candidate Bush won the majority of electoral votes necessary to win the election. Although such results have led to criticism of the Electoral College, the system continues to be used, in part because it encourages presidential candidates to campaign throughout the nation rather than focus exclusively on the most highly populated states and, in part because constitutional amendments are very difficult to pass.

America's presidential elections are run by the nation's primary political parties—Republicans and Democrats. Other political parties, called *third parties*, frequently develop as well, but if their ideas gain popularity, they are usually adopted by one of the two major parties. Although Americans need not become formal members of a specific political party, many prefer one party over the other. Generally, the Democratic and Republican parties stand for different principles, programs, and policies involving the powers of the federal government, the powers of the state governments, international issues, and the rights and responsibilities of individuals. These principles, however, change over time, and it is not rare for one party to assume the principles of the other.

Generally speaking, Republicans believe the federal government should exercise substantial power over military, national defense, and criminal matters but otherwise limit its authority over people and businesses, fiscal spending, and taxation. Many Republicans also believe that private businesses perform better than government programs and that social welfare programs should be limited to prevent people from becoming dependent on government aid and losing their motivation to be financially self-sufficient. Very conservative Republicans strongly support unregulated financial contributions to political candidates, capital punishment, gun ownership, and believe that Christian prayer should be permitted in public schools but sex education should not; many oppose contraception, abortion, and all welfare programs; and many believe the government should uphold social customs such as traditional families, religions, and gender roles.

Democrats believe, generally, that the federal government should exercise sufficient power to promote social equality among people and develop programs to improve people's well-being, especially the well-being of the most disadvantaged people. Democrats typically support reproductive responsibility and government insurance of medical care but oppose capital punishment, gun ownership, and prayers in school and government events because they believe the government should not impose religious beliefs on the people. Very liberal Democrats typically believe that the government should redistribute wealth to support social programs; provide jobs for the unemployed, amnesty to illegal immigrants, and legalization of marijuana; many also believe that military intervention promotes, rather than inhibits, international terrorism.

Party politics, however, frequently prevail over party principles. For example, Democratic President Clinton reduced government spending and balanced the federal budget in 2000. Once elected, his successor, Republican George W. Bush, increased the national debt by borrowing and spending more money than had any prior President. Consequently, during the 2008 presidential campaign, the Democratic candidates argued for fiscal conservatism to reduce government spending on the Iraq War while the Republican candidates argued for increased government spending to support the war.

Presidential Qualifications

No person except a natural born Citizen, or a Citizen of the United States, at the time of the Adoption of this Constitution, shall be eligible to the Office of President; neither shall any Person be eligible to that Office who shall not have attained to the Age of thirty five Years, and been fourteen Years a Resident within the United States.

The President must be *"a natural born Citizen"* of the United States who is at least 35 years of age and has resided in the United States for at least 14 years.

Removal and Succession of the President

In case of the removal of the President from Office, or of his Death, Resignation or Inability to discharge the Powers and Duties of the said Office, the Same shall devolve on the Vice President, and the Congress may by Law provide for the Case of Removal, Death, Resignation or Inability, both of the

~~President and Vice President, declaring what Officer shall then act as President, and such Officer shall act accordingly, until the disability be removed, or a President shall be elected.~~

This provision originally provided that if the President died, resigned, or was removed from office the Vice President was to assume presidential duties, but not the presidential office.

Nonetheless, nine Vice Presidents were sworn into office as President after the death or resignation of the sitting President.[24] Consequently, this provision was replaced in 1967 by the *Twenty-Fifth Amendment,* which provides: *"**In the case of the removal of the President from office or his death or resignation, the Vice President shall become President.**"* The Twenty-Fifth Amendment also designates the Vice President as one of several officials who decides if a President must be temporarily relieved from responsibilities due to a disability, and authorizes the Vice President to *"**immediately assume the powers and duties of the office as Acting President**"* until the President is able to return to office. This provision is typically invoked when a President undergoes surgery that requires anesthesia.

Although the Vice President is thought to be only "one heartbeat away from the presidency," the Constitution says little else about the vice presidential office.[25] The first Vice President, John Adams, provided this characterization of his office: "I am the Vice President. In this I am nothing, but I may be everything." Similarly, Alben Barkley, President Harry Truman's Vice President, characterized his office by telling the story of a woman who had two sons: "One son went to sea and the other son became the Vice President, and neither of them was ever heard from again."

Since the Constitution says so little about the role of the Vice President, vice presidential duties are determined by the President. Some Presidents delegate significant responsibilities to their Vice President; others do not. One major benefit of the vice presidency is that frequently the sitting Vice President is chosen to be the next presidential candidate. To date, 25 Vice Presidents have become presidential candidates of whom 14 were elected to the presidency[26] and 11 were defeated.[27]

---

[24] John Tyler, Millard Fillmore, Andrew Johnson, Chester A. Arthur, Theodore Roosevelt, Calvin Coolidge, Harry S. Truman, and Lyndon B. Johnson each became President upon the death of his predecessor. Gerald R. Ford became President after Richard Nixon resigned.

[25] One other provision of the Constitution, Article I Section 3, provides that the Vice President *"shall be President of the Senate, but shall have no Vote, unless they be evenly divided."*

[26] John Adams, Thomas Jefferson, Martin Van Buren, John Tyler, Millard Fillmore, Andrew Johnson, Chester A. Arthur, Theodore Roosevelt, Calvin Coolidge, Harry S. Truman, Lyndon B. Johnson, Richard Nixon, Gerald Ford, and George H.W. Bush

[27] Henry A. Wallace, Millard Fillmore, John C. Breckinridge, Richard Nixon, Hubert Humphrey, Walter Mondale, and Al Gore. Presidents John Adams, Martin Van Buren, Theodore Roosevelt, and George H.W. Bush were defeated when they ran for a second term of office.

Presidential Compensation

> *The President shall, at stated Times, receive for his Services, a Compensation, which shall neither be increased nor diminished during the Period for which he shall have been elected, and he shall not receive within that Period any other Emolument from the United States, or any of them.*

Congress determines the President's salary which, once set, cannot be increased or decreased during that President's term in office. The first presidential salary was $25,000. The current presidential salary is $400,000. In addition to salary, presidential compensation includes residence in the White House, health care, and a lifetime pension.

Presidential Oath of Office

> *Before he enter on the Execution of his Office, he shall take the following Oath or Affirmation:—"I do solemnly swear (or affirm) that I will faithfully execute the Office of President of the United States, and will to the best of my Ability, preserve, protect and defend the Constitution of the United States."*

The President publicly takes the *Presidential Oath of Office* at an *Inauguration Ceremony* on the steps of the United States Capitol Building.

Article II Section 2: Presidential Powers

> *The President shall be Commander in Chief of the Army and Navy of the United States, and of the Militia of the several States, when called into the actual Service of the United States;*

One of the President's primary powers, as a civilian, is to be the **"***Commander in Chief***"** of the nation's military that consists of the Army, Navy, Marine Corps, and Air Force. Although the Constitution grants Congress the power to declare war and the President the power to command the military, the President's war power is greater. Congress has formally declared war 11 times,[28] while Presidents have committed America's armed forces to more than 200 "undeclared wars" without the formal consent of Congress. The most recent "undeclared wars" have

---

[28] Declaration of War with Great Britain, 1812; Declaration of War with Mexico, 1846; Declaration of War with Spain, 1898; Declaration of War with Germany, 1917; Declaration of War with Austria-Hungary, 1917; Declaration of War with Japan, 1941; Declaration of War with Germany, 1941; Declaration of War with Italy, 1941; Declaration of War with Bulgaria, 1942; Declaration of War with Hungary, 1942; Declaration of War with Rumania, 1942.

Barack Obama took the Presidential Oath of Office as the 44th President of the United States, accompanied by his wife, Michelle Obama, on January 20, 2009. Chief Justice John Roberts administered the Presidential Oath.

included the conflicts in Korea (1950-1953), Vietnam (1965-1973), Iraq I (1990-1991), Haiti (1994), the Balkans (1995 and 1999), Serbia (1999), Iraq II (2003-2011), and Afghanistan (2001-2014). Even if Congress disagrees with a President's military decisions, it is not likely to withhold funding from the military when the nation's interests are threatened or the lives and safety of American soldiers are at stake. For example, in 1907, without informing Congress, President Theodore Roosevelt sent 16 battleships halfway around the world to demonstrate the size and strength of the United States Navy. When Congress objected to funding the return of the ships, Roosevelt's response was, "Very well, the existing appropriation will carry the Navy halfway around the world and if Congress chooses to leave it on the other side, all right."

The President is also the Commander in Chief of every state's *"Militia"*, now called the National Guard. Under normal circumstances, the Governors of each state are the commanders of their state's National Guard. However, Article II Section 2 also gives the President the authority to command each state's National Guard when necessary to enforce federal laws or assist with the national defense. Presidents have ordered state National Guards into federal service during World War II, the Korean and Vietnam Wars, and the two Iraq Wars. Presidents have also ordered state National Guard units to enforce federal laws that were being violated by state governments. For example, in 1963, President Kennedy ordered Alabama's National Guard to protect black students as they enrolled in classes at the University of Alabama against the orders of Alabama's Governor George Wallace. Governor Wallace was a *segregationist* (racial separatist) who promised his state "segregation now, segregation tomorrow, segregation forever." As a segregationist, he opposed equal treatment of racial minorities and had publicly announced that no black student would ever attend the University of Alabama. On the first day of classes, Governor Wallace stood in the university's entrance and ordered the Alabama National Guard to physically block black students from entering the school. However, once the National Guard received President Kennedy's order to protect the students, its *General* (military officer) ordered Wallace to "step aside" and allow the students to enter the school. Escorted by the Alabama National Guard, the black students enrolled in the university. Several years later, Governor Wallace renounced his support of segregation and opposition to *integration* (a legal principle requiring persons of all races to be treated equally under the law).

Governor George Wallace (second from left) was protected by members of the Alabama National Guard as he blocked the entrance to the University of Alabama while being confronted by Deputy U.S. Attorney General Nicholas Katzenbach on June 11, 1963.

Alabama National Guard General Henry Graham informs Governor Wallace that President Kennedy has ordered him to "step aside" and allow black students to enter the university.

After Governor Wallace complied with the order to "step aside," Vivian Malone Jones entered the University of Alabama and registered for classes.

Presidential Power to Administer the Executive Branch

he may require the opinion, in writing, of the principal officer in each of the
executive Departments, upon any Subject relating to the Duties of their
respective Offices,

The President has the authority to create a group of advisors called the *Cabinet*. The nation's first Cabinet consisted of only four members—the *Secretaries* (leaders) of the Departments of State, Treasury, War, and the *Attorney General* (chief law enforcement officer) of the Justice Department. Today's Cabinet consists of the Secretaries of 15 executive departments that manage federal programs. The Secretaries frequently consult with and provide advice to the President, who is free to accept or reject their advice. For example, when every member of President Abraham Lincoln's Cabinet voted to oppose one of his ideas, Lincoln responded by saying, "Seven nays, one yea; the yea votes have it."

The Fifteen Executive Departments

Agriculture	Health and Human Services	Labor
Commerce	Homeland Security	State
Defense	Housing and Urban Development	Transportation
Education	Interior	Treasury
Energy	Justice	Veterans Affairs

---

1. The Department of Agriculture administers programs involving biotechnology, pesticides, farming, food supplies, and food production.

2. The Department of Commerce is responsible for overseeing the nation's domestic and international trade, economic growth, and technological development. It also conducts a census every 10 years to count all persons living within the United States.

3. The Department of Defense is responsible for military security and national defense. It consists of the Departments of the Army, Air Force, Marines, and Navy. The highest ranking military officer of each of the armed forces serves as a member of the *Joint Chiefs of Staff*, an advisory council to the Secretary of Defense. The Defense Department's main offices are located in the *Pentagon*—a large, five-sided building located in Virginia.

The Pentagon

4. The Department of Education provides federal funding and policy proposals for many state-operated educational programs.

5. The Department of Energy is responsible for the nation's energy research and policies. It is currently researching alternative fuel sources to oil and coal in order to reduce climate change and conserve scarce natural resources.

6. The Department of Health and Human Services administers health, welfare, and *Social Security programs* (financial benefits for retired and disabled workers, their families and survivors).

7. The Department of Homeland Security is responsible for protecting the United States from terrorist threats and attacks, primarily by arranging information sharing among the *intelligence agencies* (federal agencies responsible for collecting, analyzing, and using information to support law enforcement, national security, military operations, and foreign policies).

8. The Department of Housing and Urban Development provides financial aid and housing programs to low-income people and enforces laws that protect people from illegal discrimination that deprives them of housing.

9. The Department of the Interior manages the nation's natural resources and parks, and administers programs for American Indian Tribes.

10. The Justice Department represents the legal interests of the United States in court proceedings and provides legal advice to the President and the secretaries of the executive departments. The Attorney General, who is the chief law enforcement officer of the federal government, is the head of the Justice Department. The Justice Department includes the Federal Bureau of Investigation, which enforces federal criminal laws; the Immigration and Naturalization Service, which administers laws pertaining to foreign persons seeking residence, employment, or citizenship in the United States; and the Drug Enforcement Agency, which enforces federal laws that apply to illegal drugs.

11. The Department of Labor enforces health and safety laws for American workers and protects them from illegal employment discrimination. It also provides unemployment insurance and compensation for work-related injuries.

12. The Department of State is headed by the Secretary of State, one of the most powerful Cabinet positions. The State Department is responsible for overseeing international relations, treaties, and agreements between the United States and other nations. It maintains more than 250 diplomatic posts around the world. It also represents the United States at the United Nations and within other international organizations.

13. The Department of Transportation develops and regulates the nation's transportation policies such as air traffic and interstate highway systems.

14. The Department of the Treasury informs the President and Congress about the financial conditions of the nation and the federal government. It also operates the Secret Service, an agency that provides protection for the President, Vice President, their families, visiting dignitaries and heads of state; the Internal Revenue Service, which is the federal tax collection agency; and the Customs Service, which regulates the entrance of goods and people into the nation.

15. The Department of Veterans Affairs provides medical, housing, and financial services to veterans of the United States military.

The President also works closely with the White House Staff, which consists of the Chief of Staff, Legal Counsel to the President, Legislative Liaison, and Press Secretary. The Chief of Staff advises the President and manages the President's schedule. The Legislative Liaison works with Congress to develop support for the President's legislative proposals. The Legal Counsel advises the President on legal matters related to presidential duties but does not serve as the President's personal attorney. The Press Secretary informs the media about executive branch developments.

Presidential Pardon Power

and he shall have Power to grant Reprieves and Pardons for Offences against the United States, except in Cases of Impeachment.

The Presidential *pardon power* is final, absolute, and not subject to the check and balance restraints of Congress or the federal judiciary. The pardon power enables the President to grant *"Pardons," "Reprieves"*, and sentence commutations to persons convicted of federal, but not state, crimes. A *pardon* forgives a criminal offense and cancels its penalty. A *reprieve* postpones or cancels a sentence. A *commutation* reduces a sentence or fine. Most pardons are granted when a President believes that a person was wrongfully convicted, or received an unduly harsh sentence, or has been rehabilitated, or for humanitarian reasons such as terminal illness or old age. One notable pardon was President Carter's 1977 grant of *amnesty* (a general pardon) to all Vietnam draft resisters who had violated the law by failing to register for military service. Another notable pardon occurred in 1974 when President Gerald Ford granted former President Richard Nixon "a full, free and absolute pardon . . . for offenses against the United States which he . . . has committed or may have committed" in regard to a political scandal known as "Watergate."

Presidential Treaty Power

He shall have Power, by and with the Advice and Consent of the Senate to make Treaties, provided two thirds of the Senators present concur;

A *treaty* is an agreement between two or more nations that deals with international issues such as security, economic, and humanitarian concerns. The President works with the State Department to negotiate treaties with other nations. Once a treaty has been agreed to by the President and the other nation, it must receive *"the Advice and Consent of the Senate,"* which requires the approval of *"two thirds"* of the voting Senators. As a consequence of this super-majority voting requirement, a treaty can be denied approval if it is opposed by only one-third of the Senators. For example, in 1919, 49 Senators voted in favor of the Treaty of Versailles to end World War I but 35 voted against it, thus denying the treaty the two-thirds majority needed for approval.

Presidential Appointment Power

and he shall nominate, and by and with the Advice and Consent of the Senate, shall appoint Ambassadors, other public Ministers and Consuls, Judges of the supreme Court, and all other Officers of the United States, whose

Appointments are not herein otherwise provided for, and which shall be established by Law: but the Congress may by Law vest the Appointment of such inferior Officers, as they think proper, in the President alone, in the Courts of Law, or in the Heads of Departments.

The Presidential appointment power involves a two-step process by which the President submits nominations of federal officials (such as ambassadors, Supreme Court Justices, Cabinet members, executive department secretaries, prosecutors, and military officers) to the Senate, which must then provide its *"Advice and Consent"* to confirm the appointments. During this *confirmation process,* the Senate conducts hearings to interview, question, and investigate the nominees before voting to approve or disapprove their appointments.

Presidential Recess Appointment Power

The President shall have Power to fill up all Vacancies that may happen during the Recess of the Senate, by granting Commissions which shall expire at the End of their next Session.

The President is permitted to avoid the Senate's confirmation process by making appointments during a *"Recess of the Senate."* A *recess appointment,* however, lasts only until the end of the current congressional session. Presidents typically make recess appointments in order to fill positions when nominees have been denied approval by the Senate. Sometimes Congress will refuse to declare a formal recess, even though it is not conducting meetings, in order to prevent a President from making an unwanted appointment.

Although most Presidents have made recess appointments, such appointments frequently reflect a poor relationship between the President and the Senate. For example, in 2004 and 2005, President George W. Bush twice nominated John Bolton to be the United States Ambassador to the United Nations despite Mr. Bolton's repeated criticism of the United Nations as ineffective and unnecessary. After researching Mr. Bolton's record, the Senate decided not to confirm his appointment. However, once Congress recessed, President Bush appointed Mr. Bolton to be the United States Representative, but not the Ambassador, to the United Nations. Mr. Bolton's appointment lasted only until the beginning of the next congressional session, when, once again, the Senate rejected his confirmation to be the United Nations Ambassador.

Article II Section 3: Presidential Duties

He shall from time to time give to the Congress Information of the State of the Union, and recommend to their Consideration such Measures as he shall judge necessary and expedient;

Each President makes an annual *State of the Union Address* in January to present executive plans and goals to the Congress, Supreme Court Justices, and Cabinet secretaries. The speech is simultaneously broadcast to the public on television, radio, and the Internet.[29]

The President's Duty to Convene and Adjourn Congress

he may on extraordinary Occasions, convene both Houses, or either of them, and in Case of Disagreement between them, with Respect to the Time of Adjournment, he may adjourn them to such Time as he shall think proper;

The President has the power to *"convene"* a congressional session on *"extraordinary Occasions,"* and to *"adjourn"* Congress if the two chambers cannot agree on an adjournment date.

Presidential Diplomatic Duties

he shall receive Ambassadors and other Public Ministers;

The President has the duty to formally receive foreign leaders and recognize the sovereignty of their nations. *Recognition* between the United States and another nation means that both nations acknowledge the legitimacy of the other, and both agree to participate in diplomatic relations with the other. It does not mean that the nations agree with each other's conduct or policies. For example, by the end of the 19th century, America and China had developed successful trade relations with each other that continued until 1949 when the Communist Party gained control of the Chinese government. For the next 30 years, each government refused to formally recognize the other until 1972 when President Richard Nixon went to China to meet with Chairman Mao Zedong. By 1979, under President Jimmy Carter, the United States and China established full diplomatic relations with each other.

To withdraw recognition of a nation, the President recalls American diplomats who are residing in that nation, and instructs that nation's diplomats who reside in the United States to return home. The withdrawal of diplomatic recognition often means that the nations will no longer deal with each other, and sometimes may be a step toward war.

---

[29] Most State of the Union Addresses were written rather than oral presentations until 1913 when President Wilson made the first oral presentation to Congress.

Chairman Mao Zedong and President Richard M. Nixon meet in China on February 29, 1972

Presidential Law Enforcement Duties

he shall take Care that the Laws be faithfully executed, and shall Commission all the Officers of the United States.

As the chief law enforcement officer of the United States, the President has the duty to ensure that the federal government complies with the nation's laws. The President, also, must obey the nation's laws. The *Clinton v. Jones* case explains why a sitting President is not protected from a private lawsuit that alleges illegal private conduct. The case of *U.S. v. Nixon* explains why a sitting President must obey court orders. Here is that story:

Richard Nixon was first elected as President in 1968 and ran for re-election in 1972. His re-election campaign manager, John Mitchell, hired a former Central Intelligence Agency agent, G. Gordon Liddy, to serve as the attorney for the Committee to Re-Elect the President, ironically referred to as CREEP ("Creep" is American slang for someone or something that is untrustworthy and nasty). Liddy instructed CREEP to illegally install wiretaps inside the Democratic National Campaign headquarters (DNC) so that CREEP could overhear its strategy discussions. The DNC was located in the Watergate Complex, a large group of buildings located in Washington, D.C.

The Watergate Complex, located in Washington, D.C.

In the early morning of June 17, 1972, a security guard for the Watergate Complex noticed that the door to the DNC headquarters was slightly open, although the office lights were off and the office door was closed. When he entered the office, the guard saw five men who were repairing broken wiretap equipment. They had brought with them burglary tools, eavesdropping equipment, and many $100 bills. The guard contacted the police, who arrested the men and charged them with burglary.

Although President Nixon assured the public that neither he nor his administration had anything to do to with the bungled burglary, within hours of the arrest paper shredders located inside the White House and CREEP headquarters began destroying documents that connected the burglars to the White House. To avoid disclosure of their involvement with the burglary, CREEP and White House officials agreed to *bribe* (provide illegal financial support) the burglars in exchange for their silence. As a result, all five burglars remained silent when questioned by the police and prosecutor, and all five were convicted of the burglary. Once convicted, however, one of the burglars wrote a letter to the judge confessing that all the burglars had received money in return for their silence, and all had lied to protect other people who had not directly participated in the burglary.

Soon after the burglar's letter, the Senate, Justice Department, and Washington Post newspaper all began separate investigations of the wiretaps, burglary, and bribes. The Senate created the Senate Select Committee on Watergate to investigate whether the White House had been involved in any of the events. The Justice Department appointed a *Special Prosecutor* (a nongovernmental lawyer appointed by the Attorney General to investigate a government official) to investigate whether President Nixon had been involved in any of the events. The Washington Post assigned two young reporters, Bob Woodward and Carl Bernstein, to investigate all of the events.

At a hearing conducted by the Senate Select Committee on Watergate, the White House lawyer, John Dean, testified that President Nixon had not been truthful about his administration's involvement in the Watergate burglary. A White House security guard, Anthony Ulasewicz, testified that he had left brown paper bags filled with money in secret places throughout Washington, D.C., to be picked up and delivered to the burglars. A White House staff member, Alexander Butterfield, testified that President Nixon had tape-recorded every conversation that took place in the *Oval Office* (the President's White House office). Based on this last disclosure, the Senate Select Committee on Watergate and the Special Prosecutor both issued *subpoenas* (court orders) for President Nixon to turn over the Oval Office tape recordings. When Nixon refused to obey the subpoenas, the Special Prosecutor sought a court order commanding Nixon to turn over the recordings. Instead of turning over the recordings, Nixon fired the Special Prosecutor. However, when the Justice Department appointed a second Special Prosecutor, Nixon did turn over the tape recordings. When the Senate Select Committee listened to the tape recordings, it discovered that one of them was silent for 18½ minutes. President Nixon denied any knowledge of the "18½-minute gap," which he attributed to "sinister forces." Later, his secretary claimed that she had erased the tape by mistake.

The Special Prosecutor issued a second subpoena for 64 more tape recordings. This time, instead of turning over the additional recordings, the White House turned over *transcripts* (written records) of the tape recordings. Concerned that the transcripts would not accurately contain all of the taped conversations, the Special Prosecutor refused to accept the transcripts and, instead, demanded the original tape recordings. President Nixon refused to release the recordings based on the argument that *executive privilege* absolutely barred disclosure of private conversations with a President in order to allow the persons with whom the President spoke to be forthright and candid about their concerns and disagreements with the President.

American law allows certain types of communications to be *privileged* (barred) from disclosure in judicial proceedings, even if they are *relevant* (pertinent and truthful). The reason privileged communications are not subject to courtroom testimony is to protect confidential relationships that could be damaged if the parties to such relationships are forced to testify against each other. For example, communications between lawyers and clients are privileged so that

clients can confide the truth to their lawyers, no matter how illegal their revela-
tions may be, and the lawyers can provide the necessary legal protections for their
clients. Similarly, statements made by patients to physicians and mental health
therapists are privileged so that patients will fully disclose their problems and be
properly treated; husbands and wives cannot be forced to testify against each other
because of the harm such testimony could cause to the marriage and family.

President Nixon's defense was that executive privilege served the public
interest because it encouraged and protected the candor of presidential advisors.
When a lower court rejected this argument, President Nixon filed an appeal and
the case was quickly brought to the Supreme Court. Here is the Court's response
to Nixon's arguments:

United States v. Nixon
418 U.S. 683 (1974)

Chief Justice Burger delivered the opinion of the Court.

In support of his claim of absolute privilege, the President's counsel urges
two grounds, one of which is common to all governments and one of which is
peculiar to our system of separation of powers. The first ground is the valid
need for protection of communications between high Government officials and
those who advise and assist them in the performance of their manifold duties;
the importance of this confidentiality is too plain to require further discussion.
Human experience teaches that those who expect public dissemination of their
remarks may well temper candor with a concern for appearances and for their
own interests to the detriment of the decisionmaking process. . . .

The second ground asserted by the President's counsel in support of the
claim of absolute privilege rests on the doctrine of separation of powers. Here
it is argued that the independence of the Executive Branch within its own
sphere insulates a President from a judicial subpoena in an ongoing criminal
prosecution, and thereby protects confidential Presidential communications.

However, neither the doctrine of separation of powers, nor the need for
confidentiality of high level communications, without more, can sustain an
absolute, unqualified Presidential privilege of immunity from judicial process
under all circumstances. The President's need for complete candor and
objectivity from advisers calls for great deference from the courts. However,
when the privilege depends solely on the broad, undifferentiated claim of
public interest in the confidentiality of such conversations, a confrontation with other values arises. Absent a claim of need to protect
military, diplomatic, or sensitive national security secrets, we find it
difficult to accept the argument that even the very important
interest in confidentiality of Presidential communications is significantly diminished by production of such material for in camera inspection

[confidential inspection solely by the judge] with all the protection that a district court will be obliged to provide. . . .

A President and those who assist him must be free to explore alternatives in the process of shaping policies and making decisions and to do so in a way many would be unwilling to express except privately. These are the considerations justifying a presumptive privilege for Presidential communications. The privilege is fundamental to the operation of Government and inextricably rooted in the separation of powers under the Constitution. . . .

But this presumptive privilege must be considered in light of our historic commitment to the rule of law. . . . We have elected to employ an adversary system of criminal justice in which the parties contest all issues before a court of law. The need to develop all relevant facts in the adversary system [lawsuit process] is both fundamental and comprehensive. The ends of criminal justice would be defeated if judgments were to be founded on a partial and speculative presentation of the facts. The very integrity of the judicial system and public confidence in the system depend on full disclosure of all the facts, within the framework of the rules of evidence. . . .

Thus, the Fifth Amendment to the Constitution provides that no man "shall be compelled in any criminal case to be a witness against himself." And, generally, an attorney or a priest may not be required to disclose what has been revealed in professional confidence. These and other interests are recognized in law by privileges against forced disclosure. . . . [T]hese exceptions to the demand for every man's evidence are not lightly created nor expansively construed, for they are in derogation of the search for truth.

In this case we must weigh the importance of the general privilege of confidentiality of Presidential communications in performance of his responsibilities against the inroads of such privilege on the fair administration of criminal justice. The interest in preserving confidentiality is weighty indeed and entitled to great respect. However, we cannot conclude that advisers will be moved to temper the candor of their remarks by the infrequent occasions of disclosure because of the possibility that such conversations will be called for in the context of a criminal prosecution.

On the other hand, the allowance of the privilege to withhold evidence that is demonstrably relevant in a criminal trial would cut deeply into the guarantee of due process of law and gravely impair the basic function of the courts. A President's acknowledged need for confidentiality in the communications of his office is general in nature, whereas the constitutional need for production of relevant evidence in a criminal proceeding is specific and central to the fair adjudication [legal process] of a particular criminal case in the administration of justice. Without access to specific facts a criminal prosecution may be totally frustrated. The President's broad interest in confidentiality of communications will not be vitiated [made ineffective] by disclosure of a limited number of conversations preliminarily shown to have some bearing on the pending criminal cases.

> We conclude that when the ground for asserting privilege as to subpoenaed materials sought for use in a criminal trial is based only on the generalized interests in confidentiality, it cannot prevail over the fundamental demands of due process of law in the fair administration of criminal justice. The generalized assertion of privilege must yield to the demonstrated, specific need for evidence in a pending criminal trial....
>
> [W]e affirm the order of the District Court that subpoenaed materials be transmitted to that court.

Eight hours after the Supreme Court issued this unanimous opinion, the White House announced that President Nixon would obey the Court's order and turn over all the subpoenaed tape recordings. Three days later, the House of Representatives prepared Articles of Impeachment that charged President Nixon with obstruction of the Watergate investigation, misuse of executive power, and violation of his oath of office. Facing almost certain impeachment by the House and conviction by the Senate, President Nixon resigned.

THE WHITE HOUSE
WASHINGTON

August 9, 1974

Dear Mr. Secretary:

I hereby resign the Office of President of the United States.

Sincerely,

Richard Nixon

11.35 AM

The Honorable Henry A. Kissinger
The Secretary of State
Washington, D. C. 20520

HK

President Nixon's Letter of Resignation

The Watergate scandal occurred because a President misunderstood the nature of executive power. He believed that the Constitution protected all presidential conduct, even conduct that was illegal for others. The Watergate debacle was discovered, investigated, and resolved because the doctrine of checks and balances upheld the constitutional authority of Congress to investigate the President, the authority of the Supreme Court to command the President's obedience, and the freedom of the press to investigate and publish it all.

Article II Section 4: Impeachment

The President, Vice President and all civil Officers of the United States, shall be removed from Office on Impeachment for, and Conviction of Treason, Bribery, or other high Crimes and Misdemeanors.

The President, Vice President, and other federal officials can be removed from office only if impeached by the House of Representatives and convicted by the Senate of *"Treason, Bribery, or other high Crimes and Misdemeanors."* To date, only two Presidents have been impeached: Andrew Johnson in 1868 and Bill Clinton in 1998. Neither was convicted by the Senate.

Article III of the Constitution defines *treason*[30] as engaging in war against the United States, and criminal law defines *bribery* as receiving a benefit in exchange for an illegal act. However, the phrase *high crimes and misdemeanors* has no specific legal or historical definition. Historically, high crimes and misdemeanors have ranged from neglect of political duties to theft of government funds. Currently, high crimes and misdemeanors do not include policy disagreements with the President because many people frequently disagree with presidential decisions. However, there continues to be considerable disagreement about whether an impeachable high crime or misdemeanor applies only to political misconduct that involves abuse of governmental duties, or also applies to private criminal conduct.

The impeachment of President Clinton illustrates the uncertainty about the meaning of high crimes and misdemeanors. Paula Jones accused Clinton of making inappropriate and illegal sexual advances toward her and sued him in a private civil lawsuit. During the lawsuit Clinton was required to give testimony under oath. Some of that testimony was subsequently shown to be untrue. In 1998, one of the grounds listed in the Bill of Impeachment was that President

---

[30] The Constitution defines treason in Article III, Section 3, Clause 1: *"Treason against the United States, shall consist only in levying War against them, or, in adhering to their Enemies, giving them Aid and Comfort. No Person shall be convicted of Treason unless on the Testimony of two Witnesses to the same overt Act, or on Confession in open Court."*

Clinton had committed *perjury* (lied under oath) in the Paula Jones case when he stated that he had not had sexual relations with another woman, a statement that he later recanted. Those who supported impeachment believed that Clinton's perjured testimony violated his presidential oath to "preserve, protect and defend the Constitution of the United States." Those who opposed impeachment believed that this most drastic sanction should be invoked only to protect the nation from serious political or criminal misconduct, and that lying about extramarital sexual conduct in a private lawsuit did not rise to the level of a high crime or misdemeanor that endangered the nation or prevented the President from fulfilling presidential duties. Ultimately, the House voted to impeach Clinton, but the Senate acquitted him and his presidency continued. Interestingly, President Clinton received his highest approval ratings during his impeachment proceedings.

CHAPTER 3 QUESTIONS

1. a. What is the doctrine of official immunity?
    b. Why is there official immunity?
    c. Why did President Clinton not have official immunity in Paula Jones's lawsuit against him?

2. Many Americans are dissatisfied with the Electoral College system and believe it should be eliminated so that a President can be elected directly by the people.
    a. What are the arguments for eliminating the Electoral College system?
    b. What are the arguments for continuing the Electoral College system?

3. The United States formally entered World War II after Japan attacked Pearl Harbor, Hawaii, on December 7, 1941. President Roosevelt ordered the creation of geographic "military zones" within the United States from which Japanese Americans could be excluded. Over 100,000 persons of Japanese descent who were living in those areas, many of whom were American citizens, were classified as "enemy aliens" without hearings or formal charges, and sent to live in "internment camps." Toyosaburo Korematsu, who was an American citizen born in California, was arrested when he refused to leave his home in California and enter an internment camp. In 1944, the United States Supreme Court accepted his case, *Korematsu v. United States*, to determine if the President had authority to order Mr. Korematsu's internment.

    a. What legal arguments would you have made on behalf of President Roosevelt's authority to create "military zones" and "internment camps"?

    b. What legal arguments would you have made to prevent Mr. Korematsu from being involuntarily detained in an internment camp?

    c. How do you think the Court ruled? Explain your answer.

4. Why do you think the Constitution divided the impeachment power between the House and the Senate?

5. Prepare a brief on the Supreme Court's ruling in _Clinton v. Jones_ that addresses the following questions:

    a. Why is there immunity for a President's official, but not unofficial, conduct?

    b. What did the Court mean when it said, "As our opinions have made clear, immunities are grounded in 'the nature of the function performed, not the identity of the actor who performed it.'"

    c. What cases did the Court use to support its holding in _Clinton v. Jones_? Why?

    d. Why was President Clinton not protected by these prior cases?

    e. Do you think that President Clinton's perjury in Paula Jones's private lawsuit qualified as a high crime and misdemeanor justifying impeachment?

    f. What arguments would you make in favor of President Clinton's impeachment?

    g. What arguments would you make against President Clinton's impeachment?

6. Prepare a brief that addresses the following questions regarding the Supreme Court's holding in _United States v. Nixon_:

    a. What is a privileged communication?

    b. What is executive privilege?

    c. What is absolute privilege?

    d. What reasons did the Court give for ruling against Nixon's arguments for absolute privileged communications with his aides? Do you agree or disagree with the Court's ruling? Explain your answer.

    e. What is a subpoena?

    f. What is an in camera inspection?

7. **a.** Why did the Constitution make the presidential pardon power final, absolute, and not subject to the check and balance restraints of Congress?

    b. Do you agree or disagree with this degree of presidential power? Explain your answer.

8. While testifying before a Senate investigative committee, an employee of the Justice Department refused to answer questions on the grounds that her testimony would violate her oath to protect and defend the current President, George W. Bush. Actually, her oath required her to protect and defend the Constitution and the laws of the nation. Is there any difference between an oath to protect a President and an oath to defend the Constitution? Explain your answer.

Article III: The Judicial Branch

The United States Supreme Courthouse, located in Washington, D.C.

Article III Section 1: The Establishment of the Federal Judicial System

The judicial Power of the United States, shall be vested in one supreme Court, and in such inferior Courts as the Congress may from time to time ordain and establish.

Long before the Constitutional Convention was convened, each state had established its own judicial system. Like many other issues, there was considerable disagreement among the Founding Fathers about whether the federal government would need its own court system. Those who favored a strong federal government believed that a federal judicial system was necessary because the numerous state courts would not uniformly apply or enforce federal laws. Those who favored a weak federal government believed that a federal judicial system would dominate the state court systems. The Founding Fathers resolved this conflict by agreeing that while each state would retain its individual court system, the federal government would also establish its own court system and place at least one courthouse in every state.

Article III Section 1 creates the highest federal court—the United States Supreme Court. The Supreme Court, however, is the only court specifically created by the Constitution because Article I Section 8 authorized Congress to create the lower federal courts. Today, the federal judicial system consists of the Supreme Court, 13 *circuit courts of appeals* (appellate courts), and 94 *district courts* (trial courts). The primary purpose of the federal court system is to *adjudicate* (resolve by judicial process) lawsuits by providing a *forum* (court system) by which people, businesses, and governments can bring disputes to be resolved by a neutral, independent court.

Federal District Courts

The district courts are the only *trial courts* in the federal system. *Trials* are proceedings in which the *parties* (persons and entities who sue or are sued in lawsuits) present witnesses and evidence to a judge or jury to prove their case. Trials are public proceedings, open to all who are interested in attending, including the media. A federal lawsuit is first filed in a district court, where it is presided over by one judge until a final *ruling* (decision) is made by the judge, or the lawsuit is privately *settled* (resolved) by the parties. The number of judges and district courthouses within a state is based on the state's population. Each state has at least one federal district courthouse.

Federal Circuit Courts of Appeals

A party who loses a case in a district court can *appeal* that court's decision to a federal circuit court of appeals. The appeal will then be presided over by a three-judge *panel* (group). An appeal is not a second trial. The appellate court does not accept evidence or hear witnesses. Instead, the purpose of the appellate court is to review the *transcript* (recorded verbal statements made by lawyers, witnesses, and judges during a trial) and *court record* (proceedings and rulings) of the district court proceedings to determine if the district court's ruling was correct.

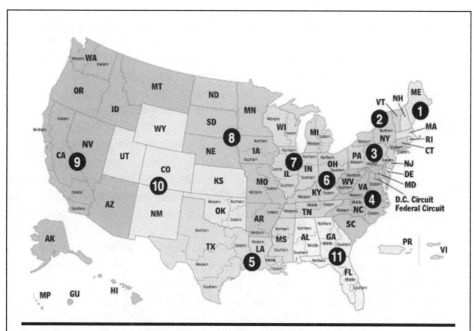

Map of the Thirteen Federal Judicial Circuit Courts of Appeals

THE FEDERAL CIRCUIT COURTS OF APPEALS AND THE DISTRICT COURTS OVER WHICH THEY PRESIDE

First Circuit:	Maine, New Hampshire, Rhode Island, Massachusetts, Puerto Rico
Second Circuit:	New York, Connecticut, Vermont
Third Circuit:	Pennsylvania, New Jersey, Delaware, Virgin Islands
Fourth Circuit:	West Virginia, Virginia, Maryland, North Carolina, South Carolina
Fifth Circuit:	Mississippi, Louisiana, Texas
Sixth Circuit:	Michigan, Ohio, Kentucky, Tennessee
Seventh Circuit:	Wisconsin, Illinois, Indiana
Eighth Circuit:	North Dakota, South Dakota, Nebraska, Minnesota, Iowa, Missouri, Arkansas
Ninth Circuit:	Washington, Oregon, California, Montana, Idaho, Nevada, Arizona, Alaska, Hawaii, Guam, Northern Mariana Islands
Tenth Circuit:	Wyoming, Utah, Colorado, New Mexico, Kansas, Oklahoma
Eleventh Circuit:	Alabama, Georgia, Florida
D.C. Circuit:	District of Columbia
Federal Circuit:	Nationwide jurisdiction over intellectual property, international trade, government contracts, and veterans' benefits cases

If the appellate court finds that the district court correctly applied the law, it will *affirm* (uphold) its decision. If the appellate court finds that the district court incorrectly applied the law, it will *reverse* (reject) its decision and *remand* (return) the case to the district court to be decided according to the appellate court's instructions.

In the federal judicial system there are 13 United States Circuit Courts of Appeals. Twelve of these circuit courts are located throughout the nation in order to preside over appeals from district courts that are geographically located within a specific circuit. For example, the Seventh Circuit Court of Appeals hears appeals from all of the federal district courts in the states of Illinois, Indiana, and Wisconsin. The Fourth Circuit Court of Appeals hears appeals from all of the federal district courts in the states of Maryland, Virginia, West Virginia, North Carolina, and South Carolina. The District of Columbia Circuit Court hears appeals only from the D.C. district courts, most of which involve federal agency matters. The Thirteenth Circuit Court, called the United States Court of Appeals for the Federal Circuit, has nationwide jurisdiction over appeals involving international trade, government contracts, intellectual property, and veterans' benefits.

The United States Supreme Court

The Supreme Court currently consists of nine Justices[1]—one *Chief Justice* who heads the Court, and eight *Associate Justices*. A decision of the Supreme Court cannot be appealed to any other court. Although parties have a right to appeal a district court decision to a circuit court of appeals, they do not have a right to appeal a circuit court decision to the United States Supreme Court. Instead, the Supreme Court has the discretion to choose which cases it will hear. A party seeking Supreme Court review will file a *writ of certiorari*, otherwise known as a *cert. petition*, asking the Court to hear its case. The cert. petition will be granted if at least four of the nine Justices agree to accept the case. The Court receives over 10,000 cert. petitions every year but grants review to fewer than 100. In choosing cases, the Court looks for disputes that only it can resolve. For example, in order to maintain uniformity in the application of federal laws, the Court grants cert. petitions when multiple circuit court cases have reached conflicting interpretations of the same federal law. Similarly, in order to maintain the supremacy of federal laws, the Court grants cert. petitions to cases decided by state supreme courts that have interpreted state laws in a manner that conflicts with federal laws.

---

[1] The Supreme Court originally had six Justices.

United States Supreme Court Justices as of 2014
Back row (left to right): Sonia Sotomayor, Stephen G. Breyer, Samuel A. Alito,
and Elena Kagan
Front row (left to right): Clarence Thomas, Antonin Scalia, Chief Justice
John G. Roberts, Anthony Kennedy, and Ruth Bader Ginsburg

Opinions

In order to avoid prejudgment of legal issues or the appearance of bias, American judges (both state and federal) may not publicly express personal views about specific laws or cases. Instead, judges "speak" only through *opinions* that they issue in cases over which they preside. The purpose of the opinion is to give the parties to the lawsuit an explanation of the court's analysis of a disputed question of law.

Supreme and appellate courts *issue* (publish) several kinds of opinions. A *majority opinion* is an opinion that receives a majority of judicial votes.[2] Only majority opinions have the force of law and are binding *precedents* (judicial opinions of higher courts that lower courts must obey). A *dissenting opinion* is written by a judge who disagrees with the majority opinion. A *concurring opinion* is written by a judge who agrees with some, but not all, of the majority opinion's analysis and ruling. A *concurring and dissenting* opinion agrees with some parts of the majority opinion's analysis but disagrees with other parts. A *plurality opinion* is written by an individual judge, or several judges, when

---

[2] Because most federal appellate court cases are ruled on by three-judge panels, a majority opinion consists of at least two votes. Because the Supreme Court consists of nine Justices, a majority opinion requires at least five votes.

there is no majority opinion. Plurality opinions do not create law, but they do disclose the basis for the judges' inability to agree on a majority opinion. *Per curiam* opinions are usually unsigned, brief, and unanimous opinions about legal issues to which a court gives less than full treatment.

Precedent

Legal *precedent* refers to higher court rulings that lower courts are required to follow. All courts must obey Supreme Court precedents because they are the "supreme law of the land"[3] that can only be overruled by the Supreme Court itself. For example, in 1896, the Supreme Court decided the case of *Plessy v. Ferguson,* 163 U.S. 537 (1896), in which Homer Plessy violated a state statute that barred black and white people from sitting in the same railroad cars. Mr. Plessy was considered to be a black man because his great-grandmother had been black. When Mr. Plessy took a seat in a "whites-only" railroad car he was arrested and charged with violating the statute. In his defense, Mr. Plessy argued that the statute denied him equal rights under the Constitution and took his case all the way to the Supreme Court, where he lost. In *Plessy v. Ferguson*, the Court upheld the "separate-but-equal" racial policy and ruled that segregation of black and white people was constitutional. As a consequence of the separate-but-equal policy, blacks and whites were required to attend separate schools, live in separate communities and use separate drinking fountains, washrooms, railroad cars, and other public facilities. Not surprisingly, the facilities for blacks were not as good as the facilities for whites. The separate-but-equal policy remained the law of the United States for 60 years until the Supreme Court overruled *Plessy* in *Brown v. Board of Education of Topeka*.

In *Brown v. Board of Education of Topeka*, the parents of African-American black students sued their local *school boards* (panels of people who are elected or appointed to manage local schools) to challenge the separate-but-equal policy of the school system. Their attorney was Thurgood Marshall, who later became the first black Supreme Court Justice. Basing his client's legal arguments on Homer Plessy's defense, Marshall argued that separate schools for white and black children deprived black children of equality as required by the *equal protection clause* of the Fourteenth Amendment. The Fourteenth Amendment was one of three amendments passed after the Civil War that ended slavery throughout the nation and granted citizenship to former slaves. One of the purposes of the Fourteenth Amendment was to provide equality to the new black citizens of the United States. Accordingly, Section 1 of the Fourteenth Amendment provides:

> *All persons born or naturalized in the United States, and subject to the jurisdiction thereof, are citizens of the United States and of the State wherein*

---

[3] Article VI states: *"This Constitution, and the Laws of the United States which shall be made in Pursuance thereof . . . shall be the supreme Law of the Land. . . ."*

Homer Plessy

they reside. No State shall make or enforce any law which shall abridge the privileges or immunities of citizens of the United States; nor shall any State deprive any person of life, liberty, or property, without due process of law; nor deny to any person within its jurisdiction the equal protection of the laws.

This section of the Fourteenth Amendment prohibits states from denying citizens the *"privileges or immunities"* of their laws; *"life, liberty, or property, without due process of law;"* and *"the equal protection of the laws."* The *equal protection clause* of the Fourteenth Amendment was the legal basis for the Court's decision in <u>*Brown v. Board of Education*</u>. Portions of the opinion follow:

Brown v. Board of Education of Topeka
347 U.S. 483 (1954)

Mr. Chief Justice Warren delivered the opinion of the Court.

These cases come to us from the States of Kansas, South Carolina, Virginia, and Delaware. They are premised on different facts and different local conditions, but a common legal question justifies their consideration together in this consolidated opinion.

In each of the cases, minors of the Negro race, through their legal representatives, seek the aid of the courts in obtaining admission to the public schools of their community on a nonsegregated basis. In each instance, they had been denied admission to schools attended by white children under laws requiring or permitting segregation according to race. This segregation was alleged to deprive the plaintiffs of the equal protection of the laws under the Fourteenth Amendment. In each of the cases other than the Delaware case, a three-judge federal district court denied relief to the plaintiffs on the so-called "separate but equal" doctrine announced by this Court in Plessy v. Ferguson, 163 U.S. 537. Under that doctrine, equality of treatment is accorded when the races are provided substantially equal facilities, even though these facilities be separate. . . .

The plaintiffs contend that segregated public schools are not "equal" and cannot be made "equal," and that hence they are deprived of the equal protection of the laws. Because of the obvious importance of the question presented, the Court took jurisdiction. . . .

In approaching this problem, we cannot turn the clock back to 1868, when the [Fourteenth] Amendment was adopted, or even to 1896, when Plessy v. Ferguson was written. We must consider public education in the light of its full development and its present place in American life throughout the Nation. Only in this way can it be determined if segregation in public schools deprives these plaintiffs of the equal protection of the laws.

Today, education is perhaps the most important function of state and local governments. Compulsory school attendance laws and the great expenditures for education both demonstrate our recognition of the importance of education to our democratic society. It is required in the performance of our most basic public responsibilities, even service in the armed forces. It is the very foundation of good citizenship. Today it is a principal instrument in awakening the child to cultural values, in preparing him for later professional training, and in helping him to adjust normally to his environment. In these days, it is doubtful that any child may reasonably be expected to succeed in life if he is denied the opportunity of an education. Such an opportunity, where the state has undertaken to provide it, is a right that must be made available to all on equal terms.

We come then to the question presented: Does segregation of children in public schools solely on the basis of race, even though the physical facilities and other "tangible" factors may be equal, deprive the children of the minority group of equal educational opportunities? We believe that it does.

In Sweatt v. Painter, 339 U.S. 629 (1950), in finding that a segregated law school for Negroes could not provide them equal educational opportunities, this Court relied in large part on "those qualities which are incapable of objective measurement but which make for greatness in a law school." In McLaurin v. Oklahoma State Regents, 339 U.S. 637 (1950), the

Court, in requiring that a Negro admitted to a white graduate school be treated like all other students, again resorted to intangible considerations: "...his ability to study, to engage in discussions and exchange views with other students, and, in general, to learn his profession." Such considerations apply with added force to children in grade and high schools. To separate them from others of similar age and qualifications solely because of their race generates a feeling of inferiority as to their status in the community that may affect their hearts and minds in a way unlikely ever to be undone. The effect of this separation on their educational opportunities was well stated by a finding in the Kansas case [the district court's decision] by a court which nevertheless felt compelled to rule against the Negro plaintiffs:

> "Segregation of white and colored children in public schools has a detrimental effect upon the colored children. The impact is greater when it has the sanction of the law; for the policy of separating the races is usually interpreted as denoting the inferiority of the negro group. A sense of inferiority affects the motivation of a child to learn. Segregation with the sanction of law, therefore, has a tendency to [retard] the educational and mental development of negro children and to deprive them of some of the benefits they would receive in a racial[ly] integrated school system."

Whatever may have been the extent of psychological knowledge at the time of <u>Plessy v. Ferguson</u>, this finding is amply supported by modern authority. Any language in <u>Plessy v. Ferguson</u> contrary to this finding is rejected.

We conclude that, in the field of public education, the doctrine of "separate but equal" has no place. Separate educational facilities are inherently unequal. Therefore, we hold that the plaintiffs and others similarly situated for whom the actions have been brought are, by reason of the segregation complained of, deprived of the equal protection of the laws guaranteed by the Fourteenth Amendment.

Brown v. Board of Education of Topeka is a landmark case in American constitutional law and political history. It stands for the principle that a nation committed to providing democracy to all its citizens cannot deprive some of its citizens of equal opportunities to participate in the benefits of its laws based on their race or ethnicity. It also stands for the proposition that the Supreme Court has the authority to change its prior precedents in order to reflect the changing values of a changing nation.

Newspaper headlines announcing the <u>Brown v. Board of Education</u> opinion

Soldiers escorting black students into the all-white Central High School in
Little Rock, Arkansas

Judicial Independence

The Judges, both of the supreme and inferior Courts, shall hold their Offices during good Behaviour,

Federal judges, including Supreme Court Justices, maintain their judicial appointments *"during good Behavior,"* which means for life, or until they resign or are removed from office.[4] Because federal judges are not elected by the people and can be removed only by impeachment, *life tenure* promotes judicial independence by protecting federal judges from angry *litigants* (parties) and powerful government officials who would try to influence a judge's decision or remove a judge because of an unpopular ruling. By protecting federal judges from political pressure and popular emotions, judicial independence upholds the autonomy and integrity of the judiciary.

Judicial Compensation

and shall, at stated Times, receive for their Services, a Compensation, which shall not be diminished during their Continuance in Office.

Last, Article III Section 1 provides that federal judges *" shall . . . receive for their Services, a Compensation, which shall not be diminished during their Continuance in Office."* This compensation provision protects judicial independence by depriving Congress of the power to punish a judge for issuing a controversial opinion, or forcing a judge to resign by reducing his or her salary.

Article III Section 2: Federal Jurisdiction

The judicial Power shall extend to all Cases, in Law and Equity, arising under this Constitution, the Laws of the United States, and Treaties made, or which shall be made, under their Authority;—to all Cases affecting Ambassadors, other public Ministers and Consuls;—to all Cases of admiralty and maritime jurisdiction; to Controversies to which the United States shall be a Party;—to Controversies between two or more States;—[between a State and Citizens of another State;—] between Citizens of different States,—between Citizens of

---

[4] Unlike federal judges, most state court judges are elected by state citizens

the same State claiming Lands under Grants of different States [and between a
State, or the Citizens there of;—and foreign States, Citizens or Subjects.][5]

Section 2 grants federal courts *jurisdiction* (authority) to preside over
"Cases" or *"Controversies"* (lawsuits). A legal dispute qualifies as a case or controversy only after it becomes *cognizable*—after the events giving rise to the
lawsuit have already occurred. Courts do not have jurisdiction over cases
based on hypothetical events or events that have not yet occurred. Additionally,
the plaintiff must have been injured by the event and must seek a remedy that the
court has legal authority to grant. The most common judicial remedy is *monetary
damages* (financial compensation), but courts also have the authority to issue
injunctions that order parties to do, or refrain from doing, specific acts.

Section 2 creates two broad categories of federal jurisdiction: *federal question
jurisdiction* and *diversity jurisdiction.* Federal question jurisdiction refers to cases
based on violations of federal statutes, treaties, or the Constitution. Diversity
jurisdiction refers to cases where the parties are citizens of different states, citizens of foreign countries, or are foreign countries. Unlike federal question cases,
diversity cases involve disputes over state laws, not federal laws.

Supreme Court Jurisdiction

> *In all Cases affecting Ambassadors, other public Ministers and Consuls, and
> those in which a State shall be Party, the supreme Court shall have original
> Jurisdiction. In all the other Cases before mentioned, the supreme Court shall
> have appellate Jurisdiction, both as Law and Fact, with such Exceptions, and
> under such Regulations as the Congress shall make.*

Section 2 also establishes two categories of Supreme Court jurisdiction. The
Supreme Court has *"original Jurisdiction"* in *"Cases affecting Ambassadors,
other public Ministers and Consuls, and those in which a State shall be
Party."* *Original jurisdiction* means that a case must be filed first in the Supreme
Court rather than in a lower district court. For all other cases, the Supreme Court
has *"appellate Jurisdiction,"* which means that a case must proceed through
district and appellate courts before it can be appealed to the Supreme Court.

Early in the nation's history, a dispute arose between the Supreme Court and
Congress as to whether Congress had the authority to pass a law that changed the
Supreme Court's appellate and original jurisdiction as defined by the Constitu-
tion. John Adams, the nation's second President, was a Federalist who believed

---

[5] These provisions were changed by the *Eleventh Amendment* enacted into law in 1795, that
prohibits federal courts from presiding over cases in which a state is sued by a person from another
state or country.

Chief Justice John Marshal

that the nation benefitted most from a strong federal government. He was defeated for re-election by Thomas Jefferson, an Anti Federalist who believed that the nation benefitted most from strong state governments and a weak federal government. To retain Federalist control over the government after his presidential term ended, Adams spent his last night in office appointing as many Federalists as possible to fill as many government positions as possible. Some of the appointment papers, however, were not delivered before midnight of his last night in office. The day after Jefferson became the President, he instructed his Secretary of State, James Madison, to treat the undelivered appointment papers as void. One of the disappointed appointees, William Marbury, filed a lawsuit in the Supreme Court asking the Court to *mandamus* (order) Madison to recognize his appointment.

Marbury filed his case directly with the Supreme Court rather than a lower district court because the *Judiciary Act of 1789* (the first act passed by the first Congress) had given the Supreme Court original jurisdiction over mandamus actions involving public officials. Consequently, the first question the Court had to resolve was whether it had original or appellate jurisdiction over Marbury's case. If the Court had original jurisdiction, then the case could continue. However, if the Court had appellate jurisdiction, then it would not have authority to preside over the case until after it had been appealed from a lower court ruling.

The nature of its jurisdiction, however, was not the Court's primary concern. As a political matter, the Court's Chief Justice, John Marshall, did not want to make any ruling in the case. If the Court ruled in Marbury's favor, President

Jefferson could ignore the ruling and, in so doing, diminish the Court's constitutional power. On the other hand, if the Court ruled in favor of President Jefferson's repudiation of Marbury's appointment, it would appear as if the Court was deferring to the greater power of the President, which would also diminish the constitutional power of the Court. To avoid either ruling, Chief Justice Marshall wrote an opinion that protected the Court's constitutional authority while neither denying former President Adams's appointment power nor yielding power to President Jefferson.

The opinion began by stating that Marbury's appointment became legally valid once it was signed by President Adams and, therefore, had to be recognized by President Jefferson. Next, however, the opinion stated that the Supreme Court had no authority to protect Marbury's appointment because it did not have original jurisdiction over the case. The opinion explained that although the Judiciary Act of 1789 allowed the Supreme Court to issue a mandamus in a case involving a public official, the Constitution's grant of original jurisdiction to the Supreme Court did not allow the Court to do so, because a mandamus was a writ issued by a higher court to a lower court. Since the Constitution was the supreme law of the land, any law passed by Congress that was inconsistent with the Constitution was void. And, since the Court had only appellate, but not original, jurisdiction over Marbury's case, it had to dismiss the suit. Here are excerpts from that opinion:

Marbury v. Madison
1 Cranch 137 (1803)

Mr. Chief Justice Marshall delivered the opinion of the court.

At the last term...a rule was granted in this case, requiring the secretary of state to...deliver to William Marbury his commission [appointment] as a justice of the peace....In the order in which the court has viewed this subject, the following questions have been considered and decided.

1. Has the applicant a right to the commission he demands?
2. If he has a right, and that right has been violated, do the laws of his country afford him a remedy?
3. If they do afford him a remedy, is it a mandamus issuing from this court?

The first object of inquiry is,

1. Has the applicant a right to the commission he demands?....

It appears from the affidavits, [written statement made under oath for use as evidence in a court proceeding] that in compliance with this law, a commission for William Marbury as a justice of peace for the county of Washington was signed by John Adams, then president of the United States;

after which the seal of the United States was affixed to it; but the commission has never reached the person for whom it was made out.

In order to determine whether he is entitled to this commission, it becomes necessary to inquire whether he has been appointed to the office.... The second section of the second article of the constitution declares, "the president shall nominate, and, by and with the advice and consent of the senate, shall appoint ambassadors, other public ministers and consuls, and all other officers of the United States, whose appointments are not otherwise provided for." The third section declares, that "he shall commission all the officers of the United States."...

The appointment being the sole act of the president.... would be made when the last act to be done by the president was performed.... The last act to be done by the president is the signature of the commission.... It is therefore decidedly the opinion of the court, that when a commission has been signed by the president, the appointment is made; and that the commission is complete when the seal of the United States has been affixed to it by the secretary of state.... Mr. Marbury, then, since his commission was signed by the president and sealed by the secretary of state, was appointed.... To withhold the commission, therefore, is an act deemed by the court not warranted by law, but violative of a vested legal right.

This brings us to the second inquiry; which is,

2. If he has a right, and that right has been violated, do the laws of his country afford him a remedy?

The very essence of civil liberty certainly consists in the right of every individual to claim the protection of the laws, whenever he receives an injury. One of the first duties of government is to afford that protection.... The government of the United States has been emphatically termed a government of laws, and not of men....

It is then the opinion of the court,

1. That by signing the commission of Mr. Marbury, the president of the United States appointed him a justice of peace ... and that the appointment conferred on him a legal right to the office for the space of five years.

2. That, having this legal title to the office, he has a consequent right to the commission; a refusal to deliver which is a plain violation of that right, for which the laws of his country afford him a remedy.

It remains to be inquired whether,

3. He is entitled to the remedy for which he applies.

This depends on ... the power of this court.... The act to establish the judicial courts of the United States [the Judiciary Act of 1789] authorizes the supreme court "to issue writs of mandamus to any courts appointed, or to persons holding office, under the authority of the United States."... In the distribution of this power it is declared that "the supreme court shall have original jurisdiction in all cases affecting ambassadors, other public ministers and consuls, and those in which a state shall be a party. In all other cases, the supreme court shall have appellate jurisdiction." . . .

If congress [pursuant to the Judiciary Act of 1789] remains at liberty to give this court appellate jurisdiction, where the constitution has declared their jurisdiction shall be original; and original jurisdiction where the constitution has declared it shall be appellate; the distribution of jurisdiction made in the constitution, is form without substance. . . .

When an instrument [law] organizing fundamentally a judicial system, divides it into one supreme, and so many inferior courts as the legislature may ordain and establish; then enumerates its powers, and proceeds . . . to define the jurisdiction of the supreme court by declaring the cases in which it shall take original jurisdiction, and that in others it shall take appellate jurisdiction, the plain import of the words seems to be, that in one class of cases its jurisdiction is original, and not appellate; in the other it is appellate, and not original. . . .

To enable this court then to issue a mandamus, it must be shown to be an exercise of appellate jurisdiction. . . . It is the essential criterion of appellate jurisdiction, that it revises and corrects the proceedings in a cause [lawsuit] already instituted, and does not create that case. . . . The authority, therefore, given to the supreme court, by the act [of 1789] establishing the judicial courts of the United States, to issue writs of mandamus to public officers, appears not to be warranted by the constitution; and it becomes necessary to inquire whether a jurisdiction, so conferred, can be exercised.

The question, whether an act, repugnant to the constitution, can become the law of the land, is a question deeply interesting to the United States. . . . The constitution is either a superior, paramount law, unchangeable by ordinary means, or it is on a level with ordinary legislative acts, and like other acts, is alterable when the legislature shall please to alter it. . . . Certainly all those who have framed written constitutions contemplate them as forming the fundamental and paramount law of the nation, and consequently the theory of every such government must be, that an act of the legislature repugnant to the constitution is void. . . .

It is emphatically the province and duty of the judicial department to say what the law is. . . . If two laws conflict with each other, the courts must decide on the operation of each. . . . [I]f both the law and the constitution apply to a particular case, so that the court must either decide that case conformably to the law, disregarding the constitution; or conformably to the constitution, disregarding the law: the court must determine which of these conflicting rules governs the case. This is of the very essence of judicial duty. . . .

There are many other parts of the constitution which serve to illustrate this subject. . . . The constitution declares that "no bill of attainder or ex post facto law shall be passed." If, however, such a bill should be passed and a person should be prosecuted under it, must the court condemn to death those victims whom the constitution endeavors to preserve?

"No person," says the constitution, "shall be convicted of treason unless on the testimony of two witnesses to the same overt act, or on confession in open court." Here the language of the constitution is addressed especially to the courts. It prescribes, directly for them, a rule of evidence not to be departed from. If the legislature should change that rule, and declare one witness, or a confession out of court, sufficient for conviction, must the constitutional principle yield to the legislative act?

From these and many other selections which might be made, it is apparent, that the framers of the constitution contemplated that instrument as a rule for the government of courts, as well as of the legislature....

[T]he constitution of the United States confirms and strengthens the principle, supposed to be essential to all written constitutions that a law repugnant to the constitution is void, and that courts, as well as other departments, are bound by that instrument.

The rule must be discharged.

Marbury v. Madison is one of the most significant cases in American political history. Chief Justice Marshall sacrificed a small dispute over Marbury's appointment in order to win a much larger battle for the Court. By invalidating a provision of the Judiciary Act of 1789 that allowed the Supreme Court to issue a mandamus, the Court asserted its authority to declare a law passed by Congress to be unconstitutional. The power of the judiciary to determine whether actions taken by the legislative and executive branches comply with the Constitution is called _judicial review_. Judicial review gave the judicial system the power to assert checks and balances over the other two branches of government and, in so doing, gave the judiciary the power to be a co-equal branch of government.

Constitutional Interpretation

Marbury v. Madison stands for the proposition that, through its power to "say what the law is," the Supreme Court has the final authority to interpret the meaning of the Constitution. But how does the Court determine what the Constitution means? The Constitution itself does not explain how it is to be interpreted. Instead, it contains many broad statements of principles that must be applied to specific cases. Consequently, interpretation of the Constitution has lent itself to several approaches.

Originalists believe that the Constitution means today exactly what it meant when it was written in 1787. Originalists ask, "What was the original intent of the

Founding Fathers when they wrote the Constitution?" Critics of originalism argue that because the Founding Fathers were not unanimous in their values and beliefs, many constitutional provisions were the result of compromise, not absolute agreement. They also argue that significant changes within the nation over the last 200 years have made it virtually impossible for a 21st century judge to think the same way as an 18th century judge.

Strict Constructionists believe that the Constitution means literally and only what its words say, and do not interpret the Constitution's words to reflect political, commercial, technological, or moral changes in American culture. Critics of strict constructionism argue that constitutional words should be interpreted to reflect contemporary realities. For example, the First Amendment guarantees a "free press," which in 1787 literally referred to manual type setters. Today's press, however, refers to radio, television, and the Internet. Similarly, in 1787, "interstate commerce" referred to trade across state borders. Today, interstate commerce also refers to airline transportation, stock exchanges, and multiple types of wireless communication.

Living Constitutionalists believe that the Constitution is an adaptable plan of government that must be interpreted to reflect changes in American values, problems, and solutions. Critics respond that the Constitution should be interpreted consistently with the original intent of the Founding Fathers and not readily altered according to the frequently changing passions and crazes of current society. For example, the Justices who decided *Plessy v. Ferguson* in 1896 may well have believed that separate railroad cars for whites and blacks reflected progress for the black race, which had only recently been emancipated from slavery. The fact that former slaves had obtained the constitutional freedom to travel anywhere within the nation by railroad was, indeed, a sign of progress. But, by 1954, legally enforced racial segregation was no longer viewed as progress, but as discrimination. What changed? In 1787, the Bill of Rights imposed restraints on the federal government's authority to deny people their freedom and liberty, but the Bill of Rights did not apply to the states. In 1787, the Constitution also did not apply to African slaves or members of the black race. After the Civil War ended in 1865, the nation passed the *Thirteenth, Fourteenth,* and *Fifteenth Amendments* to the Constitution that ended slavery, gave rights of citizenship to former slaves, and required the states to treat all citizens equally under the laws. Over the next century, these three constitutional amendments, and the statutes passed to enforce them, were extended to protect people based on race, religion, gender, and national origin—giving far broader meaning and application to the original constitutional language than the Founding Fathers ever debated. Consequently, the values that Americans identified as humanitarian and progressive after the Civil War came to be identified as inhumane racist violations of the Constitution 100 years later, but not by all.

A 19th century painting entitled "Gentlemen of the Jury," by John Morgan.

Criminal Trials

The trial of all Crimes, except in Cases of Impeachment, shall be by Jury; and such Trial shall be held in the State where the said Crimes shall have been committed; but when not committed within any State, the Trial shall be at such Place or Places as the Congress may by Law have directed.

A person accused of a federal crime is tried by a *"Jury . . . in the State where the said Crimes shall have been committed."* However, if the crime was not committed within a specific state, then Congress will determine the location for the trial. For example, a person accused of committing a federal fraud in Illinois will be tried by a jury in Illinois, whereas a person accused of conspiring to commit a federal fraud affecting multiple states will be tried in a state chosen by Congress.

Article III Section 3: Treason

Treason against the United States, shall consist only in levying War against them, or, in adhering to their Enemies, giving them Aid and Comfort. No Person shall be convicted of Treason unless on the Testimony of two Witnesses to the same overt Act, or on Confession in open Court.

> *The Congress shall have Power to declare the Punishment of Treason, but no Attainder of Treason shall work Corruption of Blood, or Forfeiture during the Life of the Person attainted.*[6]

Lastly, Article III Section 3 defines *"Treason"* as betraying the nation by waging war against the United States or giving *"Aid and Comfort"* to a national enemy. The accused person can be convicted of treason only by making a *"Confession"* in court, or if *"two Witnesses"* testify to the accused's misconduct. And, since *"Congress shall have Power to declare the Punishment of Treason," "no Attainder of Treason shall work Corruption of Blood"*—the traitor's conviction cannot be imputed to his or her family.

The Court's Role in Making National Policy

The primary function of the American judiciary is to apply laws to individual cases. In the course of applying a statute or constitutional provision, courts frequently have to determine what a law means. Consequently, lower courts often arrive at conflicting interpretations of the same law. The Supreme Court seeks out such cases in order to provide a uniform interpretation of a federal law. Once the Supreme Court decides what a law means, that interpretation becomes the supreme law of the land and applies to all cases and persons affected by the law, not just the immediate parties to the specific case.

For example, in *Brown v. Board of Education of Topeka*, the Court ruled that although a Kansas statute complied with the *Plessy v. Ferguson* separate-but-equal precedent by creating separate schools for black students and white students, it also violated the Fourteenth Amendment's equal protection clause. As a result of the Court's *Brown* ruling, all states throughout the nation were required to integrate their schools. Many people were outraged by the *Brown* decision. Some believed that laws that separated people of different races merely reflected a basic human value that the federal government should respect. Some believed that the federal judicial system did not have the constitutional authority to tell states how to operate their local schools. Some believed that no court, even the Supreme Court, had the authority to create a national policy because policy-making was a legislative, not a judicial, function.

Despite these criticisms, *Brown v. Board of Education of Topeka* became the law of the land and the primary force for promoting racial equality throughout the United States. People began bringing lawsuits to the federal courts to strike down other segregation laws, one case at a time. Universities, law schools, and graduate schools were ordered to integrate, one case at a time. Segregation in

---

[6] *Attainted* is an old English term that literally means "stained" or "dead in the eyes of the law." In this context, it figuratively means "convicted."

housing, public transportation, hotels and motels, restaurants, washrooms, drinking fountains, places of work, and the military were declared illegal, one case at a time.

Ten years after *Brown*, Congress passed and President Johnson signed the *1964 Civil Rights Act* that made all segregation laws and practices throughout the nation illegal. The era of *Brown* and the Civil Rights Act, known as the *Civil Rights Movement*, is an excellent example of how America's democracy promotes social changes that can start with the people's use of the courts and eventually reach the President and Congress. But cases won in courts, and laws passed by Congress and a President, do not guarantee equality in America. The responsibility to carry out the benefits of the civil rights laws remains with the people, who have the power to elect public officials who enforce the laws and the power to bring lawsuits to enforce violations of their own rights under those laws.

In addition to civil rights, the Supreme Court has made numerous national policies in such areas as contraception and abortion, criminal prosecution procedures, gun ownership, *capital punishment* (a criminal death sentence), speech, religion, college admissions, and sexual harassment and discrimination in the work place. Judicial critics believe that courts should neither develop nor repudiate national policies. They question the authority of judges to balance the interests of the nation as a whole against the interests of the specific parties before them. They argue that statutes reflect the will of the people as determined by their elected legislatures and that courts exceed their authority when they overrule the will of the people by declaring laws to be unconstitutional. Judicial supporters, however, believe that the primary duty of the court system is to protect the Constitution because it reflects the fundamental values of the American people more so than any unconstitutional law. Interestingly, although Congress has the authority to pass laws that reach the same result as do many judicial rulings, it sometimes does not. Instead, sometimes, members of Congress yield their policy-making authority to the court system to avoid the risk of voting on an unpopular law that will affect their ability to be re-elected.

During the Constitutional Convention, the Founding Fathers believed that because the judicial system lacked "the powers of the sword and the purse," it would be "the least dangerous branch of government" and, therefore, the least powerful. Yet the federal judiciary has become extremely powerful because it is the branch of government through which the constitutional system is interpreted and applied to everyone. In the United States, the courts can declare acts of Congress, the President, and federal and state legislatures to be invalid if they violate the Constitution. These unique characteristics of the federal judicial system are possible because federal judges have life tenure and the power of judicial review. The federal judiciary may not have the power of wealth, or the power of the military, but it does have the power of the last word.

CHAPTER 4 QUESTIONS

1. Prepare a brief for *Brown v. Board of Education of Topeka* that addresses the following questions:
    a. What was the legal issue in *Brown v. Board of Education of Topeka*?
    b. What were the primary facts that gave rise to the legal issue?
    c. How did the Court apply its prior holding in *Plessy v. Ferguson* to its decision in *Brown*?
    d. What laws did the Court apply to its holding in *Brown*?
    e. What was the Court's holding in *Brown*?
    f. Why was requiring black and white people to travel in separate train cars considered humane and progressive in 1896 but unconstitutionally discriminatory in 1954?

2. Prepare a brief of *Marbury v. Madison* that addresses the following questions:
    a. What was the legal issue in *Marbury v. Madison*?
    b. According to Chief Justice Marshall, what was the conflict between the Constitution and the Judiciary Act of 1789?
    c. What is the difference between appellate and original jurisdiction?
    d. What prevented the Court from granting Marbury the relief he requested?
    e. Explain what this language from the opinion means: "The government of the United States has been emphatically termed a government of laws, and not of men."

3. Answer the following questions regarding judicial review:
    a. What is judicial review?
    b. What is the constitutional authority for judicial review?
    c. What is the meaning of this quotation from *Marbury v. Madison?* "It is emphatically the province and duty of the judicial department to say what the law is. Those who apply the rule to particular cases, must of necessity expound and interpret that rule."
    d. How would a court system function without judicial review?
    e. In a nation based on democracy, should federal courts make national policies when judges are not elected and are not directly accountable to the people? Explain your answer.
    f. Is the judicial branch the least democratic branch of the government? Explain your answer.
    g. Do you think it is better to resolve social problems through litigation or legislation? Explain your answer.

4. Answer the following questions regarding precedent:
   a. What is precedent?
   b. How does it work?
   c. How would a judicial system function without precedent?

5. As between "Strict Constructionists," "Originalists," and "Living Constitutionalists," which approach to interpreting the Constitution do you think is the best? Explain your answer.

6. What does this quotation mean?

"The judiciary . . . has no influence over either the sword or the purse. . . . It may truly be said to have neither Force nor Will, but merely judgment. . . ."

5

The Constitutional Doctrines of Separation of Powers, Checks and Balances, and Federalism

To create a federal government of strong but limited powers, the Founding Fathers designed a constitutional plan that separated, divided, and subdivided powers on multiple levels. First, the Constitution divided the powers of the federal government into three units—the legislative, executive, and judicial branches:

Federal Government
Legislative | Executive | Judicial

Second, the Constitution divided governing powers among the state and the federal governments:

Federal Government
State Governments

Third, each state's constitution subdivided its governing powers among its own legislative, executive, and judicial branches:

State Government
Legislative | Executive | Judicial

The distribution of governing authority among the legislative, executive, and judicial branches is based on the *separation of powers doctrine.* Under this doctrine, no single branch of government has the constitutional authority to exercise *all* government powers. Instead, the Constitution distributes to each branch of government specific powers over which it has primary, but not exclusive, authority. This governing system of shared powers is based on the *doctrine of checks and balances.* According to this doctrine, the constitutional powers of the three branches overlap so that each branch has the power to restrain any unlawful or undesirable assertions of power by either of the other two branches. For example, although the President nominates people to become Justices of the Supreme Court, the Senate must approve the appointment of each nominee. Once appointed, Supreme Court Justices determine the constitutionality of federal laws passed by Congress and signed into law by the President. However, if the President vetoes a law or the Supreme Court declares a law to be unconstitutional, Congress can either rewrite the law or, in conjunction with the states, amend the Constitution to authorize the law.

The American doctrines of checks and balances and separation of powers are not intended to make governing easy or efficient. Rather, both doctrines are intended to prevent tyrannical concentrations of power in one person, or one branch of government, by requiring each branch to cooperate and compromise with the others. James Madison (the fourth President and the defendant in *Marbury v. Madison*) explained the Founding Fathers' rejection of government powers that can be exclusively exercised by one person or one branch of government when he said, "The accumulation of all powers, legislative, executive and judiciary, in the same hands . . . may justly be pronounced the very definition of tyranny." One of the consequences of governing a nation based on the doctrines of checks and balances and separation of powers, however, is that politics can cause gridlock and governing can be contentious and time-consuming.

Checks and Balances and Separation of Powers: The War Powers

The power to conduct war provides an excellent example of how the American system of government is affected by the separation of powers and checks and balances doctrines. Although war typically refers to external power struggles between nations, war can also cause internal power struggles within a nation at war. Because wars are inherently threatening, wartime pressures for funding, supplies, labor, political support, and developing alliances with other countries can challenge a nation's commitment to its own governing principles that are more easily complied with in times of peace. The following cases explore famous power struggles among the three federal branches of government in times of war.

In 1952, during the Korean Conflict,[1] American steel mill workers who were manufacturing weaponry attempted to increase their pay by threatening to *strike* (stop working). Rather than ask Congress to pass a law to resolve the dispute, President Truman issued an order requiring the federal government to seize the privately owned steel mills. In response, the steel mill owners sued the government, arguing that the President's order amounted to a statute that only Congress had the constitutional authority to pass. In *Youngstown Sheet & Tube Co. v. Sawyer*, the Supreme Court agreed with the steel mill owners. It ruled that without Congressional approval, the Constitution did not grant the President, even as Commander in Chief of the military, the authority to seize the steel mills from their owners:

Youngstown Sheet & Tube Co. v. Sawyer
343 U.S. 579 (1952)

Justice Black delivered the opinion of the Court.

We are asked to decide whether the President was acting within his constitutional power when he issued an order directing the Secretary of Commerce to take possession of and operate most of the Nation's steel mills. The mill owners argue that the President's order amounts to lawmaking, a legislative function which the Constitution has expressly confided to the Congress and not to the President. The Government's position is that the order was made on findings of the President that his action was necessary to avert a national catastrophe which would inevitably result from a stoppage of steel production, and that in meeting this grave emergency the President was acting within the aggregate of his constitutional powers as the Nation's Chief Executive and the Commander in Chief of the Armed Forces of the United States....

The indispensability of steel as a component of substantially all weapons and other war materials led the President to believe that the proposed work stoppage would immediately jeopardize our national defense and that governmental seizure of the steel mills was necessary in order to assure the continued availability of steel. Reciting these

---

[1] Prior to World War II, Korea was controlled by Japan. After World War II, the Korean peninsula was divided by the United States and Russia into two sectors—a communist sector in the north and a democratic sector in the south. The separation of the peninsula into two governments resulted in constant turmoil between the two sectors. In 1950, North Korea invaded South Korea. To prevent communism from taking over the entire peninsula, the United States and twenty other nations fought on behalf of the south, while Russia and China fought on behalf of the north. Although neither sector succeeded in overtaking the other, the war ended in 1953.

considerations for his action, the President, a few hours before the strike was to begin, issued Executive Order 10340.... The order directed the Secretary of Commerce to take possession of most of the steel mills and keep them running.... The next morning the President sent a message to Congress reporting his action. Twelve days later he sent a second message. Congress has taken no action....

The President's power, if any, to issue the order must stem either from an act of Congress or from the Constitution itself. There is no statute that expressly authorizes the President to take possession of property as he did here. Nor is there any act of Congress to which our attention has been directed from which such a power can fairly be implied. Indeed, we do not understand the Government to rely on statutory authorization for this seizure....

It is clear that if the President had authority to issue the order he did, it must be found in some provision of the Constitution. And it is not claimed that express constitutional language grants this power to the President. The contention is that Presidential power should be implied from the aggregate of his powers under the Constitution. Particular reliance is placed on provisions in Article II which say that "The executive Power shall be vested in a President..."; that "he shall take Care that the Laws be faithfully executed"; and that he "shall be Commander in Chief of the Army and Navy of the United States."

The order cannot properly be sustained as an exercise of the President's military power as Commander in Chief of the Armed Forces.... [W]e cannot with faithfulness to our constitutional system hold that the Commander in Chief of the Armed Forces has the ultimate power as such to take possession of private property in order to keep labor disputes from stopping production. This is a job for the Nation's lawmakers, not for its military authorities.

Nor can the seizure order be sustained because of the several constitutional provisions that grant executive power to the President. In the framework of our Constitution, the President's power to see that the laws are faithfully executed refutes the idea that he is to be a lawmaker. The Constitution limits his functions in the lawmaking process to the recommending of laws he thinks wise and the vetoing of laws he thinks bad. And the Constitution is neither silent nor equivocal about who shall make laws which the President is to execute. The first section of the first article says that "All legislative Powers herein granted shall be vested in a Congress of the United States...."After granting many powers to the Congress, Article I goes on to provide that Congress may "make all Laws which shall be necessary and proper for carrying into Execution the foregoing Powers, and all other Powers vested by this Constitution in the Government of the United States, or in any Department or Officer thereof."

The President's order does not direct that a congressional policy be executed in a manner prescribed by Congress—it directs that a presidential policy be executed in a manner prescribed by the President. The preamble of the order itself, like that of many statutes, sets out reasons why the President believes certain policies should be adopted, proclaims these policies as rules of conduct to be followed, and again, like a statute, authorizes a government official to promulgate additional rules and regulations consistent with the policy proclaimed and needed to carry that policy into execution. The power of Congress to adopt such public policies as those proclaimed by the order is beyond question. It can authorize the taking of private property for public use. It can make laws regulating the relationships between employers and employees, prescribing rules designed to settle labor disputes, and fixing wages and working conditions in certain fields of our economy. The Constitution does not subject this lawmaking power of Congress to Presidential or military supervision or control....

The Founders of this Nation entrusted the lawmaking power to the Congress alone in both good and bad times. It would do no good to recall the historical events, the fears of power and the hopes for freedom that lay behind their choice. Such a review would but confirm our holding that this seizure order cannot stand.

Youngstown Steel is a landmark case in American constitutional law that demonstrates the power of the judiciary to check the power of a President who, though determined to protect the nation in time of war, exceeded the constitutional authority of the presidency.

More recently, the doctrines of checks and balances and separation of powers affected America's effort to combat terrorism at home and abroad. On September 11, 2001, America was subject to four attacks by al-Qaeda (Islamist) terrorists. Al-Qaeda hijacked four passenger airplanes and flew two of them into the North and South Towers of the World Trade Center in New York City. The third airplane crashed into the Pentagon in Virginia. The fourth airplane was targeted to attack Washington, D.C. but, instead, crashed onto a field in Pennsylvania after its passengers tried to prevent the terrorists from overtaking the plane. In total, approximately 3,000 people died as a result of these attacks.

After the 9/11 terrorist attacks, the United States military invaded Afghanistan and Iraq in an attempt to eliminate the al-Qaeda and Taliban *insurgencies* (armed rebellions). President George W. Bush ordered the United States military to *detain* (imprison without judicial proceedings) the captured insurgents in *military brigs* (prisons) located in the United States and Guantanamo Bay, Cuba, a territory leased and exclusively controlled by the United States military since 1903. According to the executive branch, these detainees were neither criminals, entitled to constitutional protections, nor prisoners of war, entitled

Photo of the second airplane flying into the World Trade Center

Photo of the destroyed World Trade Center

to the protections of the *Geneva Conventions* (international warfare treaties). Instead, the executive branch referred to the detainees as *enemy combatants* because they engaged in armed warfare against the United States on behalf of a religious ideology rather than a sovereign nation. According to President Bush's theory of *executive detention,* because the enemy combatants were not protected under either the U.S. Constitution or international treaties, they could be detained until the war on terror ended—essentially, indefinitely. Consequently, the enemy combatants were imprisoned for several years without being charged with crimes or given access to legal proceedings to defend themselves. Several of the enemy combatants challenged the legality of their detentions by filing writs of habeas corpus in federal courts. In response, the executive branch argued that the American judiciary lacked jurisdiction over the enemy combatants because they were detained in Cuba, a country that was not subject to American law. The Supreme Court disagreed. In *Rasul v. Bush*, the Court upheld both the right of the enemy combatants to file writs of habeas corpus and the authority of the federal courts to preside over their cases. Excerpts from the Court's opinion follow:

Rasul v. Bush
542 U.S. 466 (2004)

Justice Stevens delivered the opinion of the Court.

On September 11, 2001, agents of the al Qaeda terrorist network hijacked four commercial airliners and used them as missiles to attack American targets. While one of the four attacks was foiled by the heroism of the plane's passengers, the other three killed approximately 3,000 innocent civilians, destroyed hundreds of millions of dollars of property, and severely damaged the U.S. economy. In response to the attacks, Congress passed a joint resolution authorizing the President to use "all necessary and appropriate force against those nations, organizations, or persons he determines planned, authorized, committed, or aided the terrorist attacks... or harbored such organizations or persons." Authorization for Use of Military Force, Pub. L. 107-40, §§1-2, 115 Stat. 224. Acting pursuant to that authorization, the President sent U.S. Armed Forces into Afghanistan to wage a military campaign against al Qaeda and the Taliban regime that had supported it....

Congress has granted federal district courts, "within their respective jurisdictions," the authority to hear applications for habeas corpus by any person who claims to be held "in custody in violation of the Constitution or laws or treaties of the United States." 28 U.S.C. §§2241(a), (c)(3). The statute traces its ancestry to the first grant of federal court jurisdiction: Section 14 of the Judiciary Act of 1789 authorized federal courts to issue the writ of habeas corpus to prisoners "in custody, under or by colour of the authority of the United States, or committed for trial before some court of the same."Act of Sept. 24, 1789, ch. 20, §14, 1 Stat. 82. In 1867, Congress extended the protections of the writ to "all cases where any person may be restrained of his or her liberty in violation of the constitution, or of any treaty or law of the United States." Act of Feb. 5, 1867, ch. 28, 14 Stat....

The question now before us is whether the habeas statute confers a right to judicial review of the legality of Executive detention of aliens in a territory over which the United States exercises plenary and exclusive jurisdiction, but not "ultimate sovereignty."...

Petitioners in these cases... are not nationals of countries at war with the United States, and they deny that they have engaged in or plotted acts of aggression against the United States; they have never been afforded access to any tribunal, much less charged with and convicted of wrongdoing; and for more than two years they have been imprisoned in territory over which the United States exercises exclusive jurisdiction and control....

In Braden v. 30th Judicial Circuit Court of Ky., 410 U.S. 484, 495 (1973), this Court held... that the prisoner's presence within the territorial jurisdiction of the district court is not "an invariable prerequisite" to the exercise of district court jurisdiction under the federal habeas statute. Rather, because "the writ of habeas corpus does not act upon the prisoner who seeks relief, but upon the person who holds him in what is alleged to be unlawful custody," a district court acts "within [its] respective jurisdiction" within the meaning of §2241 as long as "the custodian can be reached by service of process." 410 U.S., at 494-495....

[R]espondents contend that we can discern a limit on §2241 through application of the "longstanding principle of American law" that congressional legislation is presumed not to have extraterritorial application unless such intent is clearly manifested. EEOC v. Arabian American Oil Co., 499 U.S. 244, 248 (1991). Whatever traction the presumption against extraterritoriality might have in other contexts, it certainly has no application to the operation of the habeas statute with respect to persons detained within "the territorial jurisdiction" of the United States. Foley Bros., Inc. v. Filardo, 336 U.S. 281, 285 (1949). By the express terms of its agreements with Cuba, the United States exercises "complete jurisdiction and control" over the Guantanamo Bay Naval Base, and may continue to exercise such control permanently if it so chooses. 1903 Lease Agreement, Art. III; 1934 Treaty, Art. III. Respondents themselves concede that the habeas statute would create federal-court jurisdiction over the claims of an American citizen held at the base. Considering that the statute draws no distinction between Americans and aliens held in federal custody, there is little reason to think that Congress intended the geographical coverage of the statute to vary depending on the detainee's citizenship. Aliens held at the base, no less than American citizens, are entitled to invoke the federal courts' authority under §2241. . . .

In the end, the answer to the question presented is clear. Petitioners contend that they are being held in federal custody in violation of the laws of the United States. No party questions the District Court's jurisdiction over petitioners' custodians. Section 2241, by its terms, requires nothing more. We therefore hold that §2241 confers on the District Court jurisdiction to hear petitioners' habeas corpus challenges to the legality of their detention at the Guantanamo Bay Naval Base. . . .

Justice Stevens' majority opinion received six votes. Justice Scalia wrote the following dissent, which was joined by two other Justices. The dissenters disagreed with the Court's ruling that prisoners of war who were detained outside of the United States were allowed to file habeas corpus petitions to challenge their detentions.

Justice Scalia, with whom the Chief Justice and Justice Thomas join, dissenting.

As we have repeatedly said: "Federal courts are courts of limited jurisdiction. They possess only that power authorized by Constitution and statute, which is not to be expanded by judicial decree." . . . [T]his case turns on the words of §2241, a text the Court today largely ignores. . . . Section 2241(a) states: "Writs of habeas corpus may be granted by the Supreme Court, any justice thereof, the district court and any circuit judge within their respective jurisdictions." . . . [T]he statute could not be clearer that a necessary requirement for issuing the writ is that some federal district court have territorial jurisdiction over the detainee. Here, as the Court allows, the Guantanamo Bay detainees are not located within the territorial jurisdiction of any federal district court. One would think that is the end of this case. . . .

Today's opinion . . . extends the habeas statute, for the first time, to aliens held beyond the sovereign territory of the United States and beyond the territorial jurisdiction of its courts. . . . Today, the Court springs a trap on the Executive, subjecting Guantanamo Bay to the oversight of the federal courts even though it has never before been thought to be within their jurisdiction—and thus making it a foolish place to have housed alien wartime detainees. . . .

The consequence of this holding, as applied to aliens outside the country, is breathtaking. It permits an alien captured in a foreign theater of active combat to bring a [habeas] petition against the Secretary of Defense.... The Commander in Chief and his subordinates had every reason to expect that the internment of combatants at Guantanamo Bay would not have the consequence of bringing the cumbersome machinery of our domestic courts into military affairs. Congress is in session. If it wishes to change federal judges' habeas jurisdiction from what this Court had previously held that to be, it could have done so....

For this court to create such a monstrous scheme in time of war, and in frustration of our military commanders' reliance upon clearly stated prior law, is judicial adventurism of the worst sort.

In 2004, the Court also ruled on another case involving another enemy combatant who filed a habeas corpus writ. This enemy combatant, however, was an American citizen who had been detained in military brigs located in Virginia and South Carolina. Yasir Esam Hamdi was born in the United States but spent most of his life in Saudi Arabia. In 2001, he was captured in Afghanistan as a member of the Taliban and was eventually turned over to the United States military. Once imprisoned in the United States, Hamdi filed a writ of habeas corpus challenging his indefinite detention and seeking protections such as access to legal counsel, a trial to determine his guilt or innocence, and release from unlawful imprisonment. Secretary of Defense Donald Rumsfeld responded that because Hamdi was an enemy combatant, the government was justified in detaining him indefinitely, without a trial, lawyer, or an opportunity to defend himself. Once again, the Supreme Court disagreed. Five of the nine Justices held that because Hamdi was an American citizen, he was constitutionally entitled to file a writ of habeas corpus.

Hamdi v. Rumsfeld

542 U.S. 507 (2004)

Justice O'Connor announced the judgment of the Court.

At this difficult time in our Nation's history, we are called upon to consider the legality of the Government's detention of a United States citizen on United States soil as an "enemy combatant."...

On September 11, 2001, the al Qaeda terrorist network used hijacked commercial airliners to attack prominent targets in the United States.... This case arises out of the detention of a man whom the

Government alleges took up arms with the Taliban during this conflict. His name is Yaser Esam Hamdi. Born an American citizen in Louisiana in 1980, Hamdi moved with his family to Saudi Arabia as a child. By 2001, the parties agree, he resided in Afghanistan. At some point that year, he was seized by members of the Northern Alliance, a coalition of military groups opposed to the Taliban government, and eventually was turned over to the United States military. The Government asserts that it initially detained and interrogated Hamdi in Afghanistan before transferring him to the United States Naval Base in Guantanamo Bay in January 2002. In April 2002, upon learning that Hamdi is an American citizen, authorities transferred him to a naval brig in Norfolk, Virginia, where he remained until a recent transfer to a brig in Charleston, South Carolina. The Government contends that Hamdi is an "enemy combatant," and that this status justifies holding him in the United States indefinitely—without formal charges or proceedings— unless and until it makes the determination that access to counsel or further process is warranted. . . .

The [habeas corpus] petition contends that Hamdi's detention was not legally authorized. It argues that, "[a]s an American citizen . . . Hamdi enjoys the full protections of the Constitution," and that Hamdi's detention in the United States without charges, access to an impartial tribunal, or assistance of counsel "violated and continue[s] to violate the Fifth and Fourteenth Amendments to the United States Constitution." . . . Although his habeas petition provides no details with regard to the factual circumstances surrounding [Hamdi's] capture and detention, [the petition asserts that Hamdi] went to Afghanistan to do "relief work," and that he had been in that country less than two months before September 11, 2001, and could not have received military training. The 20-year-old was traveling on his own for the first time . . . and "[b]ecause of his lack of experience, he was trapped in Afghanistan once that military campaign began." . . .

There is no bar to this Nation's holding one of its own citizens as an enemy combatant. In <u>Ex parte Quirin</u>, 317 U.S. 1 (1942) one of the detainees, Haupt, alleged that he was a naturalized United States citizen. 317 U.S., at 20. We held that "[c]itizens who associate themselves with the military arm of the enemy government, and with its aid, guidance and direction enter this country bent on hostile acts, are enemy belligerents within the meaning of . . . the law of war." Id.,[2] at 37-38. . . .

[The government asserts] that Hamdi "traveled to Afghanistan" in July or August 2001, and that he thereafter "affiliated with a Taliban military unit and received weapons training." It asserts that Hamdi "remained with his Taliban unit following the attacks of September 11" and that, during the time when Northern Alliance forces were "engaged in battle with the

---

[2] *Id.* refers to the immediately preceding case cite.

Taliban," "Hamdi's Taliban unit surrendered" to those forces, after which he "surrender[ed] his Kalishnikov assault rifle" to them. . . . Hamdi was labeled an enemy combatant "[b]ased upon his interviews and in light of his association with the Taliban." . . .

The threshold question before us is whether the Executive has the authority to detain citizens who qualify as "enemy combatants." . . . The AUMF [Authorization for Use of Military Force, 115 Stat. 224] authorizes the President to use "all necessary and appropriate force" against "nations, organizations, or persons" associated with the September 11, 2001 terrorist attacks. There can be no doubt that individuals who fought against the United States in Afghanistan as part of the Taliban, an organization known to have supported the al Qaeda terrorist network responsible for those attacks, are individuals Congress sought to target in passing the AUMF. We conclude that detention of individuals falling into the limited category we are considering, for the duration of the particular conflict in which they were captured, is so fundamental and accepted an incident to war as to be an exercise of the "necessary and appropriate force" Congress has authorized the President to use. . . .

The purpose of detention is to prevent captured individuals from returning to the field of battle and taking up arms once again. Naqvi, Doubtful Prisoner-of-War Status, 84 Int'l Rev. Red Cross 571, 572 (2002) ("Captivity in war is 'neither revenge, nor punishment, but solely protective custody, the only purpose of which is to prevent the prisoners of war from further participation in the war'" (quoting decision of Nuremberg Military Tribunal, reprinted in 41 Am. J. Int'l L. 172, 229 (1947)). . . .

Hamdi objects, nevertheless, that Congress has not authorized the indefinite detention to which he is now subject. . . . We take Hamdi's objection to be not to the lack of certainty regarding the date on which the conflict will end, but to the substantial prospect of perpetual detention. . . . The prospect Hamdi raises is therefore not far-fetched. If the Government does not consider this unconventional war won for two generations, and if it maintains during that time that Hamdi might, if released, rejoin forces fighting against the United States, then . . . Hamdi's detention could last for the rest of his life. . . .

First, the Government urges . . . that because it is "undisputed" that Hamdi's seizure took place in a combat zone, the habeas determination can be made purely as a matter of law, with no further hearing or factfinding necessary. This argument is easily rejected. . . . [T]he circumstances surrounding Hamdi's seizure cannot in any way be characterized as "undisputed." . . . Under the definition of enemy combatant that we accept today as falling within the scope of Congress' authorization, Hamdi would need to be "part of or supporting forces hostile to the United States or coalition partners" and "engaged in an armed conflict against the United States" to justify his detention in the United States for the duration of the relevant conflict. The habeas petition states only that "[w]hen seized by the United States Government, Mr. Hamdi resided in Afghanistan." An assertion that one resided in a country in which combat operations are taking place is not a concession that one was "captured in a zone of active combat operations in a foreign theater of war," (emphasis added), and certainly is not a concession that one was "part of or supporting forces hostile to the United States or coalition partners" and "engaged in an armed conflict against the United States." Accordingly, we reject any [Government] argument that Hamdi has made concessions that eliminate any right to further process. . . .

[According to] the Government's second argument . . . courts should review [the Government's] determination that a citizen is an enemy combatant under a very deferential "some evidence" standard. . . . [and] assume the accuracy of the Government's articulated basis for Hamdi's detention. . . . In response, Hamdi emphasizes that this Court consistently has recognized that an individual challenging his detention may not be held at the will of the Executive without recourse to some proceeding before a neutral tribunal to determine whether the Executive's asserted justifications for that detention have basis in fact and warrant in law. . . .

Striking the proper constitutional balance here is of great importance to the Nation during this period of ongoing combat. But it is equally vital that our calculus not give short shrift to the values that this country holds dear or to the privilege that is American citizenship. It is during our most challenging and uncertain moments that . . . we must preserve our commitment at home to the principles for which we fight abroad. . . .

We therefore hold that a citizen-detainee seeking to challenge his classification as an enemy combatant must receive notice of the factual basis for his classification, and a fair opportunity to rebut the Government's factual assertions before a neutral decisionmaker. These essential constitutional promises may not be eroded. . . .

In so holding, we necessarily reject the Government's assertion that separation of powers principles mandate a heavily circumscribed role for the courts in such circumstances. Indeed, the position that the courts must forgo any examination of the individual case and focus exclusively on the legality of the broader detention scheme cannot be mandated by any reasonable view of separation of powers, as this approach serves only to condense power into a single branch of government. We have long since made clear that a state of war is not a blank check for the President when it comes to the rights of the Nation's citizens. Whatever power the United States Constitution envisions for the Executive in its exchanges with other nations or with enemy organizations in times of conflict, it most assuredly envisions a role for all three branches when individual liberties are at stake. Home Building & Loan Assn. v. Blaisdell, 290 U.S. 398, 426 (1934) (The war power "is a power to wage war successfully, and thus it permits the harnessing of the entire energies of the people in a supreme cooperative effort to preserve the nation. But even the war power does not remove constitutional limitations safeguarding essential liberties"). Likewise, we have made clear that, unless Congress acts to suspend it, the Great Writ of habeas corpus allows the Judicial Branch to play a necessary role in maintaining this delicate balance of governance, serving as an important judicial check on the Executive's discretion in the realm of detentions. . . .

We have no reason to doubt that courts faced with these sensitive matters will pay proper heed both to the matters of national security that might arise in an individual case and to the constitutional limitations safeguarding essential liberties that remain vibrant even in times of security concerns. . . .

It is so ordered.

Justice Scalia agreed with the result reached in the O'Connor opinion but disagreed with its reasons. His dissent was joined by one other Justice. Here are excerpts from Scalia's dissent:

Justice Scalia, with whom Justice Stevens joins, dissenting.

The very core of liberty secured by our Anglo-Saxon system of separated powers has been freedom from indefinite imprisonment at the will of the Executive. . . .

The allegations here, of course, are no ordinary accusations of criminal activity. Yaser Esam Hamdi has been imprisoned because the Government believes he participated in the waging of war against the United States. The relevant question, then, is whether there is a different, special procedure for imprisonment of a citizen accused of wrongdoing by aiding the enemy in wartime.

Justice O'Connor . . . asserts that captured enemy combatants (other than those suspected of war crimes) have traditionally been detained until the cessation of hostilities and then released. That is probably an accurate description of wartime practice with respect to enemy aliens. The tradition with respect to American citizens, however, has been quite different. Citizens aiding the enemy have been treated as traitors subject to the criminal process. . . . [C]itizens have been charged and tried in Article III courts for acts of war against the United States, even when their noncitizen co-conspirators were not. For example, two American citizens alleged to have participated during World War I in a spying conspiracy on behalf of Germany were tried in federal court. See United States v. Fricke, 259 F. 673 (SDNY 1919); United States v. Robinson, 259 F. 685 (SDNY 1919).

A German member of the same conspiracy was subjected to military process. See <u>United States ex rel. Wessels v. McDonald</u>, 265 F. 754 (EDNY 1920). During World War II, the famous German saboteurs of <u>Ex parte Quirin</u>, 317 U.S. 1 (1942), received military process, but the citizens who associated with them...were punished under the criminal process. See <u>Haupt v. United States</u>, 330 U.S. 631 (1947)....

Several limitations give my views in this matter a relatively narrow compass. They apply only to citizens, accused of being enemy combatants, who are detained within the territorial jurisdiction of a federal court. This is not likely to be a numerous group; currently we know of only two, Hamdi and Jose Padilla....The Government has been notably successful in securing conviction, and hence long-term custody or execution, of those who have waged war against the state.

I frankly do not know whether these tools are sufficient to meet the Government's security needs, including the need to obtain intelligence through interrogation. It is far beyond my competence, or the Court's competence, to determine that. But it is not beyond Congress's. If the situation demands it, the Executive can ask Congress to authorize suspension [elimination] of the writ [of habeas corpus]—which can be made subject to whatever conditions Congress deems appropriate....To be sure, suspension is limited by the Constitution to cases of rebellion or invasion. But whether the attacks of September 11, 2001, constitute an "invasion," and whether those attacks still justify suspension several years later, are questions for Congress rather than this Court. If civil rights are to be curtailed during wartime, it must be done openly and democratically, as the Constitution requires, rather than by silent erosion through an opinion of this Court....

Because the Court has proceeded to meet the current emergency in a manner the Constitution does not envision, I respectfully dissent.

It is interesting to note that Justice Scalia agreed with the government's argument in *Rasul* but disagreed with the government's argument in *Hamdi*. In *Rasul*, Scalia agreed that a noncitizen enemy combatant detained outside the United States did not have a right to file a habeas corpus writ in a federal court; in *Hamdi*, Scalia disagreed with the government that an American citizen who was alleged to be an enemy combatant had no right to file a habeas corpus writ in a federal court.

Only Justice Thomas agreed with the government's arguments in both *Hamdi* and *Rasul* that because the constitutional war power authorized the executive branch to protect the nation's security, such decisions "should not be subjected to judicial second-guessing."

Yaser Esam Hamdi in Guantánamo Bay, Cuba, 2002

Secretary of Defense Donald Rumsfeld, 2005

Justice Thomas, dissenting.

The Executive Branch, acting pursuant to the powers vested in the President by the Constitution and with explicit congressional approval, has determined that [Hamdi] is an enemy combatant and should be detained. This detention falls squarely within the Federal Government's war powers, and we lack the expertise and capacity to second-guess that decision. As such, petitioners' habeas challenge should fail, and there is no reason to remand the case....

The national security, after all, is the primary responsibility and purpose of the Federal Government. But because the Founders understood that they could not foresee the myriad potential threats to national security that might later arise, they chose to create a Federal Government that necessarily possesses sufficient power to handle any threat to the security of the Nation.... The Founders intended that the President have primary responsibility—along with the necessary power—to protect the national security and to conduct the Nation's foreign relations.... To this end, the Constitution vests in the President "[t]he executive Power," Art. II, §1, provides that he "shall be Commander in Chief of the" armed forces, §2, and places in him the power to recognize foreign governments, §3.

This Court has long recognized these features and has accordingly held that the President has constitutional authority to protect the national security and that this authority carries with it broad discretion....

[The] Executive's decision that a detention is necessary to protect the public need not and should not be subjected to judicial second-guessing. Indeed, at least in the context of enemy-combatant determinations, this would defeat the unity, secrecy, and dispatch that the Founders believed to be so important to the warmaking function....

Accordingly, I conclude that the Government's detention of Hamdi as an enemy combatant does not violate the Constitution. By detaining Hamdi, the President, in the prosecution of a war and authorized by Congress, has acted well within his authority. Hamdi thereby received all the process to which he was due under the circumstances....

Hamdi and *Rasul* demonstrate the authority of the judiciary to restrain unconstitutional assertions of executive power that violate the doctrines of checks and balances and separation of powers. The executive department of President George W. Bush asserted executive powers, and interpreted constitutional provisions, federal laws, and international treaties in a manner it believed to be in the best interest of the nation but which the Supreme Court repeatedly rejected as unconstitutional. Under the American rule of law, constitutional authority is not altered by war. Instead, constitutional authority must be exercised in accordance with the law, even by the President, even in times of war.

Contemporary Federalism

The United States is neither one centralized nation, like France, nor an alliance of independent states, like the European Union. Rather, the United States is a federal union of 50 individual states. These federal and state governments are able to govern the same people and the same geographic areas at the same time because they govern different matters. The individual states govern local matters occurring within their geographic borders such as industries, businesses, public utilities, family matters, and crimes. The federal government governs matters that affect the entire nation such as national defense, immigration, currency, and foreign policy. Both the federal and state governments exercise authority over taxation, crime, environmental matters, and commerce.

American *federalism* is based on three constitutional provisions. First, the *supremacy clause* of Article VI provides that the Constitution and federal laws are *"the supreme Law of the Land"* that must be obeyed by all states and all American residents. Consequently, state laws that conflict with federal laws are unconstitutional and unenforceable, even if they affect purely local matters. Second, the Tenth Amendment provides, *"The powers not delegated to the United States by the Constitution, nor prohibited by it to the States, are reserved to the States respectively, or to the people."* Consequently, the federal government is barred from exercising powers other than those specifically delegated to it by the Constitution. Third, Article IV provides, *"Full faith and Credit shall be given in each State to the Acts, Records and judicial Proceedings of every other State."* Consequently, under the *full faith and credit clause* if a person is convicted of a crime in Mississippi but flees to Texas, Texas must respect the Mississippi conviction and return the fugitive to Mississippi.

Not surprisingly, the distribution of governing authority under the federalist system has provoked numerous power struggles among the federal government and the 50 states. Here are some famous examples:

The Civil War and the Post Civil War Constitutional Amendments

The Civil War between the northern and southern states was fought from 1861-1865 over the issue of whether slavery should be permitted or banned throughout the nation. Part of the slavery dispute involved the question of which political entity - the states or the federal government - had the constitutional authority to determine the legality of slavery. The economy of the southern states was based primarily on cotton and tobacco farming, both of which were heavily dependent on slave labor. Consequently, the south believed that slavery was a local, economic matter that was most appropriately governed by the states. The northern states opposed slavery as morally reprehensible and believed that the federal government had the authority to ban it throughout the nation. When Abraham Lincoln won the presidential election in 1860, 11 southern states declared their independence from the nation and formed the Confederate States of America (the "Confederacy"). Lincoln regarded the formation of the Confederacy as an illegal rebellion against the nation. The Civil War was fought not only to end slavery but also to force the southern states back into the nation. After the northern states won the Civil War, Congress ratified the Thirteenth, Fourteenth, and Fifteenth Amendments to the Constitution. These amendments significantly modified the constitutional distribution of powers between the federal and state governments.

The Thirteenth Amendment, which ended slavery throughout the nation, provided:

Neither slavery nor involuntary servitude, except as a punishment for crime whereof the party shall have been duly convicted, shall exist within the United States, or any place subject to their jurisdiction.

The Fourteenth Amendment provided citizenship and constitutional rights to all persons born within the United States:

All persons born or naturalized in the United States and subject to the jurisdiction thereof, are citizens of the United States and of the State wherein they reside. No State shall make or enforce any law which shall abridge the privileges or immunities of citizens of the United States; nor shall any State deprive any person of life, liberty, or property, without due process of law;[3] nor deny to any person within its jurisdiction the equal protection of the laws.

The Fifteenth Amendment granted the right to vote to all former male slaves who had become national citizens[4]:

The right of citizens of the United States to vote shall not be denied or abridged by the United States or by any State on account of race, color, or previous condition of servitude.

---

[3] Prior to the Fourteenth Amendment, the due process clause applied only to the federal government pursuant to the Fifth Amendment.
[4] Women were not granted the right to vote until the *Nineteenth Amendment* was ratified in 1920.

A photo of a "Colored Waiting Room" at a Bus Depot during the Jim Crow Era

A photo of separate drinking fountains for whites and blacks during the
Jim Crow Era. Photographer Russell Lee

These post Civil War amendments imposed restraints on state powers that the southern states deeply resented and resisted. And, although the amendments ended slavery, they did not end many of the economic and racial issues associated with it. Many states continued to pass discriminatory laws, called *Jim Crow laws*, that required different treatment of the black and white races. The Jim Crow laws preserved racial segregation by forbidding blacks and whites from intermarrying, attending the same schools, living in the same towns, sitting together on buses and trains, and using the same drinking fountains, washrooms, and other public facilities. Many Jim Crow laws also prevented black people from exercising their right to vote. By the 1940s, the national *Civil Rights Movement* developed for the purpose of ending segregation and bringing legal, social, political, and economic equality to America's black citizens. That effort continues to this day.

The Supremacy Clause and Medical Marijuana

Although the supremacy clause provides that federal laws are enforceable throughout the nation, it does not eliminate potential conflicts between federal and state laws. A current example of a conflict between federal and state laws involves the legality of marijuana use and possession. For example, California passed a law in 1996 that permitted doctors to prescribe marijuana to patients who suffered from chronic pain. The California law conflicted with the federal Controlled Substances Act of 1970 that criminalized the sale, use, and possession of marijuana for any purpose. Users and growers of marijuana in California brought a *declaratory judgment action* (a judicial proceeding to declare the rights and obligations of parties when a legal dispute has arisen but injuries have not yet occurred) in federal court seeking a ruling that the California law was constitutional. The case made its way up to the Supreme Court, which, in *Gonzales v. Raich,* 545 U.S. 1 (2005), ruled against the California law. The Court held that even purely local activities, such as growing and using marijuana in one's home, could be regulated or banned by Congress if such activities violated a federal law. The *Gonzales* case, however, did not end the dispute over legalizing marijuana. At least 23 states have legalized, decriminalized, or regulated marijuana use for various purposes. Although the federal government has not modified its Controlled Substances Act to legalize marijuana, it is currently not challenging the new state statutes.

The Full Faith and Credit Clause and Same-Sex Marriage

The full faith and credit clause of Article IV Section I serves as the constitutional glue that binds together the legal systems of the 50 states by requiring every state to recognize and respect the laws of every other state. Consequently, persons married under Illinois law should be considered married in New York, and persons divorced under California law should be considered divorced in Maine. Since the Tenth Amendment states that all powers that are not specifically delegated to the federal government *"are reserved to the States, respectively, or to the people,"* each state has legalized marriage based on the terms and conditions it deems proper. Historically, most states have limited the right to marriage to opposite-sex couples. Recently, however, more than 30 states have legalized same-sex marriage. Many other states deeply oppose same-sex marriage and refuse to give full faith and credit to such marriages and divorces. The legality of same-sex marriage provides an excellent example of how constitutional provisions like the Tenth Amendment and the full faith and credit clause can create conflicts within the Constitution and among the states.

The following two judicial opinions demonstrate this conflict. Both courts based their analyses on the due process and equal protection clauses of the Fourteenth Amendment. Due process requires that laws must provide people with full and fair opportunities to defend themselves from government actions against their life, liberty, and property. Equal protection prohibits federal and state governments from denying people equal treatment under the law. Both courts questioned whether their state's legal prohibitions against same-sex marriage satisfied the *rational basis test,* a judicial standard that requires courts to deem a law constitutional if it is rationally related to a legitimate governmental purpose. Both courts addressed the historical meaning of marriage. Both courts acknowledged recent changes in public opinion and the nature of the disagreements for and against same-sex marriage. Both courts questioned whether either the judicial or legislative branches had the constitutional authority to legalize same-sex marriage. Both courts reached opposite conclusions.

Goodridge v. Department of Public Health was decided by the State Supreme Judicial Court of Massachusetts. That court determined that a Massachusetts law barring same-sex marriage failed to satisfy the rational basis test in violation of both the due process and equal protection clauses of the Massachusetts constitution. That court also determined that striking down state laws that conflicted with the state's constitution was an appropriate judicial function.

Goodridge v. Department of Public Health
440 Mass. 309 (2003)

Chief Justice Marshall

The question before us is whether, consistent with the Massachusetts Constitution, the Commonwealth may deny the protections, benefits, and obligations conferred by civil marriage to two individuals of the same sex who wish to marry. We conclude that it may not. . . .

We are mindful that our decision marks a change in the history of our marriage law. Many people hold deep-seated religious, moral, and ethical convictions that marriage should be limited to the union of one man and one woman, and that homosexual conduct is immoral. Many hold equally strong religious, moral, and ethical convictions that same-sex couples are entitled to be married, and that homosexual persons should be treated no differently than their heterosexual neighbors. Neither view answers the question before us. Our concern is with the Massachusetts Constitution as a charter of governance for every person properly within its reach. . . .

The plaintiffs challenge the marriage statute [G.L.c.207] on both equal protection and due process grounds. . . . For due process claims, rational basis analysis requires that statutes "bear a real and substantial relation to the public health, safety, morals, or some other phase of the general welfare." Coffee-Rich, Inc. v. Commissioner of Pub. Health, 348 Mass. 763 (1965), quoting Sperry & Hutchinson Co. v. Director of the Div. on the Necessaries of Life, 307 Mass. 408, 418 (1940). For equal protection challenges, the rational basis test requires that "an impartial lawmaker could logically believe that the classification would serve a legitimate public purpose that transcends the harm to the members of the disadvantaged class." English v. New England Med. Ctr., 405 Mass. 423, 429 (1989) quoting Cleburne v. Cleburne Living Ctr., Inc., 473 U.S. 432, 452 (1985) (Stevens, J., concurring). . . . For the reasons we explain below, we conclude that the marriage ban does not meet the rational basis test for either due process or equal protection. . . .

The department [of Public Health] posits three legislative rationales for prohibiting same-sex couples from marrying: (1) providing a "favorable setting for procreation"; (2) ensuring the optimal setting for child rearing, which the department defines as "a two-parent family with one parent of each sex"; and (3) preserving scarce State and private financial resources. We consider each in turn.

The judge in the Superior [trial] Court endorsed the first rationale, holding that "the state's interest in regulating marriage is based on the traditional concept that marriage's primary purpose is procreation." This is incorrect. Our laws of civil marriage do not privilege procreative heterosexual intercourse between married people above every other form of adult intimacy and every other means of creating a family.... Fertility is not a condition of marriage, nor is it grounds for divorce. People who have never consummated their marriage, and never plan to, may be and stay married.... While it is certainly true that many, perhaps most, married couples have children together (assisted or unassisted), it is the exclusive and permanent commitment of the marriage partners to one another, not the begetting of children, that is the sine qua non of civil marriage....

The department's first stated rationale, equating marriage with unassisted heterosexual procreation, shades imperceptibly into its second: that confining marriage to opposite-sex couples ensures that children are raised in the "optimal" setting. Protecting the welfare of children is a paramount State policy. Restricting marriage to opposite-sex couples, however, cannot plausibly further this policy....

The department has offered no evidence that forbidding marriage to people of the same sex will increase the number of couples choosing to enter into opposite-sex marriages in order to have and raise children. There is thus no rational relationship between the marriage statute and the Commonwealth's proffered goal of protecting the "optimal" child rearing unit. Moreover, the department readily concedes that people in same-sex couples may be "excellent" parents. These couples (including four of the plaintiff couples) have children for the reasons others do—to love them, to care for them, to nurture them. But the task of child rearing for same-sex couples is made infinitely harder by their status as outliers to the marriage laws. While establishing the parentage of children as soon as possible is crucial to the safety and welfare of children, same-sex couples must undergo the sometimes lengthy and intrusive process of second-parent adoption to establish their joint parentage. While the enhanced income provided by marital benefits is an important source of security and stability for married couples and their children, those benefits are denied to families headed by same-sex couples. While the laws of divorce provide clear and reasonably predictable guidelines for child support, child custody, and property division on dissolution of a marriage, same-sex couples who dissolve their relationships find themselves and their children in the highly unpredictable terrain of equity jurisdiction [judicial decisions based on concepts of fairness but not laws]. Given the wide range of public benefits reserved only for married couples, we do not credit the department's contention that the absence of access to civil marriage amounts to little more than an inconvenience to same-sex couples and their children.... It cannot be rational under our laws, and indeed it is not permitted, to penalize children by depriving them of State benefits because the State disapproves of their parents' sexual orientation.

The third rationale advanced by the department is that limiting marriage to opposite-sex couples furthers the Legislature's interest in conserving scarce State and private financial resources. The marriage restriction is rational, it argues, because the [state legislature] logically could assume that same-sex couples are more financially independent than married couples and thus less needy of public marital benefits, such as tax advantages, or private marital benefits, such as employer-financed health plans that include spouses in their coverage.

An absolute statutory ban on same-sex marriage bears no rational relationship to the goal of economy. First, the department's conclusory generalization—that same-sex couples are less financially dependent on each other than opposite-sex couples—ignores that many same-sex couples, such as many of the plaintiffs in this case, have children and other dependents (here, aged parents) in their care. The department does not contend, nor could it, that these dependents are less needy or deserving than the dependents of married couples. Second, Massachusetts marriage laws do not condition receipt of public and private financial benefits to married individuals on a demonstration of financial dependence on each other; the benefits are available to married couples regardless of whether they mingle their finances or actually depend on each other for support. . . .

The marriage ban works a deep and scarring hardship on a very real segment of the community for no rational reason. The absence of any reasonable relationship between, on the one hand, an absolute disqualification of same-sex couples who wish to enter into civil marriage and, on the other, protection of public health, safety, or general welfare, suggests that the marriage restriction is rooted in persistent prejudices against persons who are (or who are believed to be) homosexual. . . .

We declare that barring an individual from the protections, benefits, and obligations of civil marriage solely because that person would marry a person of the same sex violates the Massachusetts Constitution. . . .

The next case, _Jonathan P. Robicheaux v. James D. Caldwell,_ was decided by a federal district court in Louisiana. Unlike the Massachusetts Supreme Court, this court determined that both a Louisiana statue[5] and constitutional provision that banned same-sex marriage satisfied the rational basis test. This court also stated that determining the legality of same-sex marriage was more appropriately decided by the state legislature rather than by one judge.

---

[5] Article 3520(B) of the Louisiana Civil Code defines marriage as between one man and one woman.

Robicheaux v. James D. Caldwell

E.D. La. (Case 2:13-cv-05090-MLCF-ALC) 2014

Judge Feldman

[The] national same-sex marriage struggle animates a clash between convictions regarding the value of state decisions reached by way of the democratic [legislative] process as contrasted with personal, genuine, and sincere lifestyle choices.... One may be firmly resolved in favor of same-sex marriage, others may be just as determined that marriage is between a man and a woman. The challenge is how and where best to resolve these conflicting notions about what is marriage....

The Fourteenth Amendment to the Constitution commands that no state shall "deny to any person within its jurisdiction the equal protection of the laws." U.S. Const. amend. XIV, §1. "The Equal Protection Clause... essentially directs that all persons similarly situated be treated alike." Stoneburner v. Sec'y of the Army, 152 F.3d 485, 491 (5th Cir. 1998) (citing City of Cleburne, Tex. v. Cleburne Living Ctr., 473 U.S. 432, 440 (1985))....

When conducting rational basis review, the Supreme Court has instructed that "we will not overturn such [government action] unless the varying treatment of different groups or persons is so unrelated to the achievement of any combination of legitimate purposes that we can only conclude that the actions were irrational." Kimel v. Fl. Bd. of Regents, 528 U.S. 62, 84 (2000). "In the ordinary case, a law will be sustained if it can be said to advance a legitimate government interest, even if the law seems unwise or works to the disadvantage of a particular group, or if the rationale seems tenuous." Romer v. Evans, 517 U.S. 620, 632 (1996)....

Plaintiffs submit that Louisiana's constitutional amendment and Civil Code article [statute] violate the Equal Protection Clause by prohibiting same-sex marriage within Louisiana, and by declining to recognize same-sex marriages that are lawful in other states....

Louisiana's [marriage] laws and Constitution are directly related to achieving marriage's historically preeminent purpose of linking children to their biological parents.... The Court is persuaded that a meaning of what is marriage that has endured in history for thousands of years, and prevails in a majority of states today, is not universally irrational on the constitutional grid.... Because this Court concludes that Louisiana's [marriage] laws are rationally related to its legitimate state interest... they do not offend plaintiffs' rights to Equal Protection....

The Fourteenth Amendment prohibits a state from "depriv[ing] any person of life, liberty, or property, without due process of law." U.S. Const. amend. XIV, §1.... The substantive component of due process, which plaintiffs count on here, protects fundamental rights that are so "implicit in the concept of ordered liberty" that "neither liberty nor justice would exist if they were sacrificed." <u>Palko v. Connecticut</u>, 302 U.S. 319, 325-36 (1937)....[S]uch fundamental rights have been held to include "the rights to marry, to have children, to direct the education and upbringing of one's children, to marital privacy, to use contraception, to bodily integrity, and to abortion." <u>Washington v. Glucksberg</u>, 521 U.S. 702, 720 (1997)....

No authority dictates, and plaintiffs do not contend, that same-sex marriage is anchored to history or tradition....Many states have democratically chosen to recognize same-sex marriage. But until recent years, it had no place at all in this nation's history and tradition. Public attitude might be becoming more diverse, but any right to same-sex marriage is not yet so entrenched as to be fundamental. There is simply no fundamental right, historically or traditionally, to same-sex marriage....

The depth of passion inherent in the issues before this Court defies definition....Perhaps that is the next frontier, the next phase of some "evolving understanding of equality," where what is marriage will be explored....And so, inconvenient questions persist. For example, must the states permit or recognize a marriage between an aunt and niece? Aunt and nephew? Brother/brother? Father and child? May minors marry? Must marriage be limited to only two people? What about a transgender spouse? Is such a union same-gender or male-female? All such unions would undeniably be equally committed to love and caring for one another, just like the plaintiffs....

This Court is powerless to be indifferent to the unknown and possibly imprudent consequences of such a decision. A decision for which there remains the arena of democratic debate. Free and open and probing debate. Indeed, fractious debate....

Heeding those cautions, it is not for this Court to resolve the wisdom of same-sex marriage. The nation is witness to a strong conversation about what is marriage. The central question that must first be asked, is what is the fairest forum for the answer? A new right may or may not be affirmed by the democratic process....As Judge Niemeyer bluntly wrote in his insightful dissent in <u>Bostic v. Schaefer</u>, Nos. 14-1167, 14-1169 & 14-1173, 2014 U.S. App. LEXIS 14298 (4th Cir. July 28, 2014):

> Because there is no fundamental right to same-sex marriage and there are rational reasons for not recognizing it, just as there are rational reasons for recognizing it, I conclude that we, the Third Branch, must allow the States to enact legislation on the subject in accordance with their political processes. The U.S. Constitution does not, in my judgment, restrict the States' policy choices on this issue. If given the choice, some States will surely recognize same-sex marriage and some will surely not. But that is, to be sure, the beauty of federalism.

> 2014 U.S. App. LEXIS 14298, at 109. Federalism is not extinct. Federalism remains a vibrant and essential component of our nation's constitutional structure.
>
> For all of these reasons, the Court finds that Louisiana's definition of marriage as between one man and one woman and the limitation on recognition of same-sex marriages permitted by law in other states found in Article XII, Section 15 of the Louisiana Constitution and article 3520(B) of the Louisiana Civil Code do not infringe the guarantees of the Equal Protection and Due Process Clauses of the United States Constitution.... [T]he defendants have shown that Louisiana's decision to neither permit nor recognize same-sex marriage, formed in the arena of the democratic process, is supported by a rational basis....

Federalism remains a significant power struggle among states, and between states and the federal government. The United States is an extremely diverse nation. Throughout the various geographic regions people have different religious, cultural, and moral values. Because the citizens of each state elect their own governing officials, federalism allows many social, economic, and political programs to be based on the values of each local population. Consequently, many initiatives such as the abolition of slavery and the right of women to vote were introduced by some states and opposed by other states before being accepted at the federal level. Based on the nature of American federalism, the states continue to develop environmental, labor, medical, familial, and educational programs that appeal to or are opposed by other states and which sometimes are never addressed by the federal government. Because American federalism encourages innovation at both the state and the federal levels, it also provokes numerous power struggles between the state and the federal governments.

CHAPTER 5 QUESTIONS

1. a. What is the doctrine of separation of powers?
   b. What is the doctrine of checks and balances?
   c. What is the relationship between the two doctrines?

2. Prepare a brief that addresses the following question regarding the Supreme Court's ruling in *Youngstown Steel v. Sawyer*:
   a. What legal issue did the Court address?
   b. What was the steel mill owners' argument?

    c. What was the President's argument?

    d. Which argument did the Court agree with? Explain your answer.

3. Answer the following questions about the writ of habeas corpus:

    a. What is a writ of habeas corpus?

    b. Who files it?

    c. Who decides to grant or deny it?

    d. Who must obey it?

    e. What power does it give to the judiciary?

4. Prepare a brief that addresses the following questions regarding the Supreme Court's ruling in *Rasul v. Bush*:

    a. What legal issue did the Court address?

    b. Explain the Court's holding.

    c. Why did Justice Scalia disagree with the Court's holding?

    d. Which opinion do you think was correct? Explain your answer.

5. Prepare a brief that addresses the following questions regarding the Supreme Court's holding in *Hamdi v. Rumsfeld*:

    a. What legal issue did the Court address?

    b. What were the Government's arguments?

    c. What were Hamdi's arguments?

    d. Explain the Court's holding.

    e. Why did Justice Scalia agree with Justice O'Connor that Hamdi was entitled to file a writ of habeas corpus but disagree with Justice O'Connor's reasons?

    f. Why did Justice Thomas disagree with Justice O'Connor's analysis and holding?

    g. Which opinion, if any, do you agree with? Explain your answer.

6. Why did Justice Scalia agree with the Government's arguments in *Rasul* but disagree with the Government's arguments in *Hamdi*? Can his two opinions be reconciled?

7. What is the meaning of the following statement by Justice O'Connor in *Hamdi*?

"...Striking the proper constitutional balance here is of great importance to the Nation during this period of ongoing combat. But it is equally vital that our calculus not give short shrift to the values that this country holds dear or to the privilege that is American citizenship. It is during our most challenging and uncertain moments that our Nation's commitment to due process is most severely tested; and it is in those times that we must preserve our commitment at home to the principles for which we fight abroad..."

8. Answer the following questions about federalism:
   a. What is federalism?
   b. How does federalism affect the distribution of power between the individual states and the federal government?
   c. How did the post Civil War constitutional amendments shift political power from the states to the federal government?
   d. Does federalism cause constitutional provisions to conflict with each other? Explain your answer.

9. Prepare a brief that addresses the following questions regarding the State Supreme Judicial Court of Massachusetts's ruling in _Goodridge v. Department of Public Health_:
   a. What were the legal issues addressed by the court?
   b. What were the plaintiff's arguments?
   c. What were the Department of Public Health's arguments?
   d. What is the rational basis test? How did the court apply the rational basis test in its analysis?
   e. What was the court's ruling?

10. Prepare a brief that addresses the following questions regarding the federal district court of Louisiana's ruling in _Jonathan P. Robicheaux v. James D. Caldwell_:
    a. What was the legal issue addressed by the court?
    b. What were the plaintiff's arguments?
    c. What were the defendant's arguments?
    d. How did the court apply the rational basis test?
    e. What was the court's holding?

11. Compare _Goodridge_ and _Robicheaux_:
    a. Which issues did the _Goodridge_ and _Robicheaux_ opinions agree on?
    b. Which issues did the two opinions disagree on?
    c. Why did they reach opposite rulings?
    d. Which opinion do you think was correct? Explain your answer.

First Amendment Constitutional Rights

The 27 Amendments to the Constitution provide the legal framework for the political and civil rights of the American people. Although Americans appreciate the importance of political and civil rights, they frequently disagree about what those rights mean in practice: Can the government restrict political and civil rights? Do political and civil rights allow some people to assert their rights to the detriment of the rights of others? What is the government's role in resolving disputes between conflicting rights? Does the constitutional right of free speech protect statements that are critical of the government or that encourage people to violate the law? Does the constitutional right of religious freedom protect religious practices that offend others or are illegal? Does the constitutional right of a free press protect media publications of classified national security secrets over the objections of the government?

These issues, and many others, are the constant subjects of American political debate. In America's highly diverse cultures, there are always many opinions about the scope and meaning of rights and the power of the government to limit or deny their exercise. American democracy allows all persons the right to express their opinions about their own rights and those of others, and almost everyone does.

The exercise of rights also includes the exercise of the responsibilities necessary to protect those rights. People are expected to respect the rights of others, whether or not they agree with the right asserted. For example, if one person makes a statement that offends another person, the second person may not prevent the first person from speaking. Likewise, the second person may make a statement that offends the first person, but the first person also may not prevent the second person from speaking. If people could prevent each other from speaking, eventually everyone could prevent everyone else from speaking and no one would be able to speak. In America's democracy, people are expected to respect the rights of others because when one person loses a right, other people lose that right as well. It is also understood, however, that the irresponsible exercise of rights can lead to disruption and disorder. The relationship between the power of government to control rights and the responsibilities of people in the exercise of their rights is illustrated by the following examination of the First Amendment.

The First Amendment

The First Amendment protects the rights to freedom of religion, speech, and the press:

> *Congress shall make no law respecting an establishment of religion, or prohibiting the free exercise thereof; or abridging the freedom of speech, or of the press; or the right of the people peaceably to assemble, and to petition the Government for a redress of grievances.*

Freedom of Religion

The first phrase of the First Amendment, *"Congress shall make no law respecting an establishment of religion, or prohibiting the free exercise thereof,"* prohibits Congress and the states[1] from establishing a national religion, favoring one religion over others, and interfering with religious beliefs and practices. The phrase raises many questions: Does the free exercise of religion allow people to believe in any religion or to characterize any belief as religious? Does the free exercise of religion protect religious beliefs or practices of some people that deprive other people of their political or civil rights? Does freedom of religion mean that people have a right to freedom *from* religion—that is, the right not to believe in any religion?

The following two cases demonstrate the scope of religious freedom in America. In each case, the defendants sought religious exemptions from laws that applied to the general population because compliance with the laws conflicted with their religious beliefs and practices. In the first case, the Supreme Court granted the exemption in order to accommodate the defendants' religious freedom; in the second case, the Court did not.

---

[1] The Supreme Court first applied the First Amendment to the states in the case of *Gitlow v. New York*, 268 U.S. 652 (1925), in which the state of New York prosecuted Benjamin Gitlow for violating a state law that banned advocating the unlawful overthrow of the government. The Supreme Court rejected Gitlow's First Amendment defense and upheld his conviction, finding instead that although the states had to apply the First Amendment, Gitlow's advocacy created a "clear and present danger" to the nation.

In *Wisconsin v. Yoder*, the Court addressed the question of whether a state's compulsory education law violated the free exercise of religion of members of the Amish faith. The Amish live in religion-based small farming communities that highly value independence and insulation from modern American culture. The Amish do not use modern technologies such as cars, telephones, televisions, radios, computers, or electricity unless they can generate the energy themselves with windmills. The Amish also do not allow their teenagers to attend high school (grades 9 through 12), in part because they need them to work on the farms, and in part because of their concern that high school culture teaches values and behaviors that the Amish religion opposes such as competition, self-promotion, vanity, dating, dancing, drug and alcohol use. Like all Americans, however, the Amish are required to obey compulsory education and child labor laws.

All states have passed compulsory education and child labor laws. Compulsory education laws require all children to attend school until age 16 in order to develop the basic educational skills necessary to become independent and employable adults. Child labor laws prevent children younger than 16 from being removed from school and required to work as a source of cheap labor that takes jobs away from adults.

In *Wisconsin v. Yoder*, the state of Wisconsin criminally convicted three Amish parents of violating the state's compulsory education law because they had withdrawn their children from school before age 16. The parents raised the defense that the First Amendment's free exercise of religion provision protected their conduct because of the Amish belief that participation in high school endangered their children's salvation. The Wisconsin Supreme Court agreed with the parents' defense and reversed their convictions. The Supreme Court agreed with the Wisconsin Supreme Court:

Wisconsin v. Yoder
406 U.S. 205 (1972)

Chief Justice Burger delivered the opinion of the Court.

Respondents Jonas Yoder and Wallace Miller are members of the Old Order Amish religion, and respondent Adin Yutzy is a member of the Conservative Amish Mennonite Church. They and their families are residents of Green County, Wisconsin. Wisconsin's compulsory school attendance law required them to cause their children to attend public or private school until reaching age 16, but the respondents declined to send their children, ages 14 and 15, to public school after they completed the eighth grade.... [R]espondents were charged, tried, and convicted of violating the compulsory attendance law in Green County Court, and were fined the sum of $5 each. Respondents defended on the ground that the application of the compulsory attendance law violated their rights under the First and Fourteenth Amendments. . . . They believed that, by sending their children to high school, they would not only expose themselves to the danger of the censure of the church community, but . . . also endanger their own salvation and that of their children. . . . They object to the high school, and higher education generally, because the values they teach are in marked variance with Amish values and the Amish way of life; they view secondary school education as an impermissible exposure of their children to a "worldly" influence in conflict with their beliefs. The high school tends to emphasize intellectual and scientific accomplishments, self-distinction, competitiveness, worldly success, and social life with other students. Amish society emphasizes informal "learning through doing;" a life of "goodness," rather than a life of intellect; wisdom, rather than technical knowledge; community welfare, rather than competition; and separation from, rather than integration with, contemporary worldly society. . . .

The Amish do not object to elementary education through the first eight grades as a general proposition, because they agree that their children must have basic skills . . . in order to read the Bible, to be good farmers and citizens, and to be able to deal with non-Amish people when necessary in the course of daily affairs. They view such a basic education as acceptable because it does not significantly expose their children to worldly values or interfere with their development in the Amish community during the crucial adolescent period. . . .

The record shows that the respondents' religious beliefs . . . and what we would today call "lifestyle" have not altered in fundamentals for centuries. Their way of life in a church-oriented community, separated from the outside world and "worldly" influences, their attachment to nature, and the soil, is a way inherently simple and uncomplicated, albeit difficult to preserve against the pressure to conform. Their rejection of telephones, automobiles, radios, and television, their mode of dress, of speech, their habits of manual work do indeed set them apart from much of contemporary society; these customs are both symbolic and practical. . . .

The conclusion is inescapable that secondary schooling, by exposing Amish children to worldly influences in terms of attitudes, goals, and values contrary to beliefs, and by substantially interfering with the religious development of the Amish child and his integration into the way of life of the Amish faith community at the crucial adolescent stage of development, contravenes the basic religious tenets and practice of the Amish faith, both as to the parent and the child. . . . It carries with it precisely the kind of objective danger to the free exercise of religion that the First Amendment was designed to prevent. . . .

The State advances two primary arguments in support of its system of compulsory education. It notes, as Thomas Jefferson pointed out early in our history, that some degree of education is necessary to prepare citizens to participate effectively and intelligently in our open political system if we are to preserve freedom and independence. Further, education prepares individuals to be self-reliant and self-sufficient participants in society. We accept these propositions. However, the evidence adduced by the Amish in this case is persuasively to the effect that an additional one or two years of formal high school for Amish children in place of their long-established program of informal vocational education would do little to serve those interests....

The State further argues that the requirement of compulsory schooling to age 16 must.... be viewed as aimed not merely at providing educational opportunities for children, but as an alternative to the equally undesirable consequence of unhealthful child labor displacing adult workers.... The two kinds of statutes—compulsory school attendance and child labor laws— tend to keep children of certain ages off the labor market and in school.... [The] 16-year education limit reflects, in substantial measure, the concern that children under that age not be employed under conditions hazardous to their health, or in work that should be performed by adults.... There is no intimation that the Amish employment of their children on family farms is in any way deleterious to their health, or that Amish parents exploit children at tender years....

Finally, the State ... argues that a decision exempting Amish children from the State's requirement fails to recognize the substantive right of the Amish child to a secondary education.... It is the parents who are subject to prosecution here for failing to cause their children to attend school, and it is their right of free exercise, not that of their children, that must determine Wisconsin's power to impose criminal penalties on the parent. The dissent argues that a child who expresses a desire to attend public high school in conflict with the wishes of his parents should not be prevented from doing so. There is no reason for the Court to consider that point, since it is not an issue in the case.... The state's position from the outset has been that it is empowered to apply its compulsory attendance law to Amish parents in the same manner as to other parents—that is, without regard to the wishes of the child. That is the claim we reject today....

Indeed, it seems clear that, if the State is empowered ... to "save" a child from himself or his Amish parents by requiring an additional two years of compulsory formal high school education, the State will, in large measure, influence, if not determine, the religious future of the child.... The history and culture of Western civilization reflect a strong tradition of parental concern for the nurture and upbringing of their children. This primary role of the parents in the upbringing of their children is now established beyond debate as an enduring American tradition....

For the reasons stated we hold, with the Supreme Court of Wisconsin, that the First and Fourteenth Amendments prevent the State from compelling respondents to cause their children to attend formal high school to age 16....

In response, Justice Douglas wrote the following dissent:

Justice Douglas, dissenting in part.

The Court's analysis assumes that the only interests at stake in the case are those of the Amish parents, on the one hand, and those of the State, on the other. The difficulty with this approach is that, despite the Court's claim, the parents are seeking to vindicate not only their own free exercise claims, but also those of their high-school-age children. . . .

If the parents in this case are allowed a religious exemption, the inevitable effect is to impose the parents' notions of religious duty upon their children. Where the child is mature enough to express potentially conflicting desires, it would be an invasion of the child's rights to permit such an imposition without canvassing his views. . . . As the child has no other effective forum, it is in this litigation that his rights should be considered. And if an Amish child desires to attend high school, and is mature enough to have that desire respected, the State may well be able to override the parents' religiously motivated objections. . . .

On this important and vital matter of education, I think the children should be entitled to be heard. While the parents, absent dissent, normally speak for the entire family, the education of the child is a matter on which the child will often have decided views. He may want to be a pianist or an astronaut or an oceanographer. To do so he will have to break from the Amish tradition.

It is the future of the student, not the future of the parents, that is imperiled by today's decision. If a parent keeps his child out of school beyond the grade school, then the child will be forever barred from entry into the new and amazing world of diversity that we have today. The child may decide that that is the preferred course, or he may rebel. It is the student's judgment, not his parents', that is essential if we are to give full meaning to what we have said about the Bill of Rights and of the right of students to be masters of their own destiny. If he is harnessed to the Amish way of life by those in authority over him, and if his education is truncated, his entire life may be stunted and deformed. The child, therefore, should be given an opportunity to be heard before the State gives the exemption which we honor today. . . .

In the second case, an Amish farmer employed other Amish men to work on his farm and in his carpentry shop. Under the federal Social Security laws, the farmer was an employer who was required to deduct taxes from his employees' wages and submit those payments to the social security program. The Social Security program is funded by payroll taxes and provides financial benefits for those who are retired, disabled, and deceased. It is also one of the largest and most expensive federal programs. In _United States v. Lee_, the Amish employer sought a religious exemption from the Social Security tax on the grounds that the Amish religion opposes financial dependence on the government and, instead, requires Amish communities to financially support their own financially disadvantaged members:

United States v. Lee
455 U.S. 252 (1982)

Chief Justice Burger delivered the opinion of the Court.

Appellee, a member of the Old Order Amish, is a farmer and carpenter. From 1970 to 1977, appellee employed several other Amish to work on his farm and in his carpentry shop. He failed to file the quarterly social security tax returns required of employers, withhold social security taxes from his employees, or pay the employer's share of social security taxes. In 1978, the Internal Revenue Service [federal tax agency] assessed appellee in excess of $27,000 for unpaid employment taxes; he paid $91—the amount owed for the first quarter of 1973—and then sued in the United States District Court for the Western District of Pennsylvania for a refund, claiming that imposition of the social security taxes violated his First Amendment free exercise rights and those of his Amish employees. . . .

Congress has accommodated self-employed Amish and self-employed members of other religious groups with similar beliefs by providing exemptions from social security taxes. 26 U.S.C. §1402(g). . . . The exemption provided by §1402(g) is available only to self-employed individuals, and does not apply to employers or employees. Consequently, appellee and his employees are not within the express provisions of §1402(g). . . .

The preliminary inquiry in determining the existence of a constitutionally required exemption is whether the payment of social security taxes and the receipt of benefits interfere with the free [religious] exercise rights of the Amish. The Amish believe that there is a religiously based obligation to provide for their fellow members the kind of assistance contemplated by the social security system. Although the Government does not challenge the sincerity of this belief, the Government does contend that payment of social security taxes will not threaten the integrity of the Amish religious belief or observance. . . .

Because the social security system is nationwide, the governmental interest is apparent. The social security system in the United States serves the public interest by providing a comprehensive insurance system with a variety of benefits available to all participants, with costs shared by employers and employees. The social security system is by far the largest domestic governmental program in the United States today.... The design of the system requires support by mandatory contributions from covered employers and employees. This mandatory participation is indispensable to the fiscal vitality of the social security system.... [V]oluntary participation would be almost a contradiction in terms, and difficult, if not impossible, to administer. Thus, the Government's interest in assuring mandatory and continuous participation in, and contribution to, the social security system is very high....

The difficulty in attempting to accommodate religious beliefs in the area of taxation is that "we are a cosmopolitan nation made up of people of almost every conceivable religious preference." Braunfeld v. Brown, 366 U.S. 599, 606 (1961). The Court has long recognized that balance must be struck between the values of the comprehensive social security system... and the consequences of allowing religiously based exemptions. To maintain an organized society that guarantees religious freedom to a great variety of faiths requires that some religious practices yield to the common good....

Unlike the situation presented in Wisconsin v. Yoder, it would be difficult to accommodate the comprehensive social security system with myriad exceptions flowing from a wide variety of religious beliefs.... The tax system could not function if denominations were allowed to challenge the tax system because tax payments were spent in a manner that violates their religious belief. Because the broad public interest in maintaining a sound tax system is of such a high order, religious belief in conflict with the payment of taxes affords no basis for resisting the tax....

Congress and the courts have been sensitive to the needs flowing from the Free Exercise Clause, but every person cannot be shielded from all the burdens incident to exercising every aspect of the right to practice religious beliefs.... Granting an exemption from social security taxes to an employer operates to impose the employer's religious faith on the employees. Congress drew a line in §1402(g), exempting the self-employed Amish but not all persons working for an Amish employer. The tax imposed on employers to support the social security system must be uniformly applicable to all, except as Congress provides explicitly otherwise.

The different outcomes in *Wisconsin v. Yoder* and *United States v. Lee* demonstrate that the free exercise of religion clause permits religious exemptions from some, but not all, laws. Why was an Amish exception to a compulsory education law permitted while an Amish exception to Social Security payments was not? Almost all Americans feel burdened by taxes. If tax exemptions were

An Amish Family

allowed, most Americans would object, few would pay, and government programs would collapse from lack of funds. On the other hand, as an alternative to public and private education, most state compulsory education laws allow parents to educate their children at home as long as their home schooling meets the state's educational requirements.

Freedom of Speech

The First Amendment provides that Congress shall make no law *"abridging the freedom of speech."* The *free speech clause* provides constitutional protection for speech and other forms of expression—verbal and non-verbal, accurate and inaccurate, informed and uninformed, utterly stupid and wildly bizarre. Nonetheless, like all other constitutional rights, free speech is sometimes subject to regulation.

Understanding the meaning of free speech requires an understanding of protected versus unprotected speech. *Political speech* is the most highly protected form of speech and is rarely subject to regulation because it encourages people to participate in a "marketplace of ideas" about governmental policies, politicians, and politics. Political speech sometimes includes *symbolic speech* which expresses political matters by nonverbal conduct such as flag waving or burning, or the wearing of political buttons or armbands. Other forms of speech are subject to regulation, not because the speech is inaccurate, unpopular, or contentious, but because it violates the protected right of another person or business. For example, intellectual property laws allow authors to copyright their publications to prevent others from using their work without permission. Similarly, trademark laws protect the names and titles of businesses, manufacturers, and designers from unauthorized use by others so that people are not misled about the company from which they are purchasing products. Finally, some types of criminal speech receive no constitutional protection. For example, bribery, criminal conspiracy, perjury, and child pornography are criminalized rather than protected because they victimize innocent people and provide no countervailing social value.

Speech will sometimes be protected or not protected based on the time, place, or manner in which it occurs. For example, children may be entitled to say things in the park across the street from a school that they may not be entitled to say within the school. When issues of free speech arise at a school, the school administrators must balance the educational purpose of the school and the safety of all the students against the benefit of allowing some students to express ideas that might disturb others. In the following two cases students sought free speech protection for violating school rules that barred certain forms of expression. In the first case, the Supreme Court granted the protection; in the second case, the Court did not.

In *Tinker v. Des Moines School District*, John Tinker, age 15, Christopher Eckhardt, age 16, and Mary Beth Tinker, age 13, wore black armbands while attending a public school to silently protest against America's involvement in the Vietnam War. Concerned that the armbands might disrupt classes and school activities, the school suspended the students until they removed their armbands. Insisting that their armbands were symbolic speech protected by the First Amendment, the students refused to remove them. The Supreme Court agreed:

Tinker v. Des Moines Independent Community School District
393 U.S. 503 (1969)

Justice Fortas delivered the opinion of the Court.

It can hardly be argued that either students or teachers shed their constitutional rights to freedom of speech or expression at the schoolhouse gate. This has been the unmistakable holding of this Court for almost

50 years.... Our problem lies in the area where students in the exercise of First Amendment rights collide with the rules of the school authorities....

The school officials banned and sought to punish petitioners for a silent, passive expression of opinion, unaccompanied by any disorder or disturbance.... Accordingly, this case does not concern speech or action that intrudes upon the work of the schools or the rights of other students.... There is no indication that the work of the schools or any class was disrupted. Outside the classrooms, a few students made hostile remarks to the children wearing armbands, but there were no threats or acts of violence on school premises....

It is also relevant that the school authorities did not purport to prohibit the wearing of all symbols of political or controversial significance. The record shows that students in some of the schools wore buttons relating to national political campaigns, and some even wore the Iron Cross, traditionally a symbol of Nazism. The order prohibiting the wearing of armbands did not extend to these. Instead, a particular symbol—black armbands worn to exhibit opposition to this Nation's involvement in Vietnam—was singled out for prohibition. Clearly, the prohibition of expression of one particular opinion, at least without evidence that it is necessary to avoid material and substantial interference with schoolwork or discipline, is not constitutionally permissible.

In our system, state-operated schools may not be enclaves of totalitarianism. School officials do not possess absolute authority over their students. Students in school, as well as out of school, are "persons" under our Constitution. They are possessed of fundamental rights which the State must respect, just as they themselves must respect their obligations to the State.... In the absence of a specific showing of constitutionally valid reasons to regulate their speech, students are entitled to freedom of expression of their views....

This principle has been repeated by this Court on numerous occasions during the intervening years. In Keyishian v. Board of Regents, 385 U.S. 589, 603 (1967), Mr. Justice Brennan, speaking for the Court, said:

> "The vigilant protection of constitutional freedoms is nowhere more vital than in the community of American schools." Shelton v. Tucker, 364 U.S. 479 at 487 (1960). The classroom is peculiarly the "marketplace of ideas." The Nation's future depends upon leaders trained through wide exposure to that robust exchange of ideas which discovers truth "out of a multitude of tongues, [rather] than through any kind of authoritative selection."....

A student's rights, therefore, do not embrace merely the classroom hours. When he is in the cafeteria, or on the playing field, or on the campus during the authorized hours, he may express his opinions, even on controversial subjects like the conflict in Vietnam, if he does so without "materially and substantially interfer[ing] with the requirements of appropriate discipline in the operation of the school" and without colliding with the rights of others. Burnside v. Byars, 363 F.2d 744, 749, 5th Cir. (1966). But conduct by the student, in class or out of it, which for any reason—whether it stems from time, place, or type of behavior—materially disrupts classwork or involves substantial disorder or invasion of the rights of others is, of course, not immunized by the constitutional guarantee of freedom of speech. Cf.[2] Blackwell v. Issaquena County Board of Education., 363 F.2d 740, 5th Cir. (1966). . . .

As we have discussed, the record does not demonstrate any facts which might reasonably have led school authorities to forecast substantial disruption of or material interference with school activities, and no disturbances or disorders on the school premises in fact occurred. These petitioners merely went about their ordained rounds in school. Their deviation consisted only in wearing on their sleeve a band of black cloth, not more than two inches wide. They wore it to exhibit their disapproval of the Vietnam hostilities and their advocacy of a truce, to make their views known, and, by their example, to influence others to adopt them. They neither interrupted school activities nor sought to intrude in the school affairs or the lives of others. They caused discussion outside of the classrooms, but no interference with work and no disorder. In the circumstances, our Constitution does not permit officials of the State to deny their form of expression.

In response, Justice Black wrote the following dissent:

Justice Black, dissenting.

Assuming that the Court is correct in holding that the conduct of wearing armbands for the purpose of conveying political ideas is protected by the First Amendment, the crucial remaining questions are whether students and teachers may use the schools at their whim as a platform for the exercise of free speech—"symbolic" or "pure"—and whether the courts will allocate to themselves the function of deciding how the pupils' school day will be spent. While I have always believed that, under the First and

---

[2] *Cf.* refers to a citation that is similar, but not identical, to the issue being discussed.

Fourteenth Amendments, neither the State nor the Federal Government has any authority to regulate or censor the content of speech, I have never believed that any person has a right to give speeches or engage in demonstrations where he pleases and when he pleases. . . .

While the record does not show that any of these armband students shouted, used profane language, or were violent in any manner, detailed testimony by some of them shows their armbands caused comments, warnings by other students, the poking of fun at them, and a warning by an older football player that other, nonprotesting students had better let them alone. There is also evidence that a teacher of mathematics had his lesson period practically "wrecked" chiefly by disputes with Mary Beth Tinker, who wore her armband for her "demonstration." Even a casual reading of the record shows that this armband did divert students' minds from their regular lessons, and that talk, comments, etc., made John Tinker "self-conscious" in attending school with his armband. While the absence of obscene remarks or boisterous and loud disorder perhaps justifies the Court's statement that the few armband students did not actually "disrupt" the classwork, I think the record overwhelmingly shows that the armbands did exactly what the elected school officials and principals foresaw they would, that is, took the students' minds off their classwork and diverted them to thoughts about the highly emotional subject of the Vietnam war. . . .

I wish, therefore, wholly to disclaim any purpose on my part to hold that the Federal Constitution compels the teachers, parents, and elected school officials to surrender control of the American public school system to public school students. I dissent.

Justices Fortas and Black agreed that a primary purpose of school education is to teach young students how to learn and respect authority. Justice Fortas, however, believed that even young students were entitled to First Amendment protection of their political views as long as they did not disrupt school activities. Contrarily, Justice Black believed that such political expression was of no value to students or schools and could lead to unnecessary and harmful educational disruptions.

The _Tinker_ case did not end the debate over freedom of speech in school. The Court continued to preside over many other student speech cases and recently distinguished student political speech from less meaningful speech in _Morse v. Frederick_. Here is that story:

At American sporting events, especially those that are televised, fans have great fun trying to attract the attention of television cameras by displaying

The <u>Morse v. Frederick</u> banner now hangs in the Newseum in
Washington, D.C.

banners. The banners may say "GO CUBS!" or "HAPPY BIRTHDAY!" or "WILL
YOU MARRY ME?" Sometimes the banners are quite silly and make no sense at
all. In January of 2002, the Olympic Torch Relay[3] ran across the street from a
high school in Juneau, Alaska. The high school's principal dismissed the students
and teachers early from school to attend the event as it was being televised. As the
runner passed the crowd, high school student Joseph Frederick and several of his
friends held up a large 14-foot banner printed with the words "BONG HiTS 4
JESUS."

Principal Morse thought the banner advocated illegal drug use because a
bong is a device used for smoking marijuana. Since smoking marijuana was
both a crime and a violation of school rules, she told the students to lower the
banner. All the students obeyed except Frederick, who was suspended from
school. Frederick challenged his suspension as violating his First Amendment
right to free speech by suing Principal Morse. He argued that the phrase
"BONG HiTS 4 JESUS" was "meaningless and funny," intended only to
gain the attention of the television cameras, and was not an endorsement
of illegal drug use. The issue before the Court was whether the *Tinker*
decision controlled the facts of this case:

---

[3] During the Olympic Torch Relay, one participant passes the Olympic Torch to the next
participant as they run the route from Greece to the country that will hold the next Olympic Games.

Morse v. Frederick
551 U.S. 393 (2007)

Chief Justice Roberts delivered the opinion of the Court.

At a school-sanctioned and school-supervised event, a high school principal saw some of her students unfurl a large banner conveying a message she reasonably regarded as promoting illegal drug use. Consistent with established school policy prohibiting such messages at school events, the principal directed the students to take down the banner. One student—among those who had brought the banner to the event—refused to do so. The principal confiscated the banner and later suspended the student....

Our cases make clear that students do not "shed their constitutional rights to freedom of speech or expression at the schoolhouse gate." Tinker v. Des Moines Independent Community School Dist., 393 U.S. 503, 506 (1969). At the same time, we have held that "the constitutional rights of students in public school are not automatically coextensive with the rights of adults in other settings," Bethel School Dist. No. 403 v. Fraser, 478 U.S. 675, 682 (1986), and that the rights of students "must be 'applied in light of the special characteristics of the school environment.'" Hazelwood School Dist. v. Kuhlmeier, 484 U.S. 260, 266 (1988) (quoting Tinker, at 506). Consistent with these principles, we hold that schools may take steps to safeguard those entrusted to their care from speech that can reasonably be regarded as encouraging illegal drug use. We conclude that the school officials in this case did not violate the First Amendment by confiscating the pro-drug banner and suspending the student responsible for it....

The message on Frederick's banner is cryptic. It is no doubt offensive to some, perhaps amusing to others. To still others, it probably means nothing at all. Frederick himself claimed "that the words were just nonsense meant to attract television cameras." But Principal Morse thought the banner would be interpreted by those viewing it as promoting illegal drug use and that interpretation is plainly a reasonable one....

We agree with Morse. At least two interpretations of the words on the banner demonstrate that the sign advocated the use of illegal drugs. First, the phrase could be interpreted as an imperative: "[Take] bong hits..."—a message equivalent, as Morse explained in her declaration, to "smoke marijuana" or "use an illegal drug." Alternatively, the phrase could be viewed as celebrating drug use—"bong hits [are a good thing]," or "[we take] bong hits"—and we discern no meaningful distinction between celebrating illegal drug use in the midst of fellow students and outright advocacy or promotion....

The question thus becomes whether a principal may, consistent with the First Amendment, restrict student speech at a school event, when that speech is reasonably viewed as promoting illegal drug use. We hold that she may.

In Tinker, this Court made clear that "First Amendment rights, applied in light of the special characteristics of the school environment, are available to teachers and students." 393 U. S., at 506. . . . <u>Tinker</u> held that student expression may not be suppressed unless school officials reasonably conclude that it will "materially and substantially disrupt the work and discipline of the school." Id., at 513. The essential facts of <u>Tinker</u> are quite stark, implicating concerns at the heart of the First Amendment. Political speech, of course, is "at the core of what the First Amendment is designed to protect." <u>Virginia v. Black</u>, 538 U.S. 343, 365 (2003). . . .

This Court's next student speech case was <u>Bethel School Dist. No. 403 v. Fraser</u>, 478 U.S. 675 1986. Matthew Fraser was suspended for delivering a speech before a high school assembly in which he employed what this Court called "an elaborate, graphic, and explicit sexual metaphor." Id., at 678. . . . This Court [noted] the "marked distinction between the political 'message' of the armbands in <u>Tinker</u> and the sexual content of [Fraser's] speech." Id., at 680. But the Court also reasoned that school boards have the authority to determine "what manner of speech in the classroom or in school assembly is inappropriate." Id., at 683. . . .

Our most recent student speech case, <u>Kuhlmeier</u>, concerned . . . members of a high school newspaper [who] sued their school when it chose not to publish two of their articles. . . . This Court [held] that "educators do not offend the First Amendment by exercising editorial control over the style and content of student speech in school-sponsored expressive activities so long as their actions are reasonably related to legitimate pedagogical concerns." <u>Kuhlmeier</u>, at 273. . . . <u>Kuhlmeier</u> acknowledged that schools may regulate some speech "even though the government could not censor similar speech outside the school." Id., at 266. . . .

Congress has declared that part of a school's job is educating students about the dangers of illegal drug use. It has provided billions of dollars to support state and local drug-prevention programs. . . . Thousands of school boards throughout the country . . . have adopted policies aimed at effectuating this message. . . . Student speech celebrating illegal drug use at a school event, in the presence of school administrators and teachers, thus poses a particular challenge for school officials working to protect those entrusted to their care from the dangers of drug abuse.

School principals have a difficult job, and a vitally important one. When Frederick suddenly and unexpectedly unfurled his banner, Morse had to decide to act—or not act—on the spot. It was reasonable for her to conclude that the banner promoted illegal drug use—in violation of established school policy—and that failing to act would send a powerful message to the students in her charge, including Frederick, about how serious the school was about the dangers of illegal drug use. The First Amendment does not require schools to tolerate at school events student expression that contributes to those dangers.

Justice Stevens filed the following dissent:

Justice Stevens, with whom Justice Souter and Justice Ginsburg join, dissenting.

On January 24, 2002, the Olympic Torch Relay gave those Alaska residents a rare chance to appear on national television. As Joseph Frederick repeatedly explained, he did not address the curious message— "BONG HiTS 4 JESUS"—to his fellow students. He just wanted to get the camera crews' attention. . . .

I agree with the Court that the principal should not be held liable for pulling down Frederick's banner. I would hold, however, that the school's interest in protecting its students from exposure to speech "reasonably regarded as promoting illegal drug use," cannot justify disciplining Frederick for his attempt to make an ambiguous statement to a television audience simply because it contained an oblique reference to drugs. The First Amendment demands more, indeed, much more.

The Court holds otherwise only after laboring to establish two uncontroversial propositions: first, that the constitutional rights of students in school settings are not coextensive with the rights of adults, and second, that deterring drug use by schoolchildren is a valid and terribly important interest. As to the first, I take the Court's point that the message on Frederick's banner is not necessarily protected speech, even though it unquestionably would have been had the banner been unfurled elsewhere. As to the second, I am willing to assume that the Court is correct that the pressing need to deter drug use supports [the school's] rule prohibiting willful conduct that expressly "advocates the use of substances that are illegal to minors." But it is a gross non sequitur to draw from these two unremarkable propositions the remarkable conclusion that the school may suppress student speech that was never meant to persuade anyone to do anything.

In my judgment, the First Amendment protects student speech if the message itself neither violates a permissible rule nor expressly advocates conduct that is illegal and harmful to students. This nonsense banner does neither, and the Court does serious violence to the First Amendment in upholding—indeed, lauding—a school's decision to punish Frederick for expressing a view with which it disagreed. . . .

Two cardinal First Amendment principles animate . . . the Court's opinion in Tinker . . . First, censorship based on the content of speech, particularly censorship that depends on the viewpoint of the speaker, is subject to the most rigorous burden of justification. . . . Second, punishing someone for advocating illegal conduct is constitutional only when the advocacy is likely to provoke the harm that the government seeks to avoid.

However necessary it may be to modify those principles in the school setting, <u>Tinker</u> affirmed their continuing vitality. . . . Yet today the Court fashions a test that trivializes the two cardinal principles upon which <u>Tinker</u> rests. The Court's test invites stark viewpoint discrimination. In this case, for example, the principal has unabashedly acknowledged that she disciplined Frederick because she disagreed with the pro-drug viewpoint she ascribed to the message on the banner—a viewpoint, incidentally, that Frederick has disavowed. . . . [T]he Court's holding in this case strikes at "the heart of the First Amendment" because it upholds a punishment meted out on the basis of a listener's disagreement with her understanding (or, more likely, misunderstanding) of the speaker's viewpoint. . . .

But it is one thing to restrict speech that advocates drug use. It is another thing entirely to prohibit an obscure message with a drug theme that a third party subjectively—and not very reasonably—thinks is tantamount to express advocacy. Even the school recognizes the paramount need to hold the line between, on the one hand, non-disruptive speech that merely expresses a viewpoint that is unpopular or contrary to the school's preferred message, and on the other hand, advocacy of an illegal or unsafe course of conduct. The [school] district's prohibition of drug advocacy is a gloss on a more general rule that is otherwise quite tolerant of non-disruptive student speech:

> "Students will not be disturbed in the exercise of their constitutionally guaranteed rights to assemble peaceably and to express ideas and opinions, privately or publicly, provided that their activities do not infringe on the rights of others and do not interfere with the operation of the educational program.
>
> The Board will not permit the conduct on school premises of any willful activity . . . that interferes with the orderly operation of the educational program or offends the rights of others. The Board specifically prohibits . . . any assembly or public expression that . . . advocates the use of substances that are illegal."

There is absolutely no evidence that Frederick's banner's reference to drug paraphernalia "willful[ly]" infringed on anyone's rights or interfered with any of the school's educational programs. On its face, then, the rule gave Frederick wide berth "to express [his] ideas and opinions" so long as they did not amount to "advoca[cy]" of drug use. . . .

To the extent the Court independently finds that "BONG HiTS 4 JESUS" objectively amounts to the advocacy of illegal drug use—in other words, that it can most reasonably be interpreted as such—that conclusion practically refutes itself. This is a nonsense message, not advocacy. . . . Frederick's credible and uncontradicted explanation for the message—he just wanted to get on television—is also relevant because a speaker who does not intend to persuade his audience can hardly be said to be advocating anything. But most importantly, it takes real imagination to read a "cryptic" message (the Court's characterization, not mine) with a slanting drug reference as an incitement to drug use. Admittedly, some high school students (including those who use drugs) are dumb. Most students, however, do not shed their brains at the schoolhouse gate, and most students know dumb advocacy when they see it. The notion that the message on this banner would actually persuade either the average student or even the dumbest one to change his or her behavior is most implausible. That the Court believes such a silly message can be proscribed as advocacy underscores the novelty of its position, and suggests that the principle it articulates has no stopping point....

Although this case began with a silly, nonsensical banner, it ends with the Court inventing out of whole cloth a special First Amendment rule permitting the censorship of any student speech that mentions drugs, at least so long as someone could perceive that speech to contain a latent pro-drug message.... Even in high school, a rule that permits only one point of view to be expressed is less likely to produce correct answers than the open discussion of countervailing views. In the national debate about a serious issue, it is the expression of the minority's viewpoint that most demands the protection of the First Amendment. Whatever the better policy may be, a full and frank discussion of the costs and benefits of the attempt to prohibit the use of marijuana is far wiser than suppression of speech because it is unpopular.

I respectfully dissent.

Although the Constitution protects speech, it also allows speech to be regulated based on the time, place, and manner of what is said. It is important to note that the first sentence of Chief Justice Roberts's opinion characterized attendance at the Olympic Torch Relay as "a school-sanctioned and school-supervised event." Consequently, the school's disciplinary rules applied because the event was considered a "school event." Had the opinion characterized the Olympic Torch Relay as a public event that took place in a public park across the street from the school when school was not in session, it undoubtedly would have reached a very different result.

Freedom of the Press

The First Amendment states, *"Congress shall make no law . . . abridging the freedom . . . of the press."* Freedom of the press means that the government may not interfere with, restrain, or punish the press for investigating and publishing information, even if the government does not want the information to be published and even if the published information is false. In America, the high degree of constitutional protection provided to the press has resulted in an extremely powerful press and significant power struggles between the press and the government.

For example, to protect national security the government designates certain information as *classified* in order to maintain its secrecy and prevent its public disclosure. Consequently, disclosure of classified information is a federal crime. Sometimes, however, the press publishes information that it believes the government improperly classified, or that the government properly classified but did not properly protect from disclosure. The press's justification for its publication of classified information is that the First Amendment protects the right of the people to know what their government is doing. The conflict between the government's interest in protecting classified information and the First Amendment right of the press to publish such information is well illustrated by the celebrated "Pentagon Papers" case.

In 1967, the Defense Department wrote a classified report of the United States' involvement in the Vietnam War. Dr. Daniel Ellsberg was a Defense Department analyst whose participation in the study resulted in his opposition to the Vietnam War. Consequently, Ellsberg illegally *leaked* (disclosed) portions of the classified study to the press. On June 13, 1971, The New York Times published several sections of the study, which it called "The Pentagon Papers." The Nixon administration objected to the publication of the Pentagon Papers and obtained an injunction that prevented The New York Times from publishing more sections. Almost immediately thereafter, the Washington Post took up where The New York Times left off and published several more sections of the Pentagon Papers. When the Nixon administration sought an injunction to prevent the Washington Post from publishing more sections, the Boston Globe immediately started publishing the next set of sections. In all, 17 newspapers successively published numerous sections of the Pentagon Papers. Thirteen days after publication of the first Pentagon Papers article, the Supreme Court accepted expedited appeals of The New York Times and Washington Post cases. Four days later, the Supreme Court issued a brief per curiam opinion, in which it ruled in favor of the newspapers. The Court determined that the First Amendment imposed a heavy burden on the government to justify *prior restraint* (government censorship) of the press and had failed to meet that burden:

New York Times Co. v. United States
403 U.S. 713 (1971)

Per Curiam.

We granted certiorari in these cases in which the United States seeks to enjoin the New York Times and the Washington Post from publishing the contents of a classified study entitled "History of U.S. Decision-Making Process on Viet Nam Policy."

> "Any system of prior restraints of expression comes to this Court bearing a heavy presumption against its constitutional validity." Bantam Books, Inc. v. Sullivan, 372 U.S. 58, 70 (1963). The Government "thus carries a heavy burden of showing justification for the imposition of such a restraint." Organization for a Better Austin v. Keefe, 402 U.S. 415, 419 (1971). The District Court for the Southern District of New York in the New York Times case and the District Court for the District of Columbia and the Court of Appeals for the District of Columbia Circuit in the Washington Post case held that the Government had not met that burden.

> We agree.

Several Justices wrote concurrences:

Justice Black, with whom Justice Douglas joins, concurring.

I believe that every moment's continuance of the injunctions against these newspapers amounts to a flagrant, indefensible, and continuing violation of the First Amendment.... In my view it is unfortunate that some of my Brethren are apparently willing to hold that the publication of news may sometimes be enjoined. Such a holding would make a shambles of the First Amendment.

Our Government was launched in 1789 with the adoption of the Constitution. The Bill of Rights, including the First Amendment, followed in 1791. Now, for the first time in the 182 years since the founding of the Republic, the federal courts are asked to hold that the First Amendment does not mean what it says, but rather means that the Government can halt the publication of current news of vital importance to the people of this country....

In the First Amendment the Founding Fathers gave the free press the protection it must have to fulfill its essential role in our democracy. The press was to serve the governed, not the governors. The Government's power to censor the press was abolished so that the press would remain forever free to censure the Government. The press was protected so that it could bare the secrets of government and inform the people. Only a free and unrestrained press can effectively expose deception in government.... In my view, far from deserving condemnation for their courageous reporting, the New York Times, the Washington Post, and other newspapers should be commended for serving the purpose that the Founding Fathers saw so clearly....

Justice Brennan, concurring.

So far as I can determine, never before has the United States sought to enjoin a newspaper from publishing information in its possession.... More important, the First Amendment stands as an absolute bar to the imposition of judicial restraints in circumstances of the kind presented by these cases....

The entire thrust of the Government's claim throughout these cases has been that publication of the material sought to be enjoined "could," or "might," or "may" prejudice the national interest in various ways. But the First Amendment tolerates absolutely no prior judicial restraints of the press predicated upon surmise or conjecture that untoward consequences may result. Our cases, it is true, have indicated that there is a single, extremely narrow class of cases in which the First Amendment's ban on prior judicial restraint may be overridden.... [S]uch cases may arise only when the Nation "is at war," Schenck v. United States, 249 U.S. 47, 52 (1919), during which times "[n]o one would question but that a government might prevent actual obstruction to its recruiting service or the publication of the sailing dates of transports or the number and location of troops." Near v. Minnesota, 283 U.S. 697, 716 (1931).... [I]n neither of these actions has the Government presented or even alleged that publication of items from or based upon the material at issue would cause the happening of an event of that nature.... And therefore, every restraint issued in this case, whatever its form, has violated the First Amendment—and not less so because that restraint was justified as necessary to afford the courts an opportunity to examine the claim more thoroughly. Unless and until the Government has clearly made out its case, the First Amendment commands that no injunction may issue.

Justice White, with whom Justice Stewart joins, concurring.

I concur in today's judgments, but only because of the concededly extraordinary protection against prior restraints enjoyed by the press under our constitutional system. I do not say that in no circumstances would the First Amendment permit an injunction against publishing information about government plans or operations. Nor, after examining the materials the Government characterizes as the most sensitive and destructive, can I deny that revelation of these documents will do substantial damage to public interests. Indeed, I am confident that their disclosure will have that result. But I nevertheless agree that the United States has not satisfied the very heavy burden which it must meet to warrant an injunction against publication in these cases....

Notwithstanding the Supreme Court decision, the saga continued. Although the Nixon administration failed to prevent the newspapers from publishing the Pentagon Papers, it ordered the Justice Department to prosecute Dr. Ellsberg for illegally leaking classified information. Understanding that he had violated the law, and expecting to spend the rest of his life in prison, Dr. Ellsberg surrendered himself to the Justice Department. To ensure Ellsberg's conviction, the White House organized an investigative unit called "the Plumbers" to illegally search the office of Ellsberg's psychiatrist for mental health records that could be used to convict him. When the Plumbers failed to find the records, they illegally wiretapped conversations between Ellsberg and his lawyer. Next, a close advisor to President Nixon offered the judge who presided over Ellsberg's case the directorship of the FBI. The judge refused the offer, disclosed the bribe, and forced the government to dismiss the case, thereby ending the prosecution of Ellsberg and the possibility of his conviction.

Dr. Daniel Ellsberg

Although the Pentagon Papers episode demonstrates the function of the free press in promoting government accountability, sometimes a free press also frustrates government accountability. For example, most states authorize a *reporter's privilege*, a law that protects reporters from disclosing the identity of their confidential sources in state legal proceedings. The federal government, however, does not. Consequently, reporters are required to disclose the identities of their confidential sources in federal lawsuits. Many reporters oppose the federal disclosure requirement and believe, instead, that the First Amendment protects their agreements to maintain the confidentiality of their sources' identities. In 2005, a highly regarded New York Times reporter refused to obey a federal grand jury subpoena ordering her to disclose the identity of a high-level government official from whom she was thought to have received classified information. Here is that story:

In his 2003 State of the Union Address, President George W. Bush discussed the importance of countering terrorism and reducing the expansion of nuclear weapons throughout the world. He stated that the United States might have to take military action against Iraq's President, Saddam Hussein, who was thought to be developing weapons of mass destruction by obtaining uranium from Africa:

> "The British government has learned that Saddam Hussein recently sought significant quantities of uranium from Africa.... [L]et there be no misunderstanding: If Saddam Hussein does not fully disarm, for the safety of our people and for the peace of the world, we will lead a coalition to disarm him.... We seek peace. We strive for peace. And sometimes peace must be defended. A future lived at the mercy of terrible threat is no peace at all. If war is forced upon us, we will fight in a just cause and by just means—sparing, in every way we can, the innocent. And if war is forced upon us, we will fight with the full force and might of the United States military—and we will prevail."

Two months later, the United States military invaded Iraq. Many people publicly disputed the President's reasons for the Iraq invasion. Joseph Wilson, a former United States ambassador, published an article in the New York Times explaining that in 2002 he had been sent by the *Central Intelligence Agency* (the "CIA" is a federal intelligence agency that investigates international issues) to investigate whether Hussein had sought uranium from Niger, Africa, but found no facts to support the claim. His article stated: "If my information was deemed inaccurate, I understand. If the information was ignored because it did not fit certain preconceptions about Iraq, then a legitimate argument can be made that we went to war under false pretenses."

One week later, two White House officials contacted several reporters and told them that Wilson's wife, Valerie Plame, was a CIA agent who had been involved in the decision to send her husband to Niger. Much of this statement was true. Ms. Plame really was a CIA agent who specialized in investigating the development of weapons of mass destruction in the Middle East. More importantly, she was a *covert operative* (CIA secret spy), which meant her work was classified. Unauthorized disclosure of a covert operative's identity is considered a serious threat to national security because it can endanger the spy's life, the lives of the spies with whom she or he works, end the spies' careers, and, most importantly, endanger national safety. Wilson accused the White House of purposefully disclosing his wife's CIA identity to reporters to retaliate against his article because they knew the disclosure would be published and the publications would end her career.

In response to the disclosure, the Attorney General appointed a *Special Counsel* (a lawyer appointed to investigate governmental misconduct) to investigate the validity of Wilson's accusation against the White House. The Special Counsel convened a *grand jury* to conduct the investigation. A grand jury is a group of citizens to whom a prosecutor presents evidence of a possible crime. If the grand jury finds sufficient evidence to charge a suspected person with a crime, it will issue an *indictment* (criminal charge) against the person. The purpose of a grand jury is to protect a suspected person from the government by allowing the grand jurors, not the government prosecutor, to decide whether or not to charge the suspect with a crime. Grand jury proceedings are conducted in secret to protect the suspect's identity from adverse publicity, and also to protect witnesses who testify before the grand jury from being harassed by the suspect.

Judith Miller, a Pulitzer Prize-winning New York Times reporter, was subpoenaed by the grand jury to disclose the identity of the person from whom she had learned of Plame's CIA affiliation. Miller refused to obey the subpoena. Instead, she asserted the reporter's privilege as a First Amendment defense, arguing that the information was disclosed to her in exchange for her promise not to reveal the source's identity and that without the cooperation of confidential sources, the press could not serve its constitutional purpose of reporting important government information to the public. Miller's arguments were rejected by a federal district court. Instead, the court ruled that the reporter's privilege defense was not recognized under federal law and ordered Miller to disclose the identity of her source. When she again refused, the court held her in *contempt of court* (willful violation of a court order) and ordered her jailed until she obeyed the subpoena. Miller appealed the district court's contempt ruling to the Court of Appeals for the District of Columbia. The issue before the court of appeals involved a conflict between two American truth-seeking institutions—the grand jury and the press. The legal duty to provide truthful testimony and the right of a free press to challenge government accountability are both deeply rooted in the Constitution. Here are excerpts from that opinion:

In re: Grand Jury Subpoena, Judith Miller
397 F.3d 964 (2005)

Sentelle, Circuit Judge.

[T]he controversy giving rise to this litigation began with a political and news media controversy over a sixteen-word sentence in the State of the Union Address of President George W. Bush on January 28, 2003. In that address, President Bush stated: "The British government has learned that Saddam Hussein recently sought significant quantities of uranium from Africa." The ensuing public controversy focused... on the accuracy of the proposition that Saddam Hussein had sought uranium, a key ingredient in the development of nuclear weaponry, from Africa. Many publications on the subject followed. On July 6, 2003, the New York Times published an op-ed piece by former Ambassador Joseph Wilson, in which he claimed to have been sent to Niger in 2002 by the Central Intelligence Agency ("CIA") in response to inquiries from Vice President Cheney to investigate whether Iraq had been seeking to purchase uranium from Niger. Wilson claimed that he had conducted the requested investigation and reported on his return that there was no credible evidence that any such effort had been made.

On July 14, 2003, columnist Robert Novak published a column in the Chicago Sun-Times in which he asserted that... "two senior administration officials" told him that Wilson's selection was at the suggestion of Wilson's wife, Valerie Plame, whom Novak described as a CIA "operative on weapons of mass destruction." Robert Novak, The Mission to Niger, Chi. SUN-TIMES, July 14, 2003, at 31. After Novak's column was published, various media accounts reported that other reporters had been told by government officials that Wilson's wife worked at the CIA monitoring weapons of mass destruction, and that she was involved in her husband's selection for the mission to Niger....

Other media accounts reported that "two top White House officials called at least six Washington journalists and disclosed the identity and occupation of Wilson's wife." Mike Allen & Dana Priest, Bush Administration is Focus of Inquiry; CIA Agent's Identity was Leaked to Media, Wash. Post, Sept. 28, 2003. The Department of Justice undertook an investigation into whether government employees had violated federal law by the unauthorized disclosure of the identity of a CIA agent. As the investigation proceeded, in December of 2003, the Attorney General... appointed Patrick J. Fitzgerald... as Special Counsel and delegated full authority concerning the investigation to him.... In cooperation with Special Counsel Fitzgerald, the grand jury conducted an extensive investigation.... [S]ubpoenas were issued to Judith Miller, seeking documents and testimony related to conversations between her and a specified government official...concerning Valerie Plame Wilson....Miller refused to comply with the subpoenas....Thereafter, the court found that Miller had refused to comply without just cause and held her in civil contempt of court....

[Miller asserts] that the First Amendment affords journalists a constitutional right to conceal their confidential sources even against the subpoenas of grand juries....In Branzburg v. Hayes, 408 U.S. 665 (1972), the Highest Court considered and rejected the same claim of First Amendment privilege on facts materially indistinguishable from those at bar....The named petitioner, Branzburg, had been held in contempt in two related proceedings....The first arose from an article published by his employer, a daily newspaper, describing his observation of two Kentucky residents synthesizing hashish from marijuana as part of a profitable illegal drug operation....A Kentucky grand jury subpoenaed the journalist who...claimed privilege both under the First Amendment of the United States Constitution and various state statutory and constitutional provisions. He was held in contempt and the proceeding eventually made its way to the Supreme Court.

The second case involving petitioner Branzburg arose out of a later article published by the same newspaper describing the use of drugs in Frankfort, Kentucky. According to the article...its author had seen some of his sources smoking marijuana....Branzburg was again subpoenaed to appear before a Kentucky grand jury "to testify in the matter of violation of statutes concerning use and sale of drugs," Id. at 669....[Branzburg argued] "that if he were forced to go before the grand jury or to answer questions regarding the identity of informants or disclose information given him in confidence, his effectiveness as a reporter would be greatly damaged." Id. at 670. The Kentucky courts rejected Branzburg's claim of a First Amendment privilege. Again, he petitioned for certiorari in the Supreme Court....The Supreme Court in no uncertain terms rejected the existence of such a privilege. As we said at the outset of this discussion, the Supreme Court has already decided the First Amendment issue before us today.

In rejecting the claim of privilege, the Supreme Court made its reasoning transparent and forceful....The grand juries and the courts operate under the "longstanding principle that 'the public has a right to every man's evidence,' except for those persons protected by constitutional, common law, or statutory privilege." Id....

We have pressed appellants for some distinction between the facts before the Supreme Court in Branzburg and those before us today. They have offered none, nor have we independently found any. Unquestionably, the Supreme Court decided in Branzburg that there is no First Amendment

> privilege protecting journalists from appearing before a grand jury or from
> testifying before a grand jury or otherwise providing evidence to a grand
> jury regardless of any confidence promised by the reporter to any source.
> The Highest Court has spoken and never revisited the question. Without
> doubt, that is the end of the matter.

The Supreme Court refused to hear Miller's appeal. Miller sat in jail for 85 days until she received permission from her confidential source to disclose his identity. She then testified before the grand jury that her confidential source had been I. Lewis "Scooter" Libby, chief of staff to Vice President Cheney. She was then released from jail. Nonetheless, the story continued.

Libby was criminally charged with obstructing the efforts of the FBI to determine if a government official had leaked Valerie Plame's CIA identity to the media, although he, himself, was not charged with being the leaker. Libby's defense was that his involvement in far more important national security matters prevented him from remembering any specific conversations with reporters about Valerie Plame. Several reporters, however, including Judith Miller, did remember their conversations with Libby and testified about his references to Valerie Plame as a CIA operative who was also the wife a prominent critic of the Iraq War. The jury did not believe Libby's defense and convicted him. President Bush then partially commuted Libby's sentence.

CHAPTER 6 QUESTIONS

1. In *Wisconsin v. Yoder*, the Supreme Court granted members of the Amish faith a religious exemption from a law that applied to everyone else. In *United States v. Lee*, the Court denied members of the Amish faith a religious exemption from a law that applied to everyone else. Why did the Court reach different results in these two cases?

2. Assume the following facts: Anne and Samuel are twelve-year-old Amish children who have just completed grammar school (grades 1-8) and are looking forward to attending high school (grades 9-12). Anne is a serious and excellent student and wants to study science. Samuel is an amusing and delightful boy who loves to debate current events, dance, and play musical instruments. Anne and Samuel's Amish parents want them to immediately discontinue their education and return to the Amish community. Base your responses to the following questions on the *Yoder* decision:
   a. What legal arguments will you make on the parents' behalf if you are their lawyer?

   b. What legal arguments will you make on Anne and Samuel's behalf if you are their lawyer?

   c. What legal arguments will you make on the school board's behalf if you are its lawyer?

3. Assume you are an appellate judge in the following case: An Arkansas state criminal court convicted Gregory Holt of stabbing his former girlfriend and sentenced him to life imprisonment. Prior to his conviction, Holt converted to the Muslim religion and changed his name to Abdul Maalik Mujahmad. As a Muslim, Mujahmad believed that he was religiously required to grow a half-inch beard but was prohibited from doing so by an Arkansas state law that barred prison inmates from growing beards. In the federal criminal system, however, several laws allowed prisoners to freely exercise their religious beliefs and practices as long as doing so did not impair the safety or security of the prison system. Should either *Wisconsin v. Yoder* or *United States v. Lee* be the controlling precedent in Mujahmad's case? Explain your answer.

4. Based on the Supreme Court's decisions in *Wisconsin v. Yoder* and *United States v. Lee*, which of these two statements is correct? "Freedom of religion is a fundamental constitutional right that cannot be interfered with by American laws." Or, "Freedom of religion is a fundamental constitutional right only when it does not conflict with generally applicable law." Explain your answer.

5. Consider the following questions about *Tinker v. Des Moines Independent Community School District*:

   a. What legal test did the Supreme Court apply to support its holding in favor of the students?

   b. What did Justice Fortas mean by the statement, "It can hardly be argued that either students or teachers shed their constitutional rights to freedom of speech or expression at the schoolhouse gate"?

   c. What did Justice Black mean by the statement, "Uncontrolled and uncontrollable liberty is an enemy to domestic peace"?

   d. Which opinion do you think correctly applied the First Amendment? Explain your answer.

   e. Which opinion, if either, do you agree with? Explain your answer.

6. Consider the following questions about *Morse v. Frederick*:

   a. What legal test did the Supreme Court apply to support its holding in favor of Principal Morse?

   b. Do you think the Court would have reached the same result if student Frederick had displayed the same banner in a public park on a day and time when the school was not in session? Explain your answer.

    c. Do you think the Court would have reached the same result if Frederick's banner had said, "Legalize bong hits 4 Jesus"? Explain your answer.

    d. What did Justice Stevens mean in his dissent when he said: "The Court fashions a test that trivializes the two cardinal principles upon which *Tinker* rests. The Court's test invites stark viewpoint discrimination."

    e. Which opinion do you think correctly applied the First Amendment? Explain your answer.

    f. Do you personally agree with either opinion? Explain your answer.

7. How to interpret the Constitution:

    a. Should the Constitution be read and interpreted word by word, provision by provision, or as a unified plan of government?

    b. Is the First Amendment right to free speech consistent with the duty of the President to protect the nation from terrorism or the authority of Congress to pass laws that criminalize certain types of speech?

8. Consider the following questions about *New York Times v. United States*:

    a. What was the Court's holding?

    b. What was each Justice's position in his opinion?

    c. Do you agree with any of the Justices' opinions? If so, whose? Explain your answer.

9. Consider the following questions about *In re Grand Jury Subpoena, Judith Miller*:

    a. What was the constitutional conflict between freedom of the press and the grand jury investigation?

    b. How did the court rule? Explain your answer.

10. Think back to the Watergate event discussed in Chapter 3: While the Special Prosecutor and the Senate were investigating the burglary of the Democratic National Committee Headquarters, reporters Bob Woodward and Carl Bernstein were also conducting an investigation for the Washington Post. Unlike the government that had the power to subpoena witnesses to talk about investigated matters, Woodward and Bernstein's only means of obtaining information was to convince people who worked for the government to talk to them. Given the political sensitivity of the Watergate matter, many government workers did not want to talk to them. Eventually, Woodward and Bernstein were able to access several confidential sources, one of whom was a very high level federal employee who had exceptional knowledge about the efforts of the Nixon White House to obstruct the Watergate investigation. Woodward and Bernstein named this confidential source "Deep Throat"—a joking reference to the title of a pornographic movie from that time period. Woodward and Deep Throat held secret meetings in late evenings and early mornings in the basement of a garage where Deep Throat would disclose the

White House's most recent plans to obstruct the Watergate investigation. Woodward and Bernstein would then publish Deep Throat's disclosures in the Washington Post and the congressional investigating committees and Special Prosecutor would use the Washington Post's reports to issue subpoenas in furtherance of their own investigations. Woodward and Bernstein promised Deep Throat that they would not reveal his identity to anyone except their employer, Ben Bradlee, the editor of the Washington Post. Without this assurance of confidentiality, Deep Throat would not have agreed to talk to Woodward. Woodward and Bernstein kept their promise to Deep Throat for 32 years, until 2005, when Mark Felt publicly announced that he had been Deep Throat during the Watergate Investigation while he was also the Assistant Director of the FBI was jailed.

Three decades after Watergate, when reporter Judith Miller refused to identify her confidential source, both Woodward and Bernstein publicly stated that they would not have been able to investigate Watergate if they had been ordered to reveal any of their sources' identities. To date, they have not disclosed the identities of their other sources.

Do you think the federal government should recognize a reporter's privilege that allows reporters to withhold the identities of their confidential sources from federal investigations?

Mark Felt

The American Litigation System

The American judiciary is unique, and uniquely complicated by its multiple judicial systems. The federal government has a judicial system with courthouses located within each of the 50 states. Each of the 50 states also has its own judicial system with courthouses located throughout each state. Although the federal and state systems are organized and funded independently, they function cooperatively. Each system has the authority to preside over cases involving the laws, residents, organizations, and business entities of the other court systems.

Four doctrines make the relationship between the federal and state court systems possible. The *supremacy clause* of Article VI states:

> **This Constitution, and the Laws of the United States which shall be made in Pursuance thereof; and all Treaties made, or which shall be made, under the Authority of the United States, shall be the supreme Law of the land; and the Judges in every State shall be bound thereby, any Thing in the Constitution or Laws of any State to the contrary notwithstanding.**

The purpose of the supremacy clause is to maintain uniformity in the interpretation and application of federal laws throughout the entire nation. To do so, the supremacy clause provides that the Constitution and federal laws are the *"supreme Law of the land"* that must be obeyed by all state courts. Consequently, if a state law conflicts with a federal law, the state must apply the federal law, not its own conflicting state law. The supremacy clause also bars state courts from modifying or rejecting federal court interpretations of federal laws.

The *full faith and credit clause* of Article IV Section 1 states:

> **Full faith and Credit shall be given in each State to the public Acts, Records, and judicial Proceedings of every other State. And the Congress may by**

general Laws prescribe the Manner in which such Acts, Records and Proceedings shall be proved and the Effect thereof.

The full faith and credit clause requires every state to respect and apply the laws of every other state. For example, if a case about a car accident that occurred in New York is filed in an Illinois state court, the Illinois court must apply New York's law to the case, not Illinois's law. As a result, the full faith and credit clause prevents states from disregarding each other's laws while preventing litigants from filing cases in states that have the most favorable laws for their dispute.

The doctrine of *concurrent jurisdiction* authorizes the federal and state court systems to preside over cases that involve the laws of the other court system. Consequently, federal courts can preside over cases involving state laws and state courts can preside over cases involving federal laws. Concurrent jurisdiction promotes the efficient use of judicial resources because many lawsuits involve both state and federal laws. Without concurrent jurisdiction, litigants would have to bring separate lawsuits involving the same dispute in both federal and state courts, which could reach different results. Concurrent jurisdiction prevents inconsistent rulings on the same dispute by allowing the parties to include all legal issues that are related to the same dispute in one lawsuit within one court system.

The one exception to concurrent jurisdiction is when a law is within the *exclusive jurisdiction* of only one judicial system. For example, only federal courts have jurisdiction over patent, immigration, antitrust, and bankruptcy cases; only state courts have jurisdiction over state criminal cases, divorce cases, and worker's compensation cases that allege work-related injuries. Consequently, a lawsuit involving a law within the exclusive jurisdiction of one court system can be presided over only by a court within that system.

Organization of the State and Federal Court Systems

The state and federal court systems are organized like a triangle:

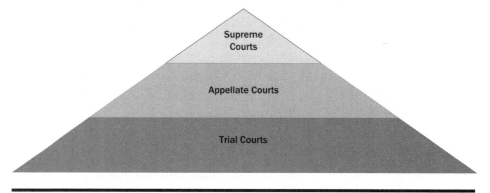

All courts, state and federal, are open to the public and the media. A case typically stays within the court system in which it is originally filed.[1] For example, a case that is filed in a state court will stay within the trial, appellate, and supreme courts of that state. Similarly, a case filed within the federal system will stay within the district, circuit, and Supreme Court. The following **COURT SYSTEMS** chart illustrates the relationships of the courts to each other within each system:

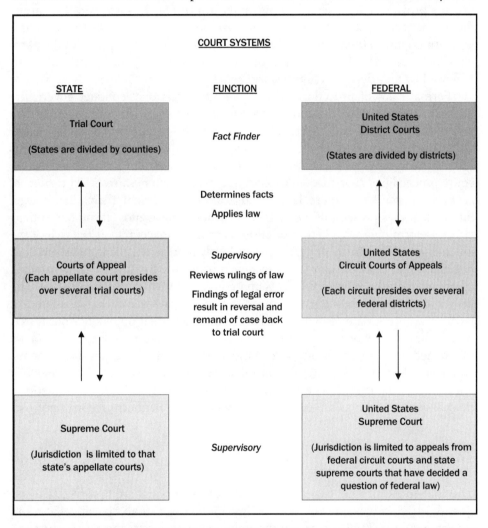

COURT SYSTEMS

STATE	FUNCTION	FEDERAL
Trial Court (States are divided by counties)	*Fact Finder*	**United States District Courts** (States are divided by districts)
	Determines facts Applies law	
Courts of Appeal (Each appellate court presides over several trial courts)	*Supervisory* Reviews rulings of law Findings of legal error result in reversal and remand of case back to trial court	**United States Circuit Courts of Appeals** (Each circuit presides over several federal districts)
Supreme Court (Jurisdiction is limited to that state's appellate courts)	*Supervisory*	**United States Supreme Court** (Jurisdiction is limited to appeals from federal circuit courts and state supreme courts that have decided a question of federal law)

---

[1] The most common exception to this general rule is the U.S. Supreme Court's jurisdiction over state supreme courts that have ruled on federal legal issues. See **COURT SYSTEMS** chart.

The Litigation Process

The manner in which lawsuits are prepared and presented is called the *litigation process.* The purpose of the litigation process is to provide a dispute resolution system in which parties to a lawsuit are represented by licensed attorneys who present their clients' cases to an impartial judge or jury. At the trial, the litigation process provides all parties an opportunity to present the facts and legal arguments that are most favorable to their positions and to discredit the facts and legal arguments of their opponents. The litigation process also provides the party who loses the case in the trial court an opportunity to have the judgment reviewed by an *appellate* (supervisory) *court.*

Formal rules of procedure, evidence, and professional conduct govern the litigation process. It is the judge's role to enforce these rules throughout the proceedings. The *rules of procedure* determine who plaintiffs may sue as defendants, the legal theories for the parties' allegations and defenses, and the remedy the court can provide. The *rules of evidence* allow lawyers to present evidence in court proceedings that meet reliability and trustworthiness tests. The *rules of professional conduct* require lawyers to zealously represent their client's legal interests, always presenting the facts in a manner that is most favorable to their client. Determining what is true or false, accurate or inaccurate, is the role of the judge or jury. The ethical obligation to zealously represent a client, however, does not mean that a lawyer can falsify evidence or distort the law. Legal arguments must be supported by provable facts and consistent with the applicable law. The lawyer's legal arguments must persuade the court that their client's position is a lawful and appropriate resolution of the dispute while their opponent's position is not. Unless they violate the rules of professional conduct, lawyers cannot be disciplined for aggressively and forcefully asserting their clients' legal arguments. Nor can a lawyer's legal arguments made on behalf of a client be personally attributed to the lawyer. The litigation system assumes that lawyers sometimes must assert arguments on behalf of clients whom they neither agree with nor like.

Trial Courts

The trial courts are the entry-level courts where lawsuits are first filed. Consequently, trial courts preside over many more cases than the appellate and supreme courts. Trial courts are the only courts in which the parties have an opportunity to present their evidence to a judge or jury that observes the witnesses, examines the evidence, and decides the outcome of the case.

The Courtroom

Each trial courtroom is staffed by a *judge, legal secretary, law clerk, minute clerk, court reporter,* and *law enforcement officer.* The judge presides over the entire case until it is ruled upon or privately *settled* (resolved and removed from the court) by the parties. The *legal secretary* manages the *judicial chambers* (office), maintains the records and documents that are kept in the chambers, accepts official court documents, formally prepares opinions and orders, and schedules the judge's appointments. The *law clerk* is a recent law school graduate who is hired for a one-or two-year period to research the law and prepare written memoranda to assist the judge's decision-making. Clerking is considered an honor because of the unique opportunity the clerkship provides for a new and inexperienced lawyer to work under the close guidance of a judge. The *court reporter* records every word that is spoken by the lawyers, witnesses, and judge in the courtroom during a proceeding. If the case is appealed, the court reporter prepares a *transcript* (record) of the proceedings that will be submitted to the appellate court for review. The *minute clerk* maintains the court's calendar of hearings, trials, ruling dates, and prepares the judge's orders to be signed and issued. Every courtroom is protected by a law enforcement officer who is responsible for preventing disruption and disorder in the courtroom. The law enforcement officer also escorts criminal defendants in and out of the courtroom and guards the jury room while jurors *deliberate* (decide the outcome of a case).

The Judges

A judge is a licensed attorney who serves as the neutral and independent supervisor of the litigation process. Federal judges are appointed by Congress for life or until they resign or are removed from office. State judges are either appointed by state legislatures or elected by state citizens for a specified period of time. The primary function of a judge is to make *legal rulings* (decisions) on disputed issues of laws and facts to ensure that the legal proceedings comply with the rules of evidence, procedure, and professionalism. Despite their control over lawsuits, judges are prohibited from talking about the cases they preside over to anyone other than their staff members, other judges, and the case attorneys.

The Lawyers

Lawyers and their legal practices are regulated by *bar associations,* organizations within each state that are operated by lawyers to regulate professional standards, not by the state or federal governments. Consequently, bar associations determine who is qualified to receive a law license or should be disciplined for professional misconduct after receiving a license. Lawyers receive their licenses after graduating from college, receiving a *Juris Doctor degree* ("J.D.") from a law school, and passing a *bar exam* (a test to determine if a law school graduate is qualified to practice law) in the state in which they will practice. Once licensed, lawyers are not required to select specific areas of practice, although many choose to specialize. The primary role of a lawyer is to protect a client's legal

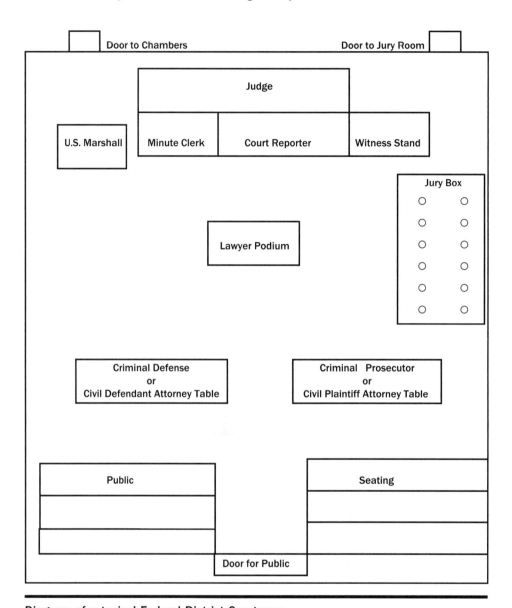

Diagram of a typical Federal District Courtroom

interests by researching the applicable law, investigating the pertinent facts, and representing the client throughout a transactional or litigation proceeding.

The Parties

In a civil case, a plaintiff files a *complaint* against a defendant that alleges the plaintiff's *rights* and the defendant's *liabilities*. A right refers to conduct, beliefs, and status to which people are entitled and which are legally protected when violated by other people, entities, or the government. A liability is a breached duty that violates a right owed to another person, entity, or government that can require the violator to compensate the injured party for the loss of the right. The most common types of compensation are *monetary damages* (money), which reimburse the injured party for financial losses and pain and suffering caused by the injuries, and *injunctive relief,* which orders a party to do or refrain from doing a specific act. Typically, the plaintiff alleges that the defendant breached a duty owed to the plaintiff pursuant to a private contract, personal injury law, commercial statute, or constitutional provision for which the plaintiff is entitled to relief.

The Proceedings

The first stage of a civil law suit is called the *pleadings.* The plaintiff initiates the pleadings by *filing* (submitting) a *complaint* in a court that has *jurisdiction* (authority) to preside over the case. The complaint will contain *allegations* (accusations) of the plaintiff's rights that were *breached* (violated) by the defendant, the harms suffered by the plaintiff as a result of the breaches, and the *relief* (remedy) sought by the plaintiff as compensation for the injuries. The defendant may respond to the complaint by filing a *motion to dismiss,* a document that asks the court to terminate the lawsuit either because it was filed in the wrong court or failed to allege a *cognizable claim* (a legal issue over which the court has authority to preside). If the court grants the motion to dismiss, the lawsuit will be terminated and qualify for *appeal* (review and reconsideration) to an appellate court. If the court denies the motion to dismiss, the defendant will file an *answer* to the complaint in which the defendant admits or denies the plaintiff's allegations, asserts *defenses* (arguments) challenging the allegations, and alleges *counter-claims* (allegations) against the plaintiff.

Once the answer is submitted, the pleading stage is complete and the parties proceed to the *discovery stage* of the lawsuit. During the discovery stage, the parties investigate their opponent's version of the case by analyzing documents, *evidence* (disputed facts), and questioning the opposing parties and their witnesses to determine their knowledge and *credibility* (believability and truthfulness). By the end of the discovery stage, the parties should know the strengths and weaknesses of their own evidence and that of their opponents and, based on such information, may agree to privately settle the case and voluntarily dismiss it from the court.

However, if the parties do not settle the case it will proceed to the trial stage. The parties will issue *subpoenas* (court orders requiring attendance) to witnesses to *testify* (answer questions) on the *witness stand* (witness chair) in front of the jury. Before testifying, each witness will take an *oath* (promise) to tell the truth. Each witness will then be questioned by the attorney for the party who requested his or her attendance at the trial. This form of questioning is called *direct examination*. During direct examination, the attorney will ask questions about the witness's observation and memory of the disputed facts. When the direct examination is finished, the attorney for the opposing party will *cross-examine* the witness. The purpose of cross-examination is to *impeach* (discredit) the witness's version of the facts, truthfulness, and reliability. Throughout the trial, the court reporter will *transcribe* (record) each witness's testimony, each lawyer's questions and objections to the opposing lawyer's questions, and the judge's statements, rulings, and orders.

To illustrate this process, assume that Mr. Ben and Mr. Mike each drive through an intersection when their cars collide. Mr. Ben sues Mr. Mike to recover monetary damages as compensation for his personal injuries and the property damage to his car. Mr. Ben's complaint alleges that Mr. Mike caused the accident by *negligently* (violating a legal standard of conduct) driving his car through a red light. In his answer, Mr. Mike denies Mr. Ben's negligence allegation and counterclaims that it was actually Mr. Ben who drove through the red light and caused the car accident, resulting in Mr. Mike's personal injuries and property damage, for which he is entitled to compensation:

Trial Court in the State of Florida

Mr. Ben

      Plaintiff   **Complaint for Negligence**

v.   **Civil Action No: 12345**

Mr. Mike

      Defendant

COMPLAINT

Plaintiff Mr. Ben sues Defendant Mr. Mike as follows:

1. **Plaintiff resides in Maine.**

2. **Defendant resides in Florida.**

3. **This action arises from a car accident that occurred on December 13, 2014, in the City of Waterville, Maine, at the intersection of Main Street and Colby Avenue.**

FACTS

4. **On December 13, 2014, at 5 p.m., Plaintiff drove his car through a green light at the intersection between Colby Avenue and Main Street when his car was struck by a car driven by Defendant who sped through a red light while crossing Colby Avenue.**

COUNT ONE

5. The collision was caused by negligence on the part of Defendant who sped through a red light at an illegally high rate of speed.

6. As a result of Defendant's negligence, Plaintiff suffered injuries to his hips, knees, and feet that required several surgeries and prevented from him from employment. Plaintiff continues to experience pain and suffering despite the numerous surgeries.

7. In addition, Plaintiff's car was substantially damaged and required extensive repairs.

PRAYER FOR RELIEF

WHEREFORE, Plaintiff seeks Two Hundred and Fifty Thousand Dollars ($250,000) in damages.

Respectfully submitted,
Matthew Rooney
Attorney for Plaintiff
300 Barnard Drive
Waterville, Maine
490-872-3541
mrooney@lawfirm.com

Trial Court in the State of Florida

Mr. Ben

    Plaintiff   **ANSWER and COUNTERCLAIM**

v.   Civil Action No: 12345

Mr. Mike

    Defendant

Defendant Mr. Mike answers the complaint of Plaintiff Mr. Ben as follows:

1. Defendant admits the allegations of paragraph 1.

2. Defendant admits the allegations of paragraph 2.

3. Defendant admits the allegations of paragraph 3.

4. Defendant admits that at 5 p.m. on December 13, 2014, Plaintiff was driving a car through the intersection at Main Street and Colby Avenue when there was a collision between the cars driven by Plaintiff and Defendant and, except as admitted, denies the other allegations of paragraph 4 of the complaint.

5. Defendant denies the allegations of paragraph 5.

6.   Defendants states that he is without information sufficient to form a belief as to the truth of the allegations of paragraph 6 of the complaint and, therefore, denies the allegations of paragraph 6.

7.   Defendants states that he is without information sufficient to form a belief as to the truth of the allegations of paragraph 7 of the complaint and, therefore, denies the allegations of paragraph 7.

DEFENSE

8.   Defendant alleges that Plaintiff drove his car negligently and recklessly through a red light while crossing the intersection between Main Street and Colby Avenue, which was the cause of the accident.

COUNTERCLAIM

9.   On December 13, 2014, at 5 p.m., Plaintiff drove his car through a red light at the intersection at Main Street and Colby Avenue in a negligent and reckless manner, which caused the collision with the car driven by Defendant.

10.   As a result of said collision, Defendant suffered serious injuries to his neck and shoulder and his car was damaged, resulting in expenses for medical treatments and car repairs in the amount of $25,000.

WHEREFORE, Defendant seeks judgment on his counterclaim in the amount of $25,000 and dismissal of Plaintiff's complaint.

Respectfully submitted,
Sherry Guthrie
Attorney for Defendant
123 Grande Ave.
Sarasota, Florida
804-293-5489
sguthrie@lawfirm.com

During discovery, Mr. Ben and Mr. Mike investigate each other's evidence and witnesses. However, once discovery concludes, neither agrees to settle because each is convinced of the strength of his case and the weakness of his opponent's case. Consequently, the case proceeds to trial and both parties issue subpoenas to their witnesses. Assume Ms. Jessica is Mr. Ben's primary witness because, during discovery, it was learned that she stood on the street corner of the intersection where the accident occurred and Mr. Ben's attorney, Mr. Rooney, believes that Ms. Jessica's testimony will be favorable to Mr. Ben. Mr. Rooney calls Ms. Jessica to the witness stand and, through direct examination, asks her a series of questions about her observations of the car accident:

Attorney Rooney:	Ms. Jessica, were you present at the scene of the car accident?
Ms. Jessica:	Yes.
Attorney Rooney:	Where were you located?
Ms. Jessica:	I was standing on the corner of Main Street and across the street from Colby Avenue when the accident occurred.
Attorney Rooney:	Was your view of the accident obstructed by anything?
Ms. Jessica:	No. There were no other cars crossing through the intersection and no other people in the area.
Attorney Rooney:	Would you please tell us what you observed?
Ms. Jessica:	As Mr. Mike sped through the red light on Colby Avenue, he was bending his neck to hold a cell phone to his ear and smoking a cigarette and drinking out of a paper cup. And he had a dog in his lap. I also heard loud music coming from his car.

On cross-examination, Mr. Mike's attorney, Ms. Guthrie, successfully impeaches the accuracy and reliability of Ms. Jessica's testimony:

Attorney Guthrie:	Ms. Jessica, do you wear eyeglasses?
Ms. Jessica:	Yes.
Attorney Guthrie:	For what purpose?
Ms. Jessica:	For all purposes. I'm basically legally blind without them.
Attorney Guthrie:	Were you wearing your glasses when you observed the car accident?
Ms. Jessica:	No. It was sunny and I was wearing my non-prescription sunglasses.
Attorney Guthrie:	What, if anything, were you doing when you observed the car accident?
Ms. Jessica:	I was adjusting my cell phone earpiece to hear music and sending a text message as I pushed my baby's stroller.
Attorney Guthrie:	I have no further questions for this witness.

The Evidence

As the lawyers present testimony and evidence during the trial, the judge determines whether such information is *admissible* (legally competent) and may be presented to the jury or *inadmissible* and may not be presented to the jury. There are three primary rules of evidence. To be presented to a jury, evidence must be *relevant* (pertinent) and may not be *hearsay* or *privileged*. To be relevant, evidence must be logically related to the proof or disproof of a disputed issue in the case. However, even relevant evidence may be inadmissible if it is either hearsay or privileged. Hearsay evidence is information that is not within the personal knowledge of a witness. For example, assume that Ms. Jessica is out of the country and unavailable to testify at the trial but that Ms. Jessica told Ms. Kathryn about the car accident. Ms. Kathryn cannot be called to testify that Ms. Jessica told her that Mr. Mike drove through a red light because she, Ms. Kathryn, did not personally observe the collision. Only Ms. Jessica, herself, can testify to what she personally observed at the accident site. Hearsay is inadmissible because it permits one person to repeat something told to them by another person but which he or she did not personally observe or experience. Hearsay is also inadmissible because the actual witness is not in the courtroom and, therefore, is not available to be cross-examined.

Unlike hearsay evidence, which is inadmissible because it is not reliable, privileged evidence is inadmissible even if it is reliable, relevant, and truthful. Privileged evidence is inadmissible in courtroom proceedings to protect socially important relationships that require trust and confidentiality. For example, Mr. Mike may confide to Attorney Guthrie that he was distracted when he drove through the intersection because he was trying to text a message on his cell phone. The jury, however, will never learn of that conversation. The *attorney-client privilege* protects confidential communications between attorneys and clients so that clients can tell the truth to their attorneys (no matter how incriminating it may be) without fear that their attorneys will be required to testify against them in court. Without such assurance, clients would not be fully truthful to their attorneys, attorneys would provide less effective legal representation, and the judicial system would be a less successful system for resolving disputes.

The case of <u>*People v. Belge*</u> provides an excellent example of the high value the legal system places on the attorney-client privilege. Robert Garrow was originally charged with committing one murder. Garrow confided to his attorney, Francis Belge, that he had committed several other murders as well and told Belge where the bodies were buried. Belge investigated and found the bodies, but because of the attorney-client privilege he could not disclose the information to the police. However, Garrow's confession to Attorney Belge was eventually disclosed during his trial and the government criminally *indicted* (charged) Belge for violating public health laws relating to the disposal of human remains. Belge defended his silence on the grounds that the attorney-client privilege prevented him from disclosing his client's confession. Excerpts from the opinion follow:

People of the State of New York v. Belge
372 N.Y.S.2d 798 (1975)[2]

Gale, Judge

In the summer of 1973 Robert F. Garrow, Jr., stood charged in Hamilton County with the crime of murder.... A defense of insanity had been interposed by counsel for Mr. Garrow. During the course of the discussions between Garrow and his two counsel, three other murders were admitted by Garrow.... Mr. Belge conducted his own investigation based upon what his client had told him and ... the body of Alicia Hauck was found in Oakwood Cemetery in Syracuse. Mr. Belge personally inspected the body and was satisfied, presumably, that this was the Alicia Hauck that his client had told him that he murdered.

This discovery was not disclosed to the authorities, but became public during the trial of Mr. Garrow in June of 1974, when to affirmatively establish the defense of insanity, these three other murders were brought before the jury.... Public indignation reached the fever pitch, statements were made by the District Attorney of Onondaga County relative to the situation and he caused the Grand Jury of Onondaga County, then sitting, to conduct a thorough investigation. As a result of this investigation ... Indictment No. 75-55 was returned as against Francis R. Belge, Esq., accusing him of having violated subdivision 1 of section 4200 of the Public Health Law, which, in essence, requires that a decent burial be accorded the dead, and section 4143 of the Public Health Law, which, in essence, requires anyone knowing of the death of a person without medical attendance, to report the same to the proper authorities. Defense counsel moves for a dismissal of the indictment on the grounds that a confidential, privileged communication existed between him and Mr. Garrow, which should excuse the attorney from making full disclosure to the authorities.

The National Association of Criminal Defense Lawyers, as amicus curiae [a non party who is allowed to provide advice to a court on a matter of law], succinctly state the issue in the following language: If this indictment stands, "The attorney-client privilege will be effectively destroyed. No defendant will be able to freely discuss the facts of his case with his attorney. No attorney will be able to listen to those facts without being faced with the ... choice of violating the law or violating his professional code of Ethics.".....

Our system of criminal justice is an adversary system and the interests of the State are not absolute, or even paramount. "The dignity of the individual is respected to the point that even when the citizen is known by

---

[2] The citation 372 N.Y.S.2d 798 (1975) refers to the New York State trial court.

the state to have committed a heinous offense, the individual is nevertheless accorded such rights as counsel, trial by jury, due process, and the privilege against self incrimination.". . . .

The effectiveness of counsel is only as great as the confidentiality of its client-attorney relationship. If the lawyer cannot get all the facts about the case, he can only give his client half of a defense. This, of necessity, involves the client telling his attorney everything remotely connected with the crime. . . . For the client to disclose not only everything about this particular crime but also everything about other crimes which might have a bearing upon his defense, requires the strictest confidence in, and on the part of, the attorney. . . .

In the case at bar we must weigh the importance of the general privilege of confidentiality in the performance of the defendant's duties as an attorney, against the inroads of such a privilege on the fair administration of criminal justice as well as the heart tearing that went on in the victim's family by reason of their uncertainty as to the whereabouts [of the murdered victim]. . . .

It is the decision of this court that Francis R. Belge conducted himself as an officer of the court with all the zeal at his command to protect the constitutional rights of his client. Both on the grounds of a privileged communication and in the interests of justice the indictment is dismissed.

The privilege doctrine protects confidential relationships that are considered more important to maintaining the stability of the social order than is the disclosure of some truthful information at a trial. In the _Belge_ case, the trial judge upheld the legality of the attorney-client privilege despite the fact that truthful, relevant, and reliable information had been withheld from the jury, the police, and the victims' families.

The Jury

Throughout the trial the jurors sit together in a *jury box* (a separate area) on one side of the courtroom. After the parties present all of their evidence and witnesses, the judge instructs the jury about the law that applies to the case. *Jury instructions* inform the jurors of the standards they must apply to determine the true facts, apply the appropriate laws to the true facts, and reach a *verdict* (decision). For example, the judge will inform the jurors that under the rules of evidence a plaintiff can win a case only by satisfying the required *burden of proof*. A burden of proof refers to the evidentiary standard a party must meet to prove the facts of the case. The lowest burden of proof, called *the preponderance of evidence standard*, applies in most civil cases and requires only that the facts necessary to win the case are more likely to be true than false. The next highest burden of proof, called the *clear and convincing evidence standard*, applies to civil fraud cases and requires that the facts necessary to win the case are highly probable and substantially convincing. The highest burden of proof standard, called *proof beyond a reasonable doubt*, applies in criminal cases and requires the prosecutor to overcome the defendant's *presumption of innocence* by proving facts that leave no reasonable doubt as to the defendant's guilt. The criminal burden of proof is more difficult to achieve than the civil burdens of proof because a criminal conviction can result in the loss of personal liberty through imprisonment, whereas the loss of a civil case by a defendant usually results only in monetary damages.

Once the jury instructions are completed, the jurors go into the *jury room* (a room adjacent to the courtroom) where they select a *foreman* or *forewoman* (leader) who leads their *deliberations* (discussions) and informs the judge when the jury reaches a verdict. After the verdict is disclosed in open court the judge enters a *judgment* in favor of the winning party. In a civil case the jury will find the defendant liable or not liable for the plaintiff's injuries. In a criminal case the jury will find the defendant guilty and convict, or not guilty and *acquit*.

Appellate Courts

Appellate courts are the second level of courts in both the state and federal systems. A party who loses at the trial court level may seek review and *reversal* (rejection) of the trial court's judgment by an appellate court. Unlike trial courts, in which a single judge presides over a case, appellate cases are presided over by three-judge panels.

The Appeal Process

The party who seeks to reverse the trial court judgment is called the *appellant* or *petitioner*. The party who must defend the validity of the trial court judgment is called the *appellee* or *respondent*. Unlike a trial court, an appellate court does not hear witnesses or examine evidence. Instead, the appellate court decides the appeal based entirely on the trial court's record, the parties' *legal briefs* (written legal arguments), and the attorneys' *oral arguments*. During the oral arguments, the attorneys are questioned by the three-judge panel. The appellate court will *affirm* the judgment if it finds that the trial court's rulings were correct. If the appellate court finds that the trial court made an erroneous ruling that affected the outcome of the case, it will reverse the judgment and *remand* (return) the case to the trial court with instructions to correct the mistake and enter a new judgment that is consistent with its instructions.

Let's return to Mr. Ben and Mr. Mike's car accident case: Assume that Ms. Jessica is unavailable to testify at the trial and the judge permits Ms. Kathryn to testify to what Ms. Jessica told her about the car accident. Assume also that the jury determines that Mr. Mike is liable to Mr. Ben because Mr. Mike's negligence caused the accident. On appeal, Mr. Mike's attorney argues that the trial court erred when it admitted Ms. Kathryn's hearsay testimony and that without her testimony there was no basis for the jury to conclude that Mr. Mike had been negligent. If the appellate court agrees with this hearsay argument, it will reverse the judgment and remand the case back to the trial court with instructions to retry the case without Ms. Kathryn's testimony. If the appellate court disagrees with Mr. Mike's argument, it will affirm the trial court judgment.

Opinions

Appellate courts publish their *opinions* (decisions) in *case reporters* for several reasons. First, appellate opinions inform the parties of the reasons for the court's decision. Second, appellate opinions provide instructions to the trial court for correcting its reversed ruling. Third, and most important, appellate opinions create precedents that interpret rules of law and explain how such rules must be applied by that appellate court and all of the trial courts over which it presides. For example, precedential rulings from the Federal Seventh Circuit Court of Appeals located in Illinois apply to all federal district courts located in Illinois, Indiana, and Wisconsin. Similarly, United States Supreme Court precedents apply to all federal district and appellate courts as well as all state trial, appellate, and supreme courts.

Precedents enable a judicial system to maintain consistent and uniform legal principles. Attorneys research precedents in case reporters to learn how appellate and supreme courts have interpreted and applied specific laws. The attorneys then prepare their legal arguments and briefs based on this research. Similarly, judges research case reporters to learn how other courts have ruled on the same or similar legal issues and rely on such opinions when required to do so or when doing so is helpful.

Supreme Courts

The highest and final courts of the federal and state systems are the supreme courts. Although a party who loses a lawsuit has the right to appeal a trial court ruling to an appellate court, that party does not have an automatic right to appeal an appellate court ruling to a supreme court. Instead, supreme courts usually choose the cases they accept for review since the primary purpose of a supreme court is to resolve conflicting appellate court rulings on the same legal issue in order to maintain consistency and uniformity of the law. For example, if there are three appellate courts in one state and each of the three has interpreted the same law differently, the state supreme court will accept appeals from those three cases to resolve the conflict and provide a final and uniform interpretation of the disputed law.

Supreme courts consist of several judges who sit together as a panel to decide cases. Like other appellate courts, supreme courts issue opinions that explain their rulings. Once a state supreme court has decided an issue of state law, its decision is final, unappealable, and binding precedent on all of the courts of that state. The only exception to this *rule of finality* is when a state supreme court opinion interprets the meaning of a federal law or a provision of the federal Constitution. The United States Supreme Court, as the final authority of the meaning of federal and constitutional laws, may accept an appeal of such a decision.

The appellate authority of the United States Supreme Court over a state supreme court is well demonstrated in the case of <u>Bush v. Gore</u>. The Constitution grants each of the 50 states the authority to conduct elections, including presidential elections, according to their individual election laws.[3] Under these state laws, citizens vote in the county in which they reside. In the presidential election of the year 2000, the two candidates were Vice President Albert Gore and Texas Governor George W. Bush. After every state except Florida had determined its vote counts, the nationwide totals were so close that neither candidate had acquired the 270 electoral votes necessary to win the election. Consequently, the outcome of the election depended on the vote count in Florida.

Florida, however, had a problem. Its vote totals were also very close— 2,909,135 for Bush and 2,907,351 for Gore. Because the totals were so close, the Florida election law required an automatic recount of all the *ballots* (papers or computer forms on which voters cast their votes). The recount reduced Bush's lead from 1,784 to 327 votes. Believing that the voting machines in some counties were defective and had miscounted some ballots, Gore filed a lawsuit in a Florida state court requesting additional time to allow ballots in four of Florida's 67 counties to be manually recounted. Bush opposed the request. The case quickly made its way up to the Florida Supreme Court, which ruled in Gore's favor by holding that Florida's election code permitted each county's *election board* (organization of local persons appointed to supervise elections and voting procedures) to manually recount and interpret the meaning of disputed ballots. By this time, Bush's vote margin had increased to 930 votes.

Candidate Bush appealed the Florida Supreme Court decision to the United States Supreme Court, arguing that its ruling violated the equal protection clause of the Fourteenth Amendment. The equal protection clause requires states to apply laws equally to all similarly situated persons and forbids states from treating some persons less favorably than others. The Supreme Court agreed with Bush's argument, finding that Florida's decision allowed identical ballots to be counted differently by each election board. The Court also ruled that the time

---

[3] Article I Section 4 states: *"The Times, Places and Manner of holding Elections for Senators and Representatives, shall be prescribed in each State by the Legislature thereof."*

had expired for Florida to correct its unconstitutional election procedures and ordered the recounting to stop. President Bush was sworn into office the next month. Excerpts from the opinion follow:

George W. Bush v. Albert Gore, Jr.
531 U.S. 98 (2000)

Per Curiam[4]

    On November 8, 2000, the day following the Presidential election, the Florida Division of Elections reported that petitioner, Governor Bush, had received 2,909,135 votes, and respondent, Vice President Gore, had received 2,907,351 votes, a margin of 1,784 for Governor Bush. Because Governor Bush's margin of victory was less than "one-half of a percent... of the votes cast," an automatic machine recount was conducted under §102.141(4) of the Florida Election Code, the results of which showed Governor Bush still winning the race but by a diminished margin.... Vice President Gore then sought manual recounts in Volusia, Palm Beach, Broward, and Miami-Dade Counties, pursuant to Florida's election protest provisions....

    Noting the closeness of the election, the [Florida Supreme] Court explained that "[o]n this record, there can be no question that there are legal votes within the 9,000 uncounted votes sufficient to place the results of this election in doubt.".... The [Florida] Supreme Court also determined that both Palm Beach County and Miami-Dade County, in their earlier manual recounts, had identified a net gain of 215 and 168 legal votes respectively, for Vice President Gore.... [T]he Court concluded that although the 168 votes identified were the result of a partial recount, they were "legal votes [that] could change the outcome of the election."....

    The question before us... is whether the recount procedures the Florida Supreme Court has adopted are consistent with its obligation to avoid arbitrary and disparate treatment of the members of its electorate....

    The recount mechanisms implemented in response to the decisions of the Florida Supreme Court do not satisfy the minimum requirement for nonarbitrary treatment of voters necessary to secure the fundamental right. Florida's basic command for the count of legally cast votes is to consider the "intent of the voter." This is unobjectionable as an abstract proposition and

---

[4] A *per curiam opinion* is anonymously written and frequently unanimous. The *Bush v. Gore* opinion was anonymously written but not unanimously decided—five Justices voted in favor of the Court's ruling but four Justices voted against it.

a starting principle. The problem inheres in the absence of specific standards to ensure its equal application. . . .

The search for intent can be confined by specific rules designed to ensure uniform treatment. The want of those rules here has led to unequal evaluation of ballots in various respects. As seems to have been acknowledged at oral argument, the standards for accepting or rejecting contested ballots might vary not only from county to county but indeed within a single county from one recount team to another. . . .

The record provides some examples. A monitor in Miami-Dade County testified at trial that he observed that three members of the county canvassing board applied different standards in defining a legal vote. And testimony at trial also revealed that at least one county changed its evaluative standards during the counting process. . . . Broward County used a more forgiving standard than Palm Beach County, and uncovered almost three times as many new votes, a result markedly disproportionate to the difference in population between the counties. . . .

The question before the Court is not whether local entities, in the exercise of their expertise, may develop different systems for implementing elections. Instead, we are presented with a situation where a state court with the power to assure uniformity has ordered a statewide recount with minimal procedural safeguards. When a court orders a statewide remedy, there must be at least some assurance that the rudimentary requirements of equal treatment and fundamental fairness are satisfied. . . .

The Supreme Court of Florida has said that the legislature intended the State's electors to "participat[e] fully in the federal electoral process," as provided in 3 U.S.C. Section 5. That statute, in turn, requires that any controversy or contest that is designed to lead to a conclusive selection of electors be completed by December 12. That date is upon us, and there is no recount procedure in place under the State Supreme Court's order that comports with minimal constitutional standards. Because it is evident that any recount seeking to meet the December 12 date will be unconstitutional for the reasons we have discussed, we reverse the judgment of the Supreme Court of Florida ordering a recount to proceed . . . and the case is remanded for further proceedings not inconsistent with this opinion.

The *Bush v. Gore* decision is one of the most controversial opinions in Supreme Court history. Some critics argued that the Florida Supreme Court's analysis of Florida's vote recounting procedures was correct and did not violate the equal protection clause. Other critics argued that the Supreme Court should have extended the December 12 recount deadline to give Florida sufficient time to correct its election procedures in order to count all of the votes, not just those that had been recounted before the deadline expired. Despite these concerns,

Vice President Gore fully understood the power of the Supreme Court's authority. In response to its decision he said, "Let there be no doubt, while I strongly disagree with the Court's decision, I accept it. I accept the finality of this outcome which will be ratified next Monday in the Electoral College. And tonight, for the sake of the unity of the people and the strength of our democracy, I offer my concession."

United States Presidential Election, November 7, 2000

Nominee	George W. Bush	Albert Gore
Party	Republican	Democrat
Home State	Texas	Tennessee
Electoral Vote	271	266
States Carried	30	20 + District of Columbia
Popular Vote	50,456,002	50,999,897
Percentage	47.9%	48.4%

CHAPTER 7 QUESTIONS

1. Under the American theory of rights and liabilities, every legal right relates to a corresponding legal duty. What would happen to legal rights if they were not associated with legal duties?

2. What is the litigation process? Given the adversarial nature of the litigation process, do you understand why it is important to hire a good lawyer?

3. What creates uniformity between the federal and state court systems?
   a. What effect does the supremacy clause have on state courts?
   b. What effect does the full faith and credit clause have on state courts?
   c. Do the supremacy and full faith and credit clauses prevent states from developing their own laws? Explain your answer.
   d. What is concurrent jurisdiction?
   e. Why do federal and state courts have concurrent jurisdiction over cases that involve each other's laws?

4. If you were Mr. Ben's lawyer, what arguments and defenses would you have raised on his behalf? If you were Mr. Mike's lawyer, what arguments and defenses would you have raised on his behalf?

5. The purpose of a trial is to determine the true facts that caused the legal dispute. However, even truthful and relevant information can be excluded from a trial if it is hearsay or privileged.
   a. What is hearsay information? Why is hearsay information inadmissible in court proceedings? Do you agree or disagree? Explain your answer.
   b. What is privileged information? Why is privileged information inadmissible in court proceedings? Do you agree or disagree? Explain your answer.
   c. What would be the effect on the litigation process if privileged information was not legally protected?
   d. What would be the effect on the relationship between the government and its citizens if privileged information was not legally protected?

6. Consider the following questions about _Bush v. Gore_:
   a. What was the legal issue addressed by the Supreme Court?
   b. What is the purpose of the equal protection clause? Who does it protect? From what? Why?
   c. Why did the Court use the equal protection clause to protect the votes that had been recounted by December 12 but prevent the recounting of votes after December 12?
   d. Who was protected by the Court's ruling? Who was not protected by its ruling?
   e. Why did candidate Gore accept the Court's ruling? What would have happened if he had refused to accept it?

The Criminal Litigation Process

Constitutional Provisions

The Constitution grants criminal defendants specific rights that are intended to provide a full and fair opportunity to defend against government charges of criminal conduct. The Fourth, Fifth, Sixth, and Eighth Amendments provide these rights at various stages of a criminal proceeding.

The Fourth Amendment provides,

> *The right of the people to be secure in their persons, houses, papers, and effects, against unreasonable searches and seizures, shall not be violated, and no Warrants shall issue, but upon probable cause, supported by Oath or affirmation, and particularly describing the place to be searched, and the persons or things to be seized.*

The Fourth Amendment requires the police to have *"probable cause"* (reasonable belief) that a crime has been committed and a search *warrant* (court order) issued by a judge in order to protect criminal suspects from *"unreasonable searches and seizures."*

The Fifth Amendment states,

> *No person shall be held to answer for a capital, or otherwise infamous crime, unless on a presentment or indictment of a Grand Jury . . . ; nor shall any person be subject for the same offence to be twice put in jeopardy of life or limb; nor shall be compelled in any criminal case to be a witness against himself, nor be deprived of life, liberty, or property, without due process of law. . . .*

"Due process" refers to the rights and procedures the government must provide before it takes coercive action against a person's *"life, liberty, or property."* Due process guarantees criminal defendants the right to be *indicted* (formally charged) of a crime by a *"Grand Jury"* (panel of independent citizens) rather than a government or a prosecutor; the right not to *"be compelled in any criminal case to be a witness against himself"* (self-incrimination); and the right not to be *"twice put in jeopardy of life or limb"* (double jeopardy). The double jeopardy clause bars the federal and state governments from subjecting a criminal defendant to repeated trials for the same offense in order to gain a conviction. Consequently, if a government fails to gain a conviction at the first trial it cannot retry the defendant again for the same crime. The double jeopardy clause, however, does not bar the federal and state governments from separately prosecuting a defendant for conduct that violates both state and federal criminal laws, nor does it bar a government from retrying a case when a conviction has been reversed by an appellate court.

The Sixth Amendment states,

> *In all criminal prosecutions, the accused shall enjoy the right to a speedy and public trial, by an impartial jury of the State and district wherein the crime shall have been committed . . . and to be informed of the nature and cause of the accusation; to be confronted with the witnesses against him; to have compulsory process for obtaining witnesses in his favor, and to have Assistance of Counsel for his defense.*

The Sixth Amendment requires a government to provide formal notice to a criminal defendant *"of the nature and cause of the accusation"* against him; *"a speedy and public trial, by an impartial jury;"* the *"Assistance of Counsel for his defense"*; and the authority *"to have compulsory process for obtaining witnesses in his favor,"* and *" to be confronted with the witnesses against him."*

The Eighth Amendment states,

> *Excessive bail shall not be required, nor excessive fines imposed, nor cruel and unusual punishments inflicted.*

The Eighth Amendment prevents a government from imposing on criminal defendants *"Excessive bail"* (financial payment for release from prison while awaiting trial) and *"fines"* (financial penalties for criminal convictions) and *"cruel and unusual punishments"* (sentences that are disproportionate to the severity of the crime).

What Is a Crime?

In the American criminal system, a crime is a statutorily defined illegal act committed against a person, a person's property, a business, an institution, or a government that is punishable by a fine, imprisonment, or death. For a criminal law to be valid, it must be so precise and specific that the average person can understand what conduct the law prohibits or requires. Crimes range from *felonies,* to *misdemeanors,* to *infractions.* Felonies, such as murder, sexual assault and armed robbery, are the most serious crimes, for which punishments range from imprisonment for more than one year to *capital punishment* (the death penalty). Misdemeanors, such as public drunkenness and disturbing the peace, are minor crimes, for which punishments range from fines to confinement in a local jail for less than one year. Infractions, such as violation of a parking restriction, refer to local rules, for which the punishments are usually small fines.

There are five basic categories of crimes in the United States: (1) violent crimes against a person; (2) crimes against property; (3) financial crimes against businesses, institutions, or persons; (4) organized crimes; and (5) crimes by and against the government. Violent crimes against a person include murder, manslaughter, sexual assault, robbery, and assault with a weapon. Crimes against property include trespass, arson, and destruction or theft of property. Crimes against businesses include financial fraud, embezzlement, antitrust violations, false advertising, and failure to comply with environmental laws. Financial crimes include fraudulent investment schemes, market manipulation, and failure to comply with mandatory disclosure requirements. Organized crimes refer to criminal activities by groups of people who coerce other people and businesses to commit crimes due to fear, extortion, or intimidation. Such crimes frequently consist of illegal drug trafficking, gambling, prostitution, and money-lending at excessively high interest rates. Crimes by and against a government include illegal wiretapping, treason, armed rebellion, assassination, failure to pay taxes, lying to obtain welfare benefits, and obstruction of criminal investigations.

Every crime consists of two elements that must occur before the conduct can be treated as a criminal offense. The first element is the *criminal act,* which may be an *act of commission* or an *act of omission.* An act of commission means that a person engaged in conduct that is forbidden by a criminal statute, such as an armed robbery. An act of omission means that a person failed to perform an act that is required by a criminal statute, such as failing to pay taxes.

The second element of a crime is the mental state, referred to as *mens rea.* Because the criminal law distinguishes between intentional and accidental acts, an act is not a crime unless the person had the required *mens rea.* For example, if a person dies in a car accident because the driver intended to kill the victim, the death will be treated as a first-degree murder. If a person dies in a car accident because the driver drove recklessly but did not intend to injure anyone, the death will be treated as a second-degree murder. If a person dies in a car accident because the driver skid on an icy road, the death will be treated as a negligent homicide. If a person dies in a car accident because an earthquake pushed one car into another car, the death will be treated as an accident, but not as a criminal act.

Pre Trial Proceedings

Search and Arrest Warrants

In the course of a police investigation, the Fourth Amendment requires a prosecutor to obtain search and arrest warrants from a judge who has reviewed the evidence and determined there is *probable cause* to believe that the suspect committed a crime or that evidence of a crime will be found in the place to be searched. The prosecutor establishes probable cause by submitting an *affidavit* (a written statement made under oath) to a judge that presents evidence of the suspect's involvement in a crime, or that identifies the place to be searched, the reasons for the search, and the items to be seized. If the judge issues the warrant, the police will conduct the search or arrest the suspect. If the prosecutor fails to present sufficient evidence to establish probable cause, the judge will deny the request for the warrant. Warrants are not required, however, when the police personally observe a crime while it is occurring.

The Fourth Amendment also bars police from engaging in unreasonable searches and seizures. Under the *exclusionary rule,* evidence that is illegally obtained as a result of an unreasonable search or seizure will be *inadmissible* (excluded) at trial. Furthermore, under the *fruits of the poisonous tree doctrine,* any additional information the police obtain because of the illegal search will also be inadmissible.

The Supreme Court announced the exclusionary rule in the case of *Mapp v. Ohio,* 367 U.S. 643 (1961). In *Mapp,* the police suspected Dollree Mapp of hiding a criminal in her home. The first time the police knocked on Mapp's door they did not have a search warrant and she refused to let them enter. Several hours later the police returned and forced their way into her home. When Mapp again demanded to see the search warrant, one of the police officers held up a piece of paper that he claimed was a search warrant. However, when Mapp reached for the paper the officer handcuffed her. The police then proceeded to search her home. Although the suspected criminal was not found, the police did find pornographic books, pictures, and photographs for which they arrested Mapp and charged her with criminal possession of obscene materials.

Despite the fact that the government could not produce the search warrant at Mapp's trial, she was convicted of possessing obscene materials. Mapp then appealed her conviction to the United States Supreme Court. In determining whether the warrantless search of Mapp's home and the obscene materials found as a result of the search were admissible evidence at her trial, the Court held that the exclusionary rule barred courts from admitting evidence that the police had seized in violation of the Fourth Amendment.

Notwithstanding the *Mapp* case, the Fourth Amendment search warrant requirement is not absolute and, instead, is subject to many exceptions. For example, warrantless searches and seizures may not violate the Fourth Amendment if a person consents to be searched or if an officer observes evidence of a crime "in plain view," such as a gun on the seat of a car. The police may also search a person who has been arrested and the area in which the arrest took place if they reasonably believe that evidence of the crime or an accomplice to the crime is nearby. Finally, if the police have probable cause to stop a moving car, they can also search the car for objects related to the car stop without obtaining a warrant. During the car search, the police may also search a suspected person for weapons if they reasonably believe the suspect has been involved in a crime.

Grand Jury Proceedings and Preliminary Hearings

Before making an arrest, a prosecutor must present evidence of criminal conduct to a grand jury. The purpose of the grand jury is to protect a criminal suspect from inappropriate prosecutorial conduct by allowing neutral, independent citizens to decide if the government has sufficient evidence of guilt to charge the suspect with a crime. The federal government and about half of the states use grand juries. In order to protect witnesses from harassment and coercion by the suspect and to ensure the privacy of innocent persons who may be wrongfully investigated by the government, grand jury proceedings are conducted secretly and the investigations are not disclosed to the public or the media.

A grand jury consists of 16 to 23 local citizens who are selected at random from voter registration lists. A grand jury term lasts from one month to one year, during which time prosecutors present witnesses, criminal suspects, and evidence obtained through law enforcement investigations to the grand jurors. Although the witnesses and suspects may consult with attorneys before entering the grand jury room, they may not be accompanied by an attorney while being questioned inside the grand jury room. Both the prosecutor and the grand jurors may question the witnesses and suspects. If the majority of grand jurors find probable cause to believe the suspect committed a crime, they will return an indictment and the prosecutor will direct the police to arrest the suspect.

As an alternative to grand juries, about half of the states use *preliminary hearings* to determine if there is sufficient evidence to prosecute a criminal suspect. Unlike grand jury proceedings, a preliminary hearing is conducted in a public courtroom before a judge after a suspect has been arrested. Like grand jury proceedings, the purpose of the preliminary hearing is to prevent the government from prosecuting a person against whom there is insufficient evidence of guilt to obtain a conviction. Consequently, during the preliminary hearing the prosecutor must convince the judge that there is probable cause to believe the suspect committed a specified crime. If the prosecutor fails to establish probable cause, the suspect must be released. If the prosecutor successfully establishes probable cause, the criminal case will continue. Although suspects are permitted to *waive* (forfeit) their preliminary hearing, many prefer to go through the process because it allows them to learn of the prosecution's evidence before the trial.

Criminal Defense Attorneys

The Sixth Amendment right to legal counsel recognizes that criminal proceedings are complex and that criminal defendants need objective, independent lawyers to "cope with the problems of law, make skilled inquiry into the facts, insist on the regularity of proceedings, ascertain whether there is a defense case and prepare and litigate such defense." *In re Gault*, 387 U.S. 1 (1976). The Supreme Court upheld the constitutional right to counsel in criminal proceedings in the case of *Gideon v. Wainwright*. Here is that story:

In 1961, the state of Florida arrested, tried, and convicted Clarence Earl Gideon of robbing a pool hall. Before his trial started, Gideon requested that the judge appoint an attorney to represent him, a right to which he believed he was entitled under the Sixth Amendment. The judge denied Gideon's request because Florida's state law, unlike the federal law, did not recognize the right to an attorney. Gideon then defended himself *pro se* (as his own lawyer) and was convicted. While in prison, he researched the law in the prison library and prepared an appeal of his case. Eventually, his appeal made its way from the Florida state courts to the United States Supreme Court.

The Supreme Court allowed Gideon to file an *in forma pauperis petition,* which is a request by a poor person to file a lawsuit without paying court costs. The Court also assigned a lawyer, Abe Fortas, to assist Gideon. Abe Fortas was one of Washington's most prominent attorneys who later became a Supreme Court Justice. Fortas argued that under the Sixth Amendment a criminal trial could not satisfy due process requirements unless the defendant received the assistance of an attorney. The Court agreed:

Gideon v. Wainwright
372 U.S. 335 (1963)

Justice Black delivered the opinion of the Court.

Petitioner was charged in a Florida state court with having broken and entered a poolroom. . . . This offense is a felony under Florida law. Appearing in court without funds and without a lawyer, petitioner asked the court to appoint counsel for him, whereupon the following colloquy took place:

The Court: Mr. Gideon, I am sorry, but I cannot appoint Counsel to represent you in this case. Under the laws of the State of Florida, the only time the Court can appoint Counsel to represent a Defendant is when that person is charged with a capital offense. I am sorry, but I will have to deny your request to appoint Counsel to defend you in this case.

The Defendant: The United States Supreme Court says I am entitled to be represented by Counsel.

Put to trial before a jury, Gideon conducted his defense about as well as could be expected from a layman. He made an opening statement to the jury, cross-examined the State's witnesses, presented witnesses in his own defense, declined to testify himself, and made a short argument "emphasizing his innocence to the charge contained in the Information filed in this case." The jury returned a verdict of guilty, and petitioner was sentenced to serve five years in the state prison. Later, petitioner filed in the Florida Supreme Court this habeas corpus petition attacking his conviction and sentence on the ground that the trial court's refusal to appoint counsel for him denied him rights "guaranteed by the Constitution and the Bill of Rights by the United States Government."....

The Sixth Amendment provides, "In all criminal prosecutions, the accused shall enjoy the right . . . to have the Assistance of Counsel for his defense." We have construed this to mean that in federal courts counsel must be provided for defendants unable to employ counsel unless the right is competently and intelligently waived. . . .

[R]eason and reflection, require us to recognize that, in our adversary system of criminal justice, any person haled into court, who is too poor to hire a lawyer, cannot be assured a fair trial unless counsel is provided for him. This seems to us to be an obvious truth. Governments, both state and federal, quite properly spend vast sums of money to establish machinery to try defendants accused of crime. Lawyers to prosecute are everywhere deemed essential to protect the public's interest in an orderly society. Similarly, there are few defendants charged with crime, few indeed, who fail to hire the best lawyers they can get to prepare and present their defense. That government hires lawyers to prosecute and defendants who have the money hire lawyers to defend are the strongest indications of the widespread belief that lawyers in criminal courts are necessities, not luxuries. The right of one charged with crime to counsel may not be deemed fundamental and essential to fair trials in some countries, but it is in ours. From the very beginning, our state and national constitutions and laws have laid great emphasis on procedural and substantive safeguards designed to assure fair trials before impartial tribunals in which every defendant stands equal before the law. This noble ideal cannot be realized if the poor man charged with crime has to face his accusers without a lawyer to assist him. . . .

The judgment is reversed and the case is remanded to the Supreme Court of Florida for further action not inconsistent with this opinion.

Clarence Earl Gideon

In 1963, Attorney General Robert F. Kennedy made the following statement about the *Gideon* case:

> "If an obscure Florida convict named Clarence Earl Gideon had not sat down in his prison cell with a pencil and paper to write a letter to the Supreme Court, and if the Court had not taken the trouble to look for merit in that one crude petition among all the bundles of mail it must receive every day, the vast machinery of American law would have gone on functioning undisturbed. But Gideon did write that letter, the Court did look into his case; he was retried with the help of a competent defense counsel, found not guilty, and released from prison after two years of punishment for a crime he did not commit—and the whole course of American legal history has been changed."

Arrest

According to the due process clause of the Fifth Amendment, once arrested and taken into *custody* (police detention), a criminal suspect cannot be compelled to say anything to the police that could be used to convict him. Custody occurs when the police have deprived a person of his liberty and the person understands that he is not free to leave the police interrogation. These due process requirements were established by the United States Supreme Court in the case of

DIVISION OF CORRECTIONS
CORRESPONDENCE REGULATIONS

MAIL WILL NOT BE DELIVERED WHICH DOES NOT CONFORM WITH THESE RULES

No. 1 -- Only 2 letters each week, not to exceed 2 sheets letter-size 8 1/2 x 11" and written *on one side only*, and if ruled paper, do not write between lines. *Your complete name* must be signed at the close of your letter.   *Clippings, stamps, letters* from other people, *stationery or cash must not be enclosed* in your letters.

No. 2 -- All *letters* must be addressed in the *complete prison name* of the inmate. *Cell number*, where applicable, and *prison number* must be placed in lower left corner of envelope, with your complete name and address in the upper left corner.

No. 3 -- *Do not send any packages without a Package Permit.* Unauthorized *packages* will be destroyed.

No. 4 -- *Letters* must be written in English only.

No. 5 -- *Books, magazines, pamphlets,* and *newspapers* of reputable character will be delivered *only if* mailed direct from the publisher.

No. 6 -- *Money* must be sent in the form of *Postal Money Orders* only, in the inmate's complete prison name and prison number.

INSTITUTION _____   CELL NUMBER _____

NAME _____   NUMBER _____

In The Supreme Court of The United States
Washington D.C.

Clarence Earl Gideon
   Petitioner
   vs.
H.G. Cochran, Jr, as
Director, Divisions
of corrections State
of Florida

Petition for a writ
of Certiorari Directed
to The Supreme Court
State of Florida.
No. 890 Misc.
OCT. TERM 1961
U. S. Supreme Court

To: The Honorable Earl Warren, Chief
  Justice of the United States
    Comes now The petitioner, Clarence
Earl Gideon, a citizen of The United States
of America, in proper person, and appearing
as his own counsel. Who petitions this
Honorable Court for a Writ of Certiorari
directed to The Supreme Court of The State
of Florida. To review the order and Judge-
ment of the court below denying The
petitioner a writ of Habeus Corpus.
    Petitioner submits That The Supreme
Court of The United States has The authority
and jurisdiction to review The final Judge-
ment of The Supreme Court of The State
of Florida the highest court of The State
Under sec. 344 (B) Title 28 U.S.C.A. and
Because the "Due process clause" of the

Clarence Gideon's *In Forma Pauperis* Petition

DIVISION OF CORRECTIONS
CORRESPONDENCE REGULATIONS

MAIL WILL NOT BE DELIVERED WHICH DOES NOT CONFORM WITH THESE RULES

No. 1 -- Only 2 letters each week, not to exceed 2 sheets letter-size 8 1/2 x 11" and written *on one side only,* and if ruled paper, do not write between lines. *Your complete name* must be signed at the close of your letter. *Clippings, stamps, letters* from other people, *stationery* or *cash must not be enclosed* in your letters.

No. 2 -- All *letters* must be addressed in the *complete prison name* of the inmate. *Cell number,* where applicable, and *prison number* must be placed in lower left corner of envelope, with your complete name and address in the upper left corner.

No. 3 -- *Do not send any packages without a Package Permit.* Unauthorized *packages* will be destroyed.

No. 4 -- *Letters* must be written in English only.

No. 5 -- *Books, magazines, pamphlets,* and *newspapers* of reputable character will be delivered *only if* mailed direct from the publisher.

No. 6 -- *Money* must be sent in the form of *Postal Money Orders* only, in the inmate's complete prison name and prison number.

INSTITUTION _____ CELL NUMBER _____

NAME _____ NUMBER _____

fourteenth admendment of the constitution
and the fifth and sixth articales of the
Bill of rights has been violated. Further
Furthermore, the decision of the court
below denying the petitioner a Writ of
Habeus Corpus is also inconsistent and
adverse to its own previous decisions
in parelled cases.
    Attached hereto, and made a part of
this petition is a true copy of the petition
for a Writ of Habeus Corpus as presented
to the Florida Supreme Court, Petitioner
asks this Honorable Court to cosider the
same arguments and authorities cited
in the petition for Writ of Habeus Corpus
before the Florida Supreme Court, In
consideration of this petition for a
Writ of Certiorari.
    The Supreme Court of Florida did not
write any opinion, Order of that court
denying petition for Writ of Habeus
Corpus dated October 30, 1961, are
attached hereto and made a part of
this petition.
    Petitioner, contends that he has
been deprived of due process of law
Habeus Corpus petition alleging that
the lower state court has decided a

federal question of substance, in a way
not in accord with the applicable
decisions of this Honorable Court. When
at the time of the petitioners trial.
He ask the lower court for the aid of
counsel. The court refused this aid
Petitioner told the court that this
court had made decision to the effect
that all citizens tried for a felony crime
should have aid of counsel. The lower
court ignored this plea.

Petitioner alleges that prior to
petitioners convictions and sentence
for Breaking and Entering with the intent
to commit petty larceny, he had requested
aid of counsel, that, at the time of his
conviction and sentence, petitioner was
without aid of counsel. That the court
refused and did not appoint counsel, and
that he was incapable adequately of
making his own defense. In consequence
of which he was made to stand trial. Made
a Prima Facia showing of denial of
due process of law. (U.S.C.A. Const
Amend. 14) William V. Kaiser Vs.
State of Missouri 65 cT. 363
Counsel must be assigned to the
accused if he is unable to employ

one, and is incapable adequately of
making his own defense
Tomkins vs State missouri 65ct 370
on the 3rd June 1961 A.b. your
Petitioner was arrested for foresaid
crime and convicted for same, Petitioner
recieve Trial and sentence without aid
of counsel, your petitioner was deprived
'Due process of law'.
Petitioner was deprived of due
process of law in the court. Evidence
in the lower court did not show that a
crime of Breaking and Entering with
the intent To commit Petty Larceny had
been committed. Your petitioner
was compelled to make his own
defense, he was incapable
adequately of making his own defense
Petitioner did not plead no/contendler
But That is what his trial amounted
To.

Wherefore the premises considered
it is respectfully contented that the
decision of the court below was in
error and the case should be
review by this court, accordingly the
writ prepared and prayed for should
be issue.

IT is respectfully submitted

Clarence Earl Gideon
Clarence Earl Gideon
P.O. Box 221
Raiford Florida

State of Florida)
county of union) ss

Petitioner, Clarence Earl Gideon,
personally appearing before me and
being duly sworn. Affirms, that
the foregoing petition and the facts
set forth in the petition are correct
and true

Sworn and suberibed before me
this 5th. day of Jan 1962

Laurence Dwyer
Notary Public
Notary Public, State of Florida at Large
My Commission Expires Aug. 19, 1962
Bonded by American Surety Co. of N.Y.

Miranda v. Arizona, 384 U.S. 436 (1966). In _Miranda_, the police suspected Ernesto Miranda of raping and kidnapping an 18-year-old woman and brought him to the police station to participate in a _line-up_. A line-up takes place in a room at a police station that is divided by one-way glass that allows people outside the room to see into the room but prevents people inside the room from seeing outside the room. The victim looks at people through the one-way glass to try to identify the suspect. If the victim identifies the suspect, the police will arrest him. If the victim does not identify the suspect, the police must release him but may bring him back to the station if they subsequently obtain more evidence. In the _Miranda_ case, the victim identified Miranda at the line-up and he was interrogated by the police. Eventually, Miranda confessed to the crime and was convicted. The Supreme Court then reversed the conviction because the police had failed to inform Miranda of his Fifth Amendment right not **"to be a witness against himself"** and his Sixth Amendment right **"to have the Assistance of counsel for his Defence."**

Based on this decision, the Court developed _Miranda_ Warnings which are intended to discourage coercive and violent police tactics that intimidate people into making false confessions. Consequently, prior to starting an interrogation, the police must give the suspect the following _Miranda_ Warnings:

Miranda Warnings

1. You have the right to remain silent.
2. Anything you say can and will be used against you in a court of law.
3. You have the right to a lawyer and to have him present with you while you are being questioned.
4. If you cannot afford to hire a lawyer, one will be appointed to represent you before you are questioned.
5. You can decide at any time to exercise these rights and refuse to answer any questions or make any statements.

Waiver

Do you understand these rights?
Do you wish to talk to us now or assert your rights to remain silent and have an attorney represent you?

The _Miranda_ Warnings allow an arrested person to remain silent, refuse to answer police questions, and be represented by legal counsel. The _Miranda_ Warnings also inform the person that if he chooses to waive these protections and answer police questions, anything he says can be used to convict him. Once the police inform a person of his _Miranda_ protections they can proceed with the interrogation unless and until the person asserts his _Miranda_ rights. At that point, the police must stop the interrogation. Under the exclusionary rule, statements obtained by the police that violate the _Miranda_ Warnings must be excluded as evidence and cannot be used to convict the defendant.

Initially, the Supreme Court was strongly criticized for its _Miranda_ decision. Many people were concerned that the _Miranda_ Warnings would interfere with police interrogations and allow guilty criminals to be released due to unintended police mistakes. These concerns were undoubtedly correct in some cases. But for the most part, the _Miranda_ Warnings have been easy to enforce and are now a widely accepted police procedure. Ironically, when Ernesto Miranda was killed in prison, the police gave _Miranda_ Warnings to the man suspected of killing him.

Bail Hearing

After arrest, a criminal defendant will be confined to a jail unless and until he is released on _bail._ Bail is the amount of money the defendant must pay to the court to be released from jail while awaiting trial. The purpose of bail is to guarantee the defendant's appearance at trial. If the defendant appears at the trial, the bail is returned. If the defendant fails to appear at the trial, the bail is forfeited. The _bail hearing_ is held before a judge in a public courtroom within 48 hours of arrest to determine if the defendant qualifies to be released on bail. If the defendant does not qualify for bail, he will remain in jail pending the outcome of the case.

The Constitution does not require bail. The Eighth Amendment requires only that _**"Excessive bail shall not be required."**_ The judge determines the amount of bail based on the seriousness of the crime, the defendant's past criminal record, and the likelihood that the defendant will be dangerous to the public or flee to avoid prosecution if released. Consequently, bail is considered a privilege, not a right, and may be denied or revoked if the defendant violates its conditions.

Arraignment Hearing

After the arrest and bail hearing, the defendant will attend an _arraignment hearing_ conducted by a judge during which the prosecutor will state the formal criminal charges against the defendant. The defendant will then respond to the charges with a _plea_. The most common pleas are _guilty_ or _not guilty_. Most defendants initially plead not guilty. A not guilty plea does not mean that the defendant is innocent. Instead, it means that the defendant is challenging the government to prove its charges at trial. A guilty plea means that the defendant is confessing to the crime and waiving the right to a trial.

Plea Bargaining

Despite the fact that most defendants initially plead not guilty, most criminal cases do not go to trial. In both the state and federal systems, more than 90 percent of criminal cases are resolved through *plea bargaining*. Plea bargaining allows the prosecutor and defense attorney to privately debate the strengths and weaknesses of the case and negotiate an agreement as to the charges to which the defendant will plead guilty and the type of sentence the prosecutor will recommend to the judge. In effect, the prosecutor offers the defendant a less severe sentence in exchange for pleading guilty to a less serious crime. To accept a plea bargain, the defendant must confess his guilt to the new charge and waive the right to a trial, appeal, and all other constitutional protections.

   A federal judge is not required to accept a plea bargain. Instead, federal judges are required to question the defendant to determine if he is mentally competent to plead guilty; if his guilty plea is voluntary; and if he understands that by pleading guilty he is waiving his constitutional rights and cannot appeal his conviction. If the federal judge is not convinced of these matters, she must refuse to accept the guilty plea. Many state court systems follow this process as well. Other states, however, encourage judges to accept plea bargains so that they do not undermine the prosecution's ability to negotiate guilty pleas.

   Plea bargaining provides advantages and disadvantages to both the defendant and the government. Pleading guilty typically reduces the severity of the charges against the defendant and, consequently, subjects the defendant to a less severe sentence than if he were convicted at a trial of a more serious crime. In exchange, the government is saved the time and expense of conducting a trial to gain a conviction. Sometimes, however, a prosecutor will initially overcharge a defendant with a more serious crime than was actually committed in order to later offer a plea bargain for the less serious crime the defendant actually committed. As a result, the defendant will not only be deprived of any constitutional protections, but also will be deprived of the benefit of pleading guilty to a less serious crime and receiving a less severe sentence. Finally, because plea bargains are negotiated privately rather than in a public courtroom before a judge, the outcome may depend on the professional skills of the defense attorney or prosecutor rather than on the severity of the crime or constitutional principles. Consequently, sometimes, plea bargains result in the convictions of innocent people.

Trial Proceedings

Speedy and Public Trial

According to the Sixth Amendment, all criminal defendants are entitled *"to a speedy and public trial."* The constitutional right to a speedy trial prevents the government from delaying a trial in order to prolong the defendant's custody, or until defense witnesses are no longer available or have forgotten the details of their testimony, or until evidence favorable to the defendant has disappeared. But how fast is a speedy trial? The Speedy Trial Act of 1974 requires the federal government to either commence a trial within 100 days of the arrest or dismiss the criminal charges. Consequently, prosecutors try to complete their investigations and prepare their cases before formally filing criminal charges against a defendant so that they can meet the 100-day time requirement. However, the Speedy Trial Act also allows a judge to extend the 100-day period if agreed to by the defense and prosecution. Most states have similar speedy trial statutes, although the precise time periods may vary among the states.

A public trial serves two purposes. First, it prevents the government from conducting secret trials or detaining a defendant in an unknown place without public knowledge. Second, trial publicity keeps the American public informed about ongoing prosecutions.

Criminal Juries

The Sixth Amendment allows a criminal defendant's guilt or innocence to be determined by an *"impartial jury."*[1] Potential jurors receive a *summons* (court order) in the mail that instructs them to report for jury duty on a specific day at a specific courthouse. The first procedure in jury selection is called *voir dire*, a French term meaning "to speak the truth" that refers to the process by which potential jurors are questioned to determine their qualifications to serve on a jury. During voir dire, the judge, prosecutor, and defense attorney will question the potential jurors to determine which ones are qualified to serve on the jury. Persons will be eliminated from the *jury pool* (group of potential jurors) if they have pre-judged the case; have a personal relationship with the prosecutor, defense attorney, or victim; have been a victim or accused of a crime; or believe that people of certain races, religions, or ethnicities are inclined to commit crimes. The prosecutor and defense attorney will also attempt to disqualify any person whose answers suggest bias or inability to favor their version of the case. The process of questioning and challenging prospective jurors continues until the jurors are chosen. The jurors then take an oath to uphold their legal duty.

Federal and most state juries consist of 12 people who must unanimously agree on the guilt or innocence of the defendant. Some states, however, allow juries of fewer than 12 people and do not require unanimous verdicts. The jury's duty is to determine the guilt or innocence of the defendant by observing the prosecutor and defense attorney as they present the evidence, and the witnesses

---

[1] A defendant may choose to be tried by a judge rather than a jury.

as they testify. Unlike grand jurors, trial jurors may not ask questions. Trial jurors are also not allowed to discuss the case among themselves or with anyone else during the trial proceedings.

Opening Statements

Once the jury is selected, the prosecutor and defense attorney begin the trial by making *opening statements.* In their opening statements, the lawyers summarize their versions of the case, the legal issues they must prove, and the evidence and witnesses they will present to prove their case and disprove their opponent's case. Trial lawyers understand that it is important to maintain consistency between their opening statements and the actual evidence they present because the jurors will notice if the witnesses and evidence are not the same as they were portrayed in the attorney's opening statement. Consequently, the opening statements also provide trial lawyers with an opportunity to convince the jurors of their own sincerity and credibility.

Presentation of Evidence

After the completion of the opening statements, the prosecutor presents the government's case against the defendant. The prosecution case will consist of evidence obtained from the police investigation such as guns, bullets, finger-prints, clothing, blood, DNA tests, documents, and witnesses who will testify about their knowledge of the crime. Once questioned by the prosecutor, each witness will be *cross-examined* by the defense attorney. Cross-examination of adverse witnesses is based on the confrontation clause of the Sixth Amendment, which grants a criminal defendant the right to question the witnesses against him. During cross-examination, the defense attorney will question an adverse witness in an attempt to discredit his or her prior testimony. Cross-examination also gives the jury an opportunity to observe the demeanor of the challenged witness to evaluate his or her credibility. When the cross-examination is complete, the prosecutor may conduct a *redirect examination* of the witness to clarify or correct matters that arose during the cross-examination. Once the prosecution presents all of its evidence and witnesses, it *rests* (ends) its case. The defense then presents its case. The defense attorney will present evidence and witnesses who will testify in favor of the defendant and who will then be cross-examined by the prosecutor. Once the defense has presented all of its evidence and witnesses, it will rest its case.

The difference between the prosecution and defense cases lies in the evidentiary burden of proof. Under the Federal Rules of Evidence, the defendant is *presumed to be innocent* unless and until the prosecution proves the defendant's guilt *beyond a reasonable doubt*, the highest legal standard of proof that must be met in any trial. The beyond a reasonable doubt standard requires that the jurors unanimously agree that the only reasonable conclusion to be drawn from the evidence is that the defendant committed the crime. If the prosecution's evidence meets this burden of proof it will successfully refute the presumption of the defendant's innocence. The Federal Rules of Evidence, however, impose no burden of proof on the defendant and, therefore, the defense is not required to prove anything. Theoretically, the defense can remain silent throughout the trial because the entire burden of proof is on the government.

Closing Arguments

After the prosecution and defense have rested their cases, the attorneys make *closing arguments* to the jury. Closing arguments in criminal cases typically summarize the evidence in a manner that is highly emotional, highly logical, or highly insistent. For example, the prosecutor may remind the jurors of their oath to correctly apply the law; and their obligation not to substitute sympathy for the defendant with a reasoned analysis of the facts; and the importance to society of maintaining law and order. The defense attorney may fault the government's evidence, appeal to the jurors' sympathies, and remind them that they must resolve any reasonable doubt in the defendant's favor.

Jury Instructions

After the closing arguments, the judge delivers the *jury instructions*. The judge will instruct the jury that it must presume the defendant's innocence unless the government has met its burden of proving the defendant's guilt beyond a reasonable doubt. The judge will also explain the relevant laws that apply to the case and how the jury is to apply such laws to the facts. For example, if the government has charged the defendant with first-degree murder, the judge will instruct the jury that it can convict the defendant of first-degree murder only if it determines beyond a reasonable doubt that his conduct was intentional; otherwise, the jury must *acquit* (free) the defendant. Based on these instructions, if the jury finds that the evidence proved only that the defendant's conduct was accidental, but not intentional, it must follow the judge's instructions and acquit the defendant.

Jury Deliberations

After the judge delivers the jury instructions, the jurors leave the courtroom and enter the jury room to begin their *deliberations* (discussions) in complete privacy. The jurors begin their deliberations by electing a *foreman* or *forewoman* to lead their discussions. Sometimes the jurors will take a preliminary vote to determine if they are united or divided. No outsiders may enter the jury room to observe or participate in the deliberations. Although the jurors may send written questions to the judge and may look at items of evidence or sections of the trial *transcript* (record), they may not refer to anything else or speak with anyone else about the case. They may not read about the case in newspapers, watch reports about the case on television or the Internet, or discuss the trial with other people. In very important or highly publicized cases, or cases where the jury's safety may be at risk, the judge may *sequester* the jury, which means that the jurors will be moved to a hotel away from the public until they reach a *verdict* (decision).

Once the jury reaches a unanimous decision, it returns to the courtroom where the foreman or forewoman delivers the verdict. If the jury renders a not guilty verdict, the judge will discharge the defendant, who is then free to leave the courtroom and resume his or her life. If the jury renders a guilty verdict, either the prosecutor or the defense attorney may ask the judge to *poll the jury,* which means the judge will ask each juror if the verdict truly reflects his or her own decision. The purpose of polling is to determine whether each juror agrees with the verdict or whether any juror felt compelled to yield to group pressure. If the polling shows that there is still disagreement within the jury, the judge will send the jurors back to the jury room to continue their deliberations.

If the jurors cannot reach a unanimous verdict, the judge may insist that they continue their deliberations until they do reach such a verdict. However, if the judge is convinced that the jury is hopelessly *deadlocked* (not unanimous), she may declare a *mistrial* (an invalid trial), discharge the jurors, and order a new trial.

Post Trial Proceedings

Sentencing

After a defendant has been convicted, a *probation officer* investigates the defendant's personal, professional, educational, and criminal backgrounds; assesses the seriousness of the crime; and evaluates whether the defendant is likely to re-engage in criminal activity. The probation officer then submits the report to the judge along with a recommendation about the appropriate type and length of *sentence* (punishment) to be imposed on the defendant.

The least severe sentence is called *probation*. Probation means that even though the defendant is sentenced to imprisonment, the judge will not immediately impose the sentence on the defendant. Instead, the defendant will remain free as long as he obeys the conditions of probation such as participating in a drug rehabilitation program performing community service, refraining from associating with certain people or committing another crime. If the defendant violates the conditions of the probation, the judge may re-impose the original sentence and imprison the defendant for the duration of the sentence.

Judges usually offer probation only to first-time offenders who have not committed serious crimes.

If the judge finds that imprisonment is appropriate, she will impose a *range-of-years sentence*, such as 5 to 15 years. The reason for imposing a range-of-years sentence rather than a sentence of specific years is to allow the judge to impose a punishment based on the circumstances of the crime and the criminal background, behavior, and attitude of the convicted defendant. A *parole board* (a panel of people) will periodically review the prisoner's behavior to determine when the prisoner should be released.

The Eighth Amendment forbids the court from imposing a *"cruel and unusual punishments"*. A punishment will be *cruel* if it is excessively disproportionate to the severity of the crime for which the defendant was convicted. A criminal punishment will be *unusual* if it is increasingly rejected by a significant number of states. The question of whether a punishment is cruel and unusual arises primarily in *capital punishment* (death penalty) cases. American law permits capital punishment for two reasons. First, capital punishment allows society to express outrage and receive retribution for particularly heinous crimes. Second, capital punishment may deter others from committing similar crimes. The efficacy and morality of capital punishment have always been strongly debated within the United States. Some critics argue that the purpose of government is to maintain order and civility rather than seek revenge or encourage others to do so. Other critics argue that there is no proof that capital punishment actually deters people from committing murders since some of the states with the highest murder rates also have the highest capital punishment rates.

The Supreme Court has addressed the constitutionality of capital punishment in several cases. In 1972, the Court held that the death penalty was not inherently cruel and unusual punishment, *Furman v. Georgia*, 408 U.S. 238 (1972). In 1988, a plurality of Justices found that capital punishment for persons younger than 16 years of age was cruel and unusual because such young people are less mature and, therefore, less culpable for their crimes than adults, *Thompson v. Dulles*, 487 U.S. 81. However, one year later, a different plurality of Justices found that capital punishment for 16- and 17-year-old juveniles was not cruel and unusual punishment, *Stanford v. Kentucky*, 492 U.S. 361 (1989). Clearly, the *Thompson* and *Stanford* opinions viewed juveniles very differently. The *Thompson* Court viewed juveniles as vulnerable, immature children who were still developing and, therefore, capable of change. The *Stanford* Court viewed juveniles as fully responsible persons who were as culpable for their crimes as adults. Then, in 2002, a majority of Supreme Court Justices ruled that capital punishment of the mentally retarded was cruel and unusual punishment because their diminished mental capacity rendered them less culpable than adult offenders, *Atkins v. Virginia*, 536 U.S. 304. For much the same reason, in 2005 the Court revisited its decision in the *Stanford* case, and in *Roper v. Simmons* a majority of Justices ruled that capital punishment of juveniles under the age of 18 is also cruel and unusual punishment. Excerpts from that opinion follow:

Roper v. Simmons
543 U.S. 551 (2005)

Justice Kennedy delivered the opinion of the Court.

This case requires us to address, for the second time in a decade and a half, whether it is permissible under the Eighth and Fourteenth Amendments to the Constitution of the United States to execute a juvenile offender who was older than 15 but younger than 18 when he committed a capital crime. In Stanford v. Kentucky, 492 U.S. 361 (1989), a divided Court rejected the proposition that the Constitution bars capital punishment for juvenile offenders in this age group. We reconsider the question.

I

At the age of 17, when he was still a junior in high school, Christopher Simmons . . . committed murder. About nine months later, after he had turned 18, he was tried and sentenced to death. There is little doubt that Simmons was the instigator of the crime. Before its commission Simmons said he wanted to murder someone. In chilling, callous terms he talked about his plan, discussing it for the most part with two friends, Charles Benjamin and John Tessmer, then aged 15 and 16 respectively. Simmons proposed to commit burglary and murder by breaking and entering, tying up a victim, and throwing the victim off a bridge. Simmons assured his friends they could "get away with it" because they were minors.

The three met at about 2 a.m. on the night of the murder, but Tessmer left before the other two set out. . . . Simmons and Benjamin entered the home of the victim, Shirley Crook, after reaching through an open window and unlocking the back door. Simmons turned on a hallway light. Awakened, Mrs. Crook called out, "Who's there?" In response Simmons entered Mrs. Crook's bedroom, where he recognized her from a previous car accident involving them both. Simmons later admitted this confirmed his resolve to murder her.

Using duct tape to cover her eyes and mouth and bind her hands, the two perpetrators put Mrs. Crook in her minivan and drove to a state park. They reinforced the bindings, covered her head with a towel, and walked her to a railroad trestle spanning the Meramec River. There they tied her hands and feet together with electrical wire, wrapped her whole face in duct tape and threw her from the bridge, drowning her in the waters below.

By the afternoon of September 9, Steven Crook had returned home from an overnight trip, found his bedroom in disarray, and reported his wife missing. On the same afternoon fishermen recovered the victim's body from the river. Simmons, meanwhile, was bragging about the killing, telling friends he had killed a woman "because the bitch seen my face."

The next day, after receiving information of Simmons' involvement, police arrested him at his high school and took him to the police station in Fenton, Missouri. They read him his <u>Miranda</u> rights. Simmons waived his right to an attorney and agreed to answer questions. After less than two hours of interrogation, Simmons confessed to the murder and agreed to perform a videotaped reenactment at the crime scene.

The State charged Simmons with burglary, kidnaping, stealing, and murder in the first degree. As Simmons was 17 at the time of the crime, he was outside the criminal jurisdiction of Missouri's juvenile court system. He was tried as an adult. At trial the State introduced Simmons' confession and the videotaped reenactment of the crime, along with testimony that Simmons discussed the crime in advance and bragged about it later. The defense called no witnesses in the guilt phase. The jury having returned a verdict of murder, the trial proceeded to the penalty phase.

[B]oth the prosecutor and defense counsel addressed Simmons' age, which the trial judge had instructed the jurors they could consider as a mitigating factor. Defense counsel reminded the jurors that juveniles of Simmons' age cannot drink, serve on juries, or even see certain movies, because "the legislatures have wisely decided that individuals of a certain age aren't responsible enough." Defense counsel argued that Simmons' age should make "a huge difference to [the jurors] in deciding just exactly what sort of punishment to make." In rebuttal, the prosecutor gave the following response: "Age, he says. Think about age. Seventeen years old. Isn't that scary? Doesn't that scare you? Mitigating? Quite the contrary I submit. Quite the contrary."

The jury recommended the death penalty.... Accepting the jury's recommendation, the trial judge imposed the death penalty.

Simmons obtained new counsel, who moved in the trial court to set aside the conviction and sentence....

Part of the submission, was that Simmons was "very immature," "very impulsive," and "very susceptible to being manipulated or influenced." The [psychological] experts testified about Simmons' background including a difficult home environment and dramatic changes in behavior, accompanied by poor school performance in adolescence. Simmons was absent from home for long periods, spending time using alcohol and drugs with other teenagers or young adults. The contention by Simmons' postconviction counsel was that these matters should have been established in the sentencing proceeding.

The trial court found no constitutional violation by reason of ineffective assistance of counsel and denied the motion for postconviction relief... [T]he Missouri Supreme Court affirmed. <u>State v. Simmons</u>, 944 S.W.2d 165, 169 (en banc), cert. denied, 522 U.S. 953 (1997). The federal courts denied Simmons' petition for a writ of habeas corpus. <u>Simmons v. Bowersox</u>, 235 F.3d 1124, 1127 (CA8), cert. denied, 534 U.S. 924 (2001).

After these proceedings in Simmons' case had run their course, this Court held that the Eighth and Fourteenth Amendments prohibit the execution of a mentally retarded person. <u>Atkins v. Virginia</u>, 536 U.S. 304 (2002). Simmons filed a new petition for state postconviction relief, arguing that the reasoning of <u>Atkins</u> established that the Constitution prohibits the execution of a juvenile who was under 18 when the crime was committed. The Missouri Supreme Court agreed. <u>State ex rel. Simmons v. Roper</u>, 112 S.W.3d 397 (2003) (en banc). It held that since <u>Stanford</u>,

> "a national consensus has developed against the execution of juvenile offenders, as demonstrated by the fact that eighteen states now bar such executions for juveniles, that twelve other states bar executions altogether, that no state has lowered its age of execution below 18 since <u>Stanford</u>, that five states have legislatively or by case law raised or established the minimum age at 18, and that the imposition of the juvenile death penalty has become truly unusual over the last decade." 112 S. W. 3d, at 399.

On this reasoning it set aside Simmons' death sentence and resentenced him to "life imprisonment without eligibility for probation, parole, or release except by act of the Governor." Id., at 413.

We granted certiorari, 540 U.S. 1160 (2004), and now affirm.

II

The Eighth Amendment provides: "Excessive bail shall not be required, nor excessive fines imposed, nor cruel and unusual punishments inflicted." The provision is applicable to the States through the Fourteenth Amendment.... By protecting even those convicted of heinous crimes, the Eighth Amendment reaffirms the duty of the government to respect the dignity of all persons.

The prohibition against "cruel and unusual punishments," like other expansive language in the Constitution, must be interpreted according to its text, by considering history, tradition, and precedent, and with due regard for its purpose and function in the constitutional design. To implement this framework we have established the propriety and affirmed the necessity of referring to "the evolving standards of decency that mark the progress of a maturing society" to determine which punishments are so disproportionate as to be cruel and unusual. <u>Trop v. Dulles</u>, 356 U.S. 86, 100-101 (1958) (plurality opinion).

In <u>Thompson v. Oklahoma</u>, 487 U.S. 815 (1988), a plurality of the Court determined that our standards of decency do not permit the execution of any offender under the age of 16 at the time of the crime. Id., at 818-838. . . . The plurality opinion explained that no death penalty State that had given express consideration to a minimum age for the death penalty had set the age lower than 16. Id., at 826—829. . . . The opinion further noted that juries imposed the death penalty on offenders under 16 with exceeding rarity; the last execution of an offender for a crime committed under the age of 16 had been carried out in 1948, 40 years prior. Id., at 832—833.

[T]he Thompson plurality stressed that "[t]he reasons why juveniles are not trusted with the privileges and responsibilities of an adult also explain why their irresponsible conduct is not as morally reprehensible as that of an adult." Id., at 835. According to the plurality, the lesser culpability of offenders under 16 made the death penalty inappropriate as a form of retribution, while the low likelihood that offenders under 16 engaged in "the kind of cost-benefit analysis that attaches any weight to the possibility of execution" made the death penalty ineffective as a means of deterrence. Id., at 836—838. . . . [T]he Court set aside the death sentence that had been imposed on the 15-year old offender.

The next year, in Stanford v. Kentucky, 492 U.S. 361 (1989), the Court . . . referred to contemporary standards of decency in this country and concluded the Eighth and Fourteenth Amendments did not proscribe the execution of juvenile offenders over 15 but under 18. The Court noted that 22 of the 37 death penalty States permitted the death penalty for 16-year-old offenders, and, among these 37 States, 25 permitted it for 17-year-old offenders. These numbers, in the Court's view, indicated there was no national consensus "sufficient to label a particular punishment cruel and unusual." Id., at 370—371. . . .

The same day the Court decided Stanford, it held that the Eighth Amendment did not mandate a categorical exemption from the death penalty for the mentally retarded. Penry v. Lynaugh, 492 U.S. 302 (1989). In reaching this conclusion it stressed that only two States had enacted laws banning the imposition of the death penalty on a mentally retarded person convicted of a capital offense. Id., at 334. According to the Court, "the two state statutes prohibiting execution of the mentally retarded, even when added to the 14 States that have rejected capital punishment completely, [did] not provide sufficient evidence at present of a national consensus." Ibid.[2]

Three Terms ago the subject was reconsidered in Atkins. We held that standards of decency have evolved since Penry and now demonstrate that the execution of the mentally retarded is cruel and unusual punishment. . . .

Mental retardation, the Court said, diminishes personal culpability even if the offender can distinguish right from wrong. 536 U.S., at 318. The

---

[2] *Ibid.* refers to the immediately preceding case citation.

impairments of mentally retarded offenders make it less defensible to impose the death penalty as retribution for past crimes and less likely that the death penalty will have a real deterrent effect. Id., at 319-320. Based on these considerations and on the finding of national consensus against executing the mentally retarded, the Court ruled that the death penalty constitutes an excessive sanction for the entire category of mentally retarded offenders, and that the Eighth Amendment "'places a substantive restriction on the State's power to take the life' of a mentally retarded offender." Id., at 321 (quoting Ford v. Wainwright, 477 U.S. 399, 405 (1986).

Just as the Atkins Court reconsidered the issue decided in Penry, we now reconsider the issue decided in Stanford. . . .

III

A

The evidence of national consensus against the death penalty for juveniles is similar, and in some respects parallel, to the evidence Atkins held sufficient to demonstrate a national consensus against the death penalty for the mentally retarded. . . . By a similar calculation in this case, 30 States prohibit the juvenile death penalty, comprising 12 that have rejected the death penalty altogether and 18 that maintain it but, by express provision or judicial interpretation, exclude juveniles from its reach. . . . In the present case, too, even in the 20 States without a formal prohibition on executing juveniles, the practice is infrequent. Since Stanford, six States have executed prisoners for crimes committed as juveniles. In the past 10 years, only three have done so: Oklahoma, Texas, and Virginia. . . . In December 2003 the Governor of Kentucky decided to spare the life of Kevin Stanford, and commuted his sentence to one of life imprisonment without parole, with the declaration that "'[w]e ought not be executing people who, legally, were children.'" Lexington Herald Leader, Dec. 9, 2003, p. B3, 2003 WL 65043346. . . .

As in Atkins, the objective indicia of consensus in this case—the rejection of the juvenile death penalty in the majority of States; the infrequency of its use even where it remains on the books; and the consistency in the trend toward abolition of the practice—provide sufficient evidence that today our society views juveniles, in the words Atkins used respecting the mentally retarded, as "categorically less culpable than the average criminal." 536 U.S., at 316.

B

A majority of States have rejected the imposition of the death penalty on juvenile offenders under 18, and we now hold this is required by the Eighth Amendment.

Because the death penalty is the most severe punishment, the Eighth Amendment applies to it with special force. . . . Capital punishment must be limited to those offenders who commit "a narrow category of the most serious crimes" and whose extreme culpability makes them "the most deserving of execution." <u>Atkins</u>, supra[3], at 319. . . .

Three general differences between juveniles under 18 and adults demonstrate that juvenile offenders cannot with reliability be classified among the worst offenders. First, as any parent knows and as the scientific and sociological studies respondent and his amici cite tend to confirm, "[a] lack of maturity and an underdeveloped sense of responsibility are found in youth more often than in adults and are more understandable among the young. These qualities often result in impetuous and ill-considered actions and decisions." <u>Johnson v. Texas</u>, 509 U.S. 350, 359–367 (1993). It has been noted that "adolescents are overrepresented statistically in virtually every category of reckless behavior." Arnett, Reckless Behavior in Adolescence: A Developmental Perspective, 12 Developmental Review 339 (1992). In recognition of the comparative immaturity and irresponsibility of juveniles, almost every State prohibits those under 18 years of age from voting, serving on juries, or marrying without parental consent.

The second area of difference is that juveniles are more vulnerable or susceptible to negative influences and outside pressures, including peer pressure. <u>Eddings v. Oklahoma</u>, 455 U.S. 104, 110–115 (1982) ("[Y]outh is more than a chronological fact. It is a time and condition of life when a person may be most susceptible to influence and to psychological damage"). This is explained in part by the prevailing circumstance that juveniles have less control, or less experience with control, over their own environment. See Steinberg & Scott, Less Guilty by Reason of Adolescence: Developmental Immaturity, Diminished Responsibility, and the Juvenile Death Penalty, 58 Am. Psychologist 1009, 1014 (2003). . . .

The third broad difference is that the character of a juvenile is not as well formed as that of an adult. The personality traits of juveniles are more transitory, less fixed. See generally E. Erikson, Identity: Youth and Crisis (1968).

These differences render suspect any conclusion that a juvenile falls among the worst offenders. The susceptibility of juveniles to immature and irresponsible behavior means "their irresponsible conduct is not as morally reprehensible as that of an adult." <u>Thompson</u>, supra, at 835 (plurality opinion). . . . The reality that juveniles still struggle to define their identity means it is less supportable to conclude that even a heinous crime committed by a juvenile is evidence of irretrievably depraved character.

---

[3] *Supra* is a Latin word meaning "above" and is used in legal documents to refer to a prior citation of a case.

From a moral standpoint it would be misguided to equate the failings of a minor with those of an adult, for a greater possibility exists that a minor's character deficiencies will be reformed.... see also Steinberg & Scott 1014 ("For most teens, [risky or antisocial] behaviors are fleeting; they cease with maturity as individual identity becomes settled. Only a relatively small proportion of adolescents who experiment in risky or illegal activities develop entrenched patterns of problem behavior that persist into adulthood").

Once the diminished culpability of juveniles is recognized, it is evident that the penological justifications for the death penalty apply to them with lesser force than to adults. We have held there are two distinct social purposes served by the death penalty: "'retribution and deterrence of capital crimes by prospective offenders.'" Atkins, 536 U.S., at 319 (quoting Gregg v. Georgia, 428 U.S. 153, 183 (1976).... Whether viewed as an attempt to express the community's moral outrage or as an attempt to right the balance for the wrong to the victim, the case for retribution is not as strong with a minor as with an adult. Retribution is not proportional if the law's most severe penalty is imposed on one whose culpability or blameworthiness is diminished, to a substantial degree, due to youth and immaturity.

As for deterrence, it is unclear whether the death penalty has a significant or even measurable deterrent effect on juveniles, as counsel for the petitioner acknowledged at oral argument.... [T]he absence of evidence of deterrent effect is of special concern because the same characteristics that render juveniles less culpable than adults suggest as well that juveniles will be less susceptible to deterrence....

IV

Our determination that the death penalty is disproportionate punishment for offenders under 18 finds confirmation in the stark reality that the United States is the only country in the world that continues to give official sanction to the juvenile death penalty. This reality does not become controlling, for the task of interpreting the Eighth Amendment remains our responsibility. Yet at least from the time of the Court's decision in Trop, the Court has referred to the laws of other countries and to international authorities as instructive for its interpretation of the Eighth Amendment's prohibition of "cruel and unusual punishments." 356 U.S., at 102-103 (plurality opinion)....

Article 37 of the United Nations Convention on the Rights of the Child, which every country in the world has ratified save for the United States and Somalia, contains an express prohibition on capital punishment for crimes committed by juveniles under 18. United Nations Convention on the Rights of the Child, Art. 37, Nov. 20, 1989, 1577 U.N.T.S. 3, 28 I.L.M. 1448, 1468—1470 (entered into force Sept. 2, 1990)....

[O]nly seven countries other than the United States have executed juvenile offenders since 1990: Iran, Pakistan, Saudi Arabia, Yemen, Nigeria, the Democratic Republic of Congo, and China. Since then each of these countries has either abolished capital punishment for juveniles or made public disavowal of the practice. Brief for Respondent 49—50. In sum, it is fair to say that the United States now stands alone in a world that has turned its face against the juvenile death penalty.

It is proper that we acknowledge the overwhelming weight of international opinion against the juvenile death penalty, resting in large part on the understanding that the instability and emotional imbalance of young people may often be a factor in the crime. The opinion of the world community, while not controlling our outcome, does provide respected and significant confirmation for our own conclusions....

***

The Eighth and Fourteenth Amendments forbid imposition of the death penalty on offenders who were under the age of 18 when their crimes were committed. The judgment of the Missouri Supreme Court setting aside the sentence of death imposed upon Christopher Simmons is affirmed.

It is so ordered.

Justice O'Connor, dissent:

The Court's decision today establishes a categorical rule forbidding the execution of any offender for any crime committed before his 18th birthday, no matter how deliberate, wanton, or cruel the offense. Neither the objective evidence of contemporary societal values, nor the Court's moral proportionality analysis, nor the two in tandem suffice to justify this ruling.

Although the Court finds support for its decision in the fact that a majority of the States now disallow capital punishment of 17-year-old offenders, it refrains from asserting that its holding is compelled by a genuine national consensus....

Instead, the rule decreed by the Court rests, ultimately, on its independent moral judgment that death is a disproportionately severe punishment for any 17-year-old offender. I do not subscribe to this judgment. Adolescents as a class are undoubtedly less mature, and therefore less culpable for their misconduct, than adults. But the Court has adduced no evidence impeaching the seemingly reasonable conclusion reached by many state legislatures: that at least some 17-year-old murderers are sufficiently mature to deserve the death penalty in an appropriate case. Nor has it been shown that capital sentencing juries are incapable of accurately assessing a youthful defendant's maturity or of giving due weight to the mitigating characteristics associated with youth....

Justice Scalia, with whom the Chief Justice and Justice Thomas join, dissenting.

In urging approval of a constitution that gave life-tenured judges the power to nullify laws enacted by the people's representatives, Alexander Hamilton assured the citizens of New York that there was little risk in this, since "[t]he judiciary...ha[s] neither FORCE nor WILL but merely judgment." The Federalist No. 78, p. 465 (C. Rossiter ed. 1961)....What a mockery today's opinion makes of Hamilton's expectation, announcing the Court's conclusion that the meaning of our Constitution has changed over the past 15 years—not, mind you, that this Court's decision 15 years ago was wrong, but that the Constitution has changed. The Court reaches this implausible result by purporting to advert, not to the original meaning of the Eighth Amendment, but to "the evolving standards of decency" of our national society. It then finds, on the flimsiest of grounds, that a national consensus which could not be perceived in our people's laws barely 15 years ago now solidly exists. Worse still, the Court says in so many words that what our people's laws say about the issue does not, in the last analysis, matter.... The Court thus proclaims itself sole arbiter of our Nation's moral standards—and in the course of discharging that awesome responsibility purports to take guidance from the views of foreign courts and legislatures. Because I do not believe that the meaning of our Eighth Amendment, any more than the meaning of other provisions of our Constitution, should be determined by the subjective views of five Members of this Court and like-minded foreigners, I dissent.

Today's opinion provides a perfect example of why judges are ill equipped to make the type of legislative judgments the Court insists on making here. To support its opinion that States should be prohibited from imposing the death penalty on anyone who committed murder before age 18, the Court looks to scientific and sociological studies, picking and choosing those that support its position....

We need not look far to find studies contradicting the Court's conclusions. As petitioner points out, the American Psychological Association (APA), which claims in this case that scientific evidence shows persons under 18 lack the ability to take moral responsibility for their decisions, has previously taken precisely the opposite position before this very Court. In its brief in Hodgson v. Minnesota, 497 U.S. 417 (1990), the APA found a "rich body of research" showing that juveniles are mature enough to decide whether to obtain an abortion without parental involvement. Brief for APA as Amicus Curiae, O. T. 1989, No. 88-805 etc., p. 18. The APA brief, citing psychology treatises and studies too numerous to list here, asserted: "[B]y middle adolescence (age 14-15) young people develop abilities similar to adults in reasoning about moral dilemmas, understanding social rules and laws, [and] reasoning about interpersonal relationships and interpersonal problems." Id., at 19-20.... Even putting aside questions of methodology, the studies cited by the Court offer scant support for a categorical prohibition of the death penalty for murderers under 18. At most, these studies conclude that, on average, or in most cases, persons under 18 are unable to take moral responsibility for their actions. Not one of the cited studies opines that all individuals under 18 are unable to appreciate the nature of their crimes.

Moreover, the cited studies describe only adolescents who engage in risky or antisocial behavior, as many young people do. Murder, however, is more than just risky or antisocial behavior. It is entirely consistent to believe that young people often act impetuously and lack judgment, but, at the same time, to believe that those who commit premeditated murder are—at least sometimes—just as culpable as adults. Christopher Simmons, who was only seven months shy of his 18th birthday when he murdered Shirley Crook, described to his friends beforehand—"[i]n chilling, callous terms," as the Court puts it—the murder he planned to commit. He then broke into the home of an innocent woman, bound her with duct tape and electrical wire, and threw her off a bridge alive and conscious. In their amici brief, the States of Alabama, Delaware, Oklahoma, Texas, Utah, and Virginia offer additional examples of murders committed by individuals under 18 that involve truly monstrous acts. In Alabama, two 17-year-olds, one 16-year-old, and one 19-year-old picked up a female hitchhiker, threw bottles at her, and kicked and stomped her for approximately 30 minutes until she died. They then sexually assaulted her lifeless body and, when they were finished, threw her body off a cliff.... Though these cases are assuredly the exception rather than the rule, the studies the Court cites in no way justify a constitutional imperative that prevents legislatures and juries from treating exceptional cases in an exceptional way—by determining that some murders are not just the acts of happy-go-lucky teenagers, but heinous crimes deserving of death.

That "almost every State prohibits those under 18 years of age from voting, serving on juries, or marrying without parental consent," ante,[4] at 15, is patently irrelevant—and is yet another resurrection of an argument that this Court gave a decent burial in <u>Stanford</u>. As we explained in <u>Stanford</u>, 492 U.S., at 374, it is "absurd to think that one must be mature enough to drive carefully, to drink responsibly, or to vote intelligently, in order to be mature enough to understand that murdering another human being is profoundly wrong, and to conform one's conduct to that most minimal of all civilized standards."....

---

[4] *Ante* is a Latin word meaning "before" and is used in legal opinions to refer to a prior section of the opinion.

The criminal justice system, by contrast, provides for individualized consideration of each defendant. In capital cases, this Court requires the sentencer to make an individualized determination, which includes weighing aggravating factors and mitigating factors, such as youth. In other contexts where individualized consideration is provided, we have recognized that at least some minors will be mature enough to make difficult decisions that involve moral considerations. For instance, we have struck down abortion statutes that do not allow minors deemed mature by courts to bypass parental notification provisions. See, e.g., Bellotti v. Baird, 443 U.S. 622, 643-644 (1979) (opinion of Powell, J.); Planned Parenthood of Central Mo. v. Danforth, 428 U.S. 52, 74-75 (1976). It is hard to see why this context should be any different. Whether to obtain an abortion is surely a much more complex decision for a young person than whether to kill an innocent person in cold blood.

The Court concludes, however, that juries cannot be trusted with the delicate task of weighing a defendant's youth along with the other mitigating and aggravating factors of his crime. This startling conclusion undermines the very foundations of our capital sentencing system, which entrusts juries with "mak[ing] the difficult and uniquely human judgments that defy codification and that 'buil[d] discretion, equity, and flexibility into a legal system.'" Mc Cleskey v. Kemp, 481 U.S. 279, 311 (1987). The Court says that juries will be unable to appreciate the significance of a defendant's youth when faced with details of a brutal crime. This assertion is based on no evidence; to the contrary, the Court itself acknowledges that the execution of under-18 offenders is "infrequent" even in the States "without a formal prohibition on executing juveniles," suggesting that juries take seriously their responsibility to weigh youth as a mitigating factor.

The Court's contention that the goals of retribution and deterrence are not served by executing murderers under 18 is also transparently false.... The Court claims that "juveniles will be less susceptible to deterrence" because "'[t]he likelihood that the teenage offender has made the kind of cost-benefit analysis that attaches any weight to the possibility of execution is so remote as to be virtually nonexistent.'" The Court unsurprisingly finds no support for this astounding proposition, save its own case law. The facts of this very case show the proposition to be false. Before committing the crime, Simmons encouraged his friends to join him by assuring them that they could "get away with it" because they were minors. This fact may have influenced the jury's decision to impose capital punishment despite Simmons' age. Because the Court refuses to entertain the possibility that its own unsubstantiated generalization about juveniles could be wrong, it ignores this evidence entirely.

Though the views of our own citizens are essentially irrelevant to the Court's decision today, the views of other countries and the so-called international community take center stage.

The Court begins by noting that "Article 37 of the United Nations Convention on the Rights of the Child, which every country in the world has ratified save for the United States and Somalia, contains an express prohibition on capital punishment for crimes committed by juveniles under 18.".... Unless the Court has added to its arsenal the power to join and ratify treaties on behalf of the United States, I cannot see how this evidence favors, rather than refutes, its position. That the Senate and the President—those actors our Constitution empowers to enter into treaties, see Art. II, §2–have declined to join and ratify treaties prohibiting execution of under—18 offenders can only suggest that our country has either not reached a national consensus on the question, or has reached a consensus contrary to what the Court announces....

More fundamentally, however, the basic premise of the Court's argument—that American law should conform to the laws of the rest of the world—ought to be rejected out of hand. In fact the Court itself does not believe it. In many significant respects the laws of most other countries differ from our law–including not only such explicit provisions of our Constitution as the right to jury trial and grand jury indictment, but even many interpretations of the Constitution prescribed by this Court itself. The Court-pronounced exclusionary rule, for example, is distinctively American. When we adopted that rule in <u>Mapp v. Ohio</u>, 367 U. S. 643, 655 (1961), it was "unique to American Jurisprudence." <u>Bivens v. Six Unknown Fed. Narcotics Agents</u>, 403 U. S. 388, 415 (1971) (Burger, C. J., dissenting). Since then a categorical exclusionary rule has been "universally rejected" by other countries, including those with rules prohibiting illegal searches and police misconduct, despite the fact that none of these countries "appears to have any alternative form of discipline for police that is effective in preventing search violations." Bradley, Mapp Goes Abroad, 52 Case W. Res. L. Rev. 375, 399-400 (2001). England, for example, rarely excludes evidence found during an illegal search or seizure and has only recently begun excluding evidence from illegally obtained confessions. See C. Slobogin, Criminal Procedure: Regulation of Police Investigation 550 (3d ed. 2002). Canada rarely excludes evidence and will only do so if admission will "bring the administration of justice into disrepute." Id., at 550-551. The European Court of Human Rights has held that introduction of illegally seized evidence does not violate the "fair trial" requirement in Article 6, §1, of the European Convention on Human Rights.

In a system based upon constitutional and statutory text democratically adopted, the concept of "law" ordinarily signifies that particular words have a fixed meaning. Such law does not change, and this Court's pronouncement of it therefore remains authoritative until (confessing our prior error) we overrule. The Court has purported to make of the Eighth Amendment, however, a mirror of the passing and changing sentiment of American society regarding penology.... This is no way to run a legal system....

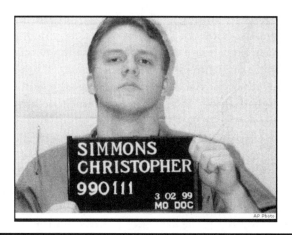

"Mug Shot" photo of Christopher Simmons taken during his arrest at the police station.

Criminal Appeal

In both the state and federal systems, a defendant who is convicted of a crime has the right to an appeal. Most criminal cases, however, are not appealed because most defendants choose to plea bargain, and plea bargains cannot be appealed. Similarly, the Fifth Amendment double jeopardy clause prevents the government from filing an appeal if a defendant is acquitted of a crime.

An appeal challenges the legal rulings made by a trial judge that resulted in a defendant's conviction. For example, a defendant may argue that the trial judge improperly admitted evidence that should have been excluded or that the judge's instructions to the jury were erroneous. A defendant who wins an appeal, however, does not necessarily win his or her freedom. Instead, the appellate court usually *remands* (returns) the case back to the trial court to conduct a new trial. At that point, the prosecution must decide whether it will retry the defendant or drop the charges against the defendant. The defendant will be freed pending the new trial only if he is released on bail by the trial judge. Many defendants whose convictions are reversed on appeal are convicted again at the second trial.

CHAPTER 8 QUESTIONS

1. Questions about due process:
   a. What is due process of law?
   b. What is its constitutional authority?
   c. What social values does it address?

2. Why must criminal statutes be written precisely and specifically?

3. What is *mens rea*? How is it used to determine criminal culpability?

4. The <u>Miranda</u> Warnings require the police to inform an arrested person of his or her constitutional rights. Do you think that it is the individual's responsibility to know what his or her rights are, or the government's responsibility to inform each individual who is arrested of his or her rights? Explain your answer.

5. Plea bargaining:
   a. What is plea bargaining?
   b. What are its benefits?
   c. Do you think plea bargaining is a good idea? Explain your answer.

6. Questions about <u>Mapp v. Ohio</u>:
   a. Was Dollree Mapp justified in preventing the police from entering her house without a warrant, or was the police search of her house without a warrant reasonable? Explain your answer.
   b. Would the police's warrantless search have been legal if they had found the person they suspected Mapp of hiding inside her home? Explain your answer.
   c. Criminal enforcement has to balance the rights of the individual to be protected from improper government intrusion against the rights of society to be protected from dangerous people. If the police had not searched Mapp's home they would not have found the pornographic materials. Do you think that Mapp's rights, or society's rights, should have been given more protection? Explain your answer.

7. Questions about the exclusionary rule:
   a. What is the purpose of the exclusionary rule?
   b. Who benefits from the exclusionary rule? Explain your answer.
   c. Who, if anyone, is harmed by the exclusionary rule? Explain your answer.
   d. Should the United States keep or abolish the exclusionary rule? Explain your answer.

8. Questions about <u>Roper v. Simmons</u>:
   a. How did the Supreme Court explain the meaning and application of "cruel and unusual punishment"?
   b. What was the Supreme Court's holding in <u>Roper v. Simmons</u>?
   c. What was the constitutional authority for the Court's ruling?
   d. What were other reasons the Court gave to support its ruling? Do you agree or disagree with these other reasons? Explain your answer.

   e. Do you think Christopher Simmons knew that killing Mrs. Crook was wrong? Do you think he killed Mrs. Crook because he was immature and impulsive? Do you think the possibility of capital execution deterred him from killing Mrs. Crook? Explain your answers.

   f. Do you agree with the majority's opinion that subjecting juveniles to the death penalty is cruel and unusual punishment because persons under age 18 are categorically less culpable of their crimes than adults? Explain your answer.

   g. What reasons did Justice O'Connor give for her dissent? Do you agree or disagree with her reasons? Explain your answer.

   h. What reasons did Justice Scalia give for his dissent? Do you agree or disagree with his reasons? Explain your answer.

   i. Is there a legally principled way to distinguish why juveniles less than 18 years of age are mature enough to decide to have an abortion but not mature enough to be treated like adults when they commit a capital crime? Explain your answer.

The Constitution of the United States

WE THE PEOPLE of the United States, in Order to form a more perfect Union, establish Justice, insure domestic Tranquility, provide for the common defence, promote the general Welfare, and secure the Blessings of Liberty to ourselves and our Posterity, do ordain and establish this Constitution for the United States of America.

Article I

Section 1.

All legislative Powers herein granted shall be vested in a Congress of the United States, which shall consist of a Senate and House of Representatives.

Section 2.

The House of Representatives shall be composed of Members chosen every second Year by the People of the several States, and the Electors in each State shall have the Qualifications requisite for Electors of the most numerous Branch of the State Legislature.

No Person shall be a Representative who shall not have attained to the Age of twenty five Years, and been seven Years a Citizen of the United States, and who shall not, when elected, be an Inhabitant of that State in which he shall be chosen.

Representatives and direct Taxes shall be apportioned among the several States which may be included within this Union, according to their respective Numbers, which shall be determined by adding to the whole Number of free Persons, including those bound to Service for a Term of Years, and excluding Indians not taxed, three fifths of all other Persons. The actual Enumeration shall be made within three Years after the first Meeting of the Congress of the United States, and within every subsequent Term of ten Years, in such Manner as they shall by Law direct. The Number of Representatives shall not exceed one for every thirty Thousand, but each State shall have at Least one Representative; and until such enumeration shall be made, the State of New Hampshire shall be entitled to chuse three, Massachusetts eight, Rhode Island and Providence Plantations one, Connecticut five, New York six, New Jersey four, Pennsylvania eight, Delaware one, Maryland six, Virginia ten, North Carolina five, South Carolina five, and Georgia three.

When vacancies happen in the Representation from any State, the Executive Authority thereof shall issue Writs of Election to fill such Vacancies.

The House of Representatives shall chuse their Speaker and other Officers; and shall have the sole Power of Impeachment.

Section 3.

The Senate of the United States shall be composed of two Senators from each State, chosen by the Legislature thereof, for six Years; and each Senator shall have one Vote.

Immediately after they shall be assembled in Consequence of the first Election, they shall be divided as equally as may be into three Classes. The Seats of the Senators of the first Class shall be vacated at the Expiration of the second Year, of the second Class at the Expiration of the fourth Year, and of the third Class at the Expiration of the sixth Year, so that one third may be chosen every second Year; and if Vacancies happen by Resignation, or otherwise, during the Recess of the Legislature of any State, the Executive thereof may make temporary Appointments until the next Meeting of the Legislature, which shall then fill such Vacancies.

No Person shall be a Senator who shall not have attained to the Age of thirty Years, and been nine Years a Citizen of the United States, and who shall not, when elected, be an Inhabitant of that State for which he shall be chosen.

The Vice President of the United States shall be President of the Senate, but shall have no Vote, unless they be equally divided.

The Senate shall chuse their other Officers, and also a President pro tempore, in the Absence of the Vice President, or when he shall exercise the Office of President of the United States.

The Senate shall have the sole Power to try all Impeachments. When sitting for that Purpose, they shall be on Oath or Affirmation. When the President of the United States is tried, the Chief Justice shall preside: And no Person shall be convicted without the Concurrence of two thirds of the Members present.

Judgment in Cases of Impeachment shall not extend further than to removal from Office, and disqualification to hold and enjoy any Office of honor, Trust, or Profit under the United States: but the Party convicted shall nevertheless be liable and subject to Indictment, Trial, Judgment, and Punishment, according to Law.

Section 4.

The Times, Places and Manner of holding Elections for Senators and Representatives shall be prescribed in each State by the Legislature thereof; but the Congress may at any time by Law make or alter such Regulations, except as to the Places of chusing Senators.

The Congress shall assemble at least once in every Year, and such Meeting shall be on the first Monday in December, unless they shall by Law appoint a different Day.

Section 5.

Each House shall be the Judge of the Elections, Returns and Qualifications of its own Members, and a Majority of each shall constitute a Quorum to do Business; but a smaller Number may adjourn from day to day, and may be authorized to compel the Attendance of absent Members, in such Manner, and under such Penalties as each House may provide.

Each House may determine the Rules of its Proceedings, punish its Members for disorderly Behaviour, and, with the Concurrence of two thirds, expel a Member.

Each House shall keep a Journal of its Proceedings, and from time to time publish the same, excepting such Parts as may in their Judgment require Secrecy; and the Yeas and Nays of the Members of either House on any question shall, at the Desire of one fifth of those Present, be entered on the Journal.

Neither House, during the Session of Congress, shall, without the Consent of the other, adjourn for more than three days, nor to any other Place than that in which the two Houses shall be sitting.

Section 6.

The Senators and Representatives shall receive a Compensation for their Services, to be ascertained by Law, and paid out of the Treasury of the United States. They shall in all Cases, except Treason, Felony and Breach of the Peace, be privileged from Arrest during their Attendance at the Session of their respective Houses, and in going to and returning from the same; and for any Speech or Debate in either House, they shall not be questioned in any other Place.

No Senator or Representative shall, during the Time for which he was elected, be appointed to any civil Office under the Authority of the United States, which shall have been created, or the Emoluments whereof shall have been increased during such time and no Person holding any Office under the United States, shall be a Member of either House during his Continuance in Office.

Section 7.

All Bills for raising Revenue shall originate in the House of Representatives; but the Senate may propose or concur with Amendments as on other Bills.

Every Bill which shall have passed the House of Representatives and the Senate, shall, before it become a Law, be presented to the President of the United States; If he approve he shall sign it, but if not he shall return it, with his Objections to that House in which it shall have originated, who shall enter the Objections at large on their Journal, and proceed to reconsider it. If after such Reconsideration two thirds of that House shall agree to pass the Bill, it shall be sent, together with the Objections, to the other House, by which it shall likewise be reconsidered, and if approved by two thirds of that House, it shall become a Law. But in all such Cases the Votes of both Houses shall be determined by Yeas and Nays, and the Names of the Persons voting for and against the Bill shall be entered on the Journal of each House respectively. If any Bill shall not be returned by the President within ten Days (Sundays excepted) after it shall have been presented to him, the Same shall be a Law, in like Manner as if he had signed it, unless the Congress by their Adjournment prevent its Return in which Case it shall not be a Law.

Every Order, Resolution, or Vote, to which the Concurrence of the Senate and House of Representatives may be necessary (except on a question of Adjournment) shall be presented to the President of the United States; and before the Same shall take Effect, shall be approved by him, or being disapproved by him, shall be repassed by two thirds of the Senate and House of Representatives, according to the Rules and Limitations prescribed in the Case of a Bill.

Section 8.

The Congress shall have Power To lay and collect Taxes, Duties, Imposts and Excises, to pay the Debts and provide for the common Defence and general Welfare of the United States; but all Duties, Imposts and Excises shall be uniform throughout the United States;

To borrow Money on the credit of the United States;

To regulate Commerce with foreign Nations, and among the several States, and with the Indian Tribes;

To establish an uniform Rule of Naturalization, and uniform Laws on the subject of Bankruptcies throughout the United States;

To coin Money, regulate the Value thereof, and of foreign Coin, and fix the Standard of Weights and Measures;

To provide for the Punishment of counterfeiting the Securities and current Coin of the United States;

To establish Post Offices and Post Roads;

To promote the Progress of Science and useful Arts, by securing for limited Times to Authors and Inventors the exclusive Right to their respective Writings and Discoveries;

To constitute Tribunals inferior to the supreme Court;

To define and punish Piracies and Felonies committed on the high Seas, and Offences against the Law of Nations;

To declare War, grant Letters of Marque and Reprisal, and make Rules concerning Captures on Land and Water;

To raise and support Armies, but no Appropriation of Money to that Use shall be for a longer Term than two Years;

To provide and maintain a Navy;

To make Rules for the Government and Regulation of the land and naval Forces;

To provide for calling forth the Militia to execute the Laws of the Union, suppress Insurrections and repel Invasions;

To provide for organizing, arming, and disciplining, the Militia, and for governing such Part of them as may be employed in the Service of the United States, reserving to the States respectively, the Appointment of the Officers, and the Authority of training the Militia according to the discipline prescribed by Congress;

To exercise exclusive Legislation in all Cases whatsoever, over such District (not exceeding ten Miles square) as may, by Cession of particular States, and the Acceptance of Congress, become the Seat of the Government of the United States, and to exercise like Authority over all Places purchased by the Consent of the Legislature of the State in which the Same shall be, for the Erection of Forts, Magazines, Arsenals, dock-Yards, and other needful Buildings;—And

To make all Laws which shall be necessary and proper for carrying into Execution the foregoing Powers, and all other Powers vested by this Constitution in the Government of the United States, or in any Department or Officer thereof.

Section 9.

The Migration or Importation of such Persons as any of the States now existing shall think proper to admit, shall not be prohibited by the Congress prior to the Year one thousand eight hundred and eight, but a Tax or duty may be imposed on such Importation, not exceeding ten dollars for each Person.

The Privilege of the Writ of Habeas Corpus shall not be suspended, unless when in Cases of Rebellion or Invasion the public Safety may require it.

No Bill of Attainder or ex post facto Law shall be passed.

No Capitation, or other direct, Tax shall be laid, unless in Proportion to the Census or Enumeration herein before directed to be taken.

No Tax or Duty shall be laid on Articles exported from any State.

No Preference shall be given by any Regulation of Commerce or Revenue to the Ports of one State over those of another: nor shall Vessels bound to, or from, one State, be obliged to enter, clear, or pay Duties in another.

No Money shall be drawn from the Treasury, but in Consequence of Appropriations made by Law; and a regular Statement and Account of the Receipts and Expenditures of all public Money shall be published from time to time.

No Title of Nobility shall be granted by the United States: And no Person holding any Office of Profit or Trust under them, shall, without the Consent of the Congress, accept of any present, Emolument, Office, or Title, of any kind whatever, from any King, Prince, or foreign State.

Section 10.

No State shall enter into any Treaty, Alliance, or Confederation; grant Letters of Marque and Reprisal; coin Money; emit Bills of Credit; make any Thing but gold and silver Coin a Tender in Payment of Debts; pass any Bill of Attainder, ex post facto Law, or Law impairing the Obligation of Contracts, or grant any Title of Nobility.

No State shall, without the Consent of the Congress, lay any Imposts or Duties on Imports or Exports, except what may be absolutely necessary for executing its inspection Laws: and the net Produce of all Duties and Imposts, laid by any State on Imports or Exports, shall be for the Use of the Treasury of the United States; and all such Laws shall be subject to the Revision and Control of the Congress.

No State shall, without the Consent of Congress, lay any Duty of Tonnage, keep Troops, or Ships of War in time of Peace, enter into any Agreement or Compact with another State, or with a foreign Power, or engage in War, unless actually invaded, or in such imminent Danger as will not admit of delay.

Article II

Section 1.

The executive Power shall be vested in a President of the United States of America. He shall hold his Office during the Term of four Years, and, together with the Vice President, chosen for the same Term, be elected, as follows:

Each State shall appoint, in such Manner as the Legislature thereof may direct, a Number of Electors, equal to the whole Number of Senators and Representatives to which the State may be entitled in the Congress; but no Senator or Representative, or Person holding an Office of Trust or Profit under the United States, shall be appointed an Elector.

The Electors shall meet in their respective States, and vote by Ballot for two Persons, of whom one at least shall not be an Inhabitant of the same State with themselves. And they shall make a List of all the Persons voted for, and of the Number of Votes for each; which List they shall sign and certify, and transmit sealed to the Seat of the Government of the United States, directed to the President of the Senate. The President of the Senate shall, in the Presence of the Senate and House of Representatives, open all the Certificates, and the Votes shall then be counted. The Person having the greatest Number of Votes shall be the President, if such Number be a Majority of the whole Number of Electors appointed; and if there be more than one who have such Majority, and have an equal Number of Votes, then the House of Representatives shall immediately chuse by Ballot one of them for President; and if no Person have a Majority, then from the five highest on the List the said House shall in like Manner chuse the President. But in chusing the President, the Votes shall be taken by States, the Representation from each State having one Vote; A quorum for this Purpose shall consist of a Member or Members from two thirds of the States, and a Majority of all the States shall be necessary to a Choice. In every Case, after the Choice of the President, the Person having the greatest Number of Votes of the Electors shall be the Vice President. But if there should remain two or more who have equal Votes, the Senate shall chuse from them by Ballot the Vice President.

The Congress may determine the Time of chusing the Electors, and the Day on which they shall give their Votes; which Day shall be the same throughout the United States.

No Person except a natural born Citizen, or a Citizen of the United States, at the time of the Adoption of this Constitution, shall be eligible to the Office of President; neither shall any Person be eligible to that Office who shall not have attained to the Age of thirty five Years, and been fourteen Years a Resident within the United States.

In Case of the Removal of the President from Office, or of his Death, Resignation or Inability to discharge the Powers and Duties of the said Office, the Same shall devolve on the Vice President, and the Congress may by Law provide for the Case of Removal, Death, Resignation or Inability, both of the President and Vice President, declaring what Officer shall then act as President, and such Officer shall act accordingly, until the Disability be removed, or a President shall be elected.

The President shall, at stated Times, receive for his Services, a Compensation, which shall neither be increased nor diminished during the Period for which he shall have been elected, and he shall not receive within that Period any other Emolument from the United States, or any of them.

Before he enter on the Execution of his Office, he shall take the following Oath or Affirmation:—"I do solemnly swear (or affirm) that I will faithfully execute the Office of President of the United States, and will to the best of my Ability, preserve, protect and defend the Constitution of the United States."

Section 2.

The President shall be Commander in Chief of the Army and Navy of the United States, and of the Militia of the several States, when called into the actual Service of the United States; he may require the Opinion, in writing, of the principal Officer in each of the executive Departments, upon any Subject relating to the Duties of their respective Offices, and he shall have Power to grant Reprieves and Pardons for Offences against the United States, except in Cases of Impeachment.

He shall have Power, by and with the Advice and Consent of the Senate to make Treaties, provided two thirds of the Senators present concur; and he shall nominate, and by and with the Advice and Consent of the Senate, shall appoint Ambassadors, other public Ministers and Consuls, Judges of the supreme Court, and all other Officers of the United States, whose Appointments are not herein otherwise provided for, and which shall be established by Law: but the Congress may by Law vest the Appointment of such inferior Officers, as they think proper, in the President alone, in the Courts of Law, or in the Heads of Departments.

The President shall have Power to fill up all Vacancies that may happen during the Recess of the Senate, by granting Commissions which shall expire at the End of their next Session.

Section 3.

He shall from time to time give to the Congress Information of the State of the Union, and recommend to their Consideration such Measures as he shall judge necessary and expedient; he may on extraordinary Occasions, convene both Houses, or either of them, and in Case of Disagreement between them, with Respect to the Time of Adjournment, he may adjourn them to such Time as he shall think proper; he shall receive Ambassadors and other Public Ministers; he shall take Care that the Laws be faithfully executed, and shall Commission all the Officers of the United States.

Section 4.

The President, Vice President and all civil Officers of the United States, shall be removed from Office on Impeachment for, and Conviction of, Treason, Bribery, or other high Crimes and Misdemeanors.

Article III

Section 1.

The judicial Power of the United States, shall be vested in one supreme Court, and in such inferior Courts as the Congress may from time to time ordain and establish. The Judges, both of the supreme and inferior Courts, shall hold their Offices during good Behaviour, and shall, at stated Times, receive for their Services, a Compensation, which shall not be diminished during their Continuance in Office.

Section 2.

The judicial Power shall extend to all Cases, in Law and Equity, arising under this Constitution, the Laws of the United States, and Treaties made, or which shall be made, under their Authority;—to all Cases affecting Ambassadors, other public Ministers and Consuls;—to all Cases of admiralty and maritime jurisdiction;—to Controversies to which the United States shall be a Party;—to Controversies between two or more States;—between a State and Citizens of another State,—between Citizens of different States,—between Citizens of the same State claiming Lands under the Grants of different States, and between a State, or the Citizens thereof;-and foreign States, Citizens or Subjects.

In all Cases affecting Ambassadors, other public Ministers and Consuls, and those in which a State shall be Party, the supreme Court shall have original Jurisdiction. In all the other Cases before mentioned, the supreme Court shall have appellate Jurisdiction, both as to Law and Fact, with such Exceptions, and under such Regulations as the Congress shall make.

The Trial of all Crimes, except in Cases of Impeachment, shall be by Jury; and such Trial shall be held in the State where the said Crimes shall have been committed; but when not committed within any State, the Trial shall be at such Place or Places as the Congress may by Law have directed.

Section 3.

Treason against the United States, shall consist only in levying War against them, or, in adhering to their Enemies, giving them Aid and Comfort. No Person shall be convicted of Treason unless on the Testimony of two Witnesses to the same overt Act, or on Confession in open Court.

The Congress shall have Power to declare the Punishment of Treason, but no Attainder of Treason shall work Corruption of Blood, or Forfeiture except during the Life of the Person attainted.

Article IV

Section 1.

Full Faith and Credit shall be given in each State to the public Acts, Records, and judicial Proceedings of every other State. And the Congress may by general Laws prescribe the Manner in which such Acts, Records and Proceedings shall be proved and the Effect thereof.

Section 2.

The Citizens of each State shall be entitled to all Privileges and Immunities of Citizens in the several States.

A Person charged in any State with Treason, Felony, or other Crime, who shall flee from Justice and be found in another State, shall on demand of the executive Authority of the State from which he fled, be delivered up, to be removed to the State having Jurisdiction of the Crime.

No Person held to Service or Labour in one state, under the Laws thereof, escaping into another, shall, in Consequence of any Law or Regulation therein, be discharged from such Service or Labour, but shall be delivered upon Claim of the Party to whom such Service or Labour may be done.

Section 3.

New States may be admitted by the Congress into this Union; but no new State shall be formed or erected within the Jurisdiction of any other State; nor any State be formed by the Junction of two or more States, or Parts of States, without the Consent of the Legislatures of the States concerned as well as of the Congress.

The Congress shall have Power to dispose of and make all needful Rules and Regulations respecting the Territory or other Property belonging to the United States; and nothing in this Constitution shall be so construed as to Prejudice any Claims of the United States, or of any particular State.

Section 4.

The United States shall guarantee to every State in this Union a Republican Form of government, and shall protect each of them against Invasion; and on Application of the Legislature, or of the Executive (when the Legislature cannot be convened) against domestic Violence.

Article V

The Congress, whenever two thirds of both Houses shall deem it necessary, shall propose Amendments to this Constitution, or, on the Application of the Legislatures of two thirds of the several states, shall call a Convention for proposing

Amendments, which, in either Case, shall be valid to all Intents and Purposes, as Part of this Constitution, when ratified by the Legislatures of three fourths of the several states, or by Conventions in three fourths thereof, as the one or the other Mode of Ratification may be proposed by the Congress; Provided that no Amendment which may be made prior to the Year One thousand eight hundred and eight shall in any Manner affect the first and fourth Clauses in the Ninth Section of the first Article; and that no State, without its Consent, shall be deprived of its equal Suffrage in the Senate.

Article VI

All Debts contracted and Engagements entered into, before the Adoption of this Constitution, shall be as valid against the United States under this Constitution, as under the Confederation.

This Constitution, and the Laws of the United States which shall be made in Pursuance thereof; and all Treaties made, or which shall be made, under the Authority of the United States, shall be the supreme Law of the Land; and the Judges in every State shall be bound thereby, any Thing in the Constitution or Laws of any State to the contrary notwithstanding.

The Senators and Representatives before mentioned, and the Members of the several State Legislatures, and all executive and judicial Officers, both of the United States and of the several States, shall be bound by Oath or Affirmation, to support this Constitution; but no religious Test shall ever be required as a Qualification to any Office or public Trust under the United States.

Article VII

The Ratification of the Conventions of nine States shall be sufficient for the Establishment of this Constitution between the States so ratifying the Same.

Done in Convention by the Unanimous Consent of the States present the Seventeenth Day of September in the Year of our Lord one thousand seven hundred and Eighty seven and of the Independence of the United States of America the Twelfth In witness whereof We have hereunto subscribed our Names,

G°. Washington
Presidt and deputy from Virginia

Delaware
Geo: Read
Gunning Bedford jun

John Dickinson
Richard Bassett
Jaco: Broom

Maryland
James McHenry
Dan of St. Thos. Jenifer
Danl Carroll

Virginia
John Blair
James Madison jr.

North Carolina
Wm. Blount
Richd. Dobbs Spaight
Hu Williamson

South Carolina
J. Rutledge
Charles Cotesworth Pinckney
Charles Pinckney
Pierce Butler

Georgia
William Few
Abr Baldwin

New Hampshire
John Langdon
Nicholas Gilman

Massachusetts
Nathaniel Gorham
Rufus King

Connecticut
Wm. Saml. Johnson
Roger Sherman

New York
Alexander Hamilton

New Jersey
Wil: Livingston
David Brearley
Wm. Paterson
Jona: Dayton

Pensylvania
B Franklin
Thomas Mifflin
Robt. Morris
Geo. Clymer
Thos. Fitz Simons
Jared Ingersoll
James Wilson
Gouv Morris

ATTEST William Jackson Secretory

The Declaration of Independence

IN CONGRESS, July 4, 1776.

The unanimous Declaration of the thirteen United States of America

When in the Course of human Events, it becomes necessary for one People to dissolve the Political Bands which have connected them with another, and to assume among the Powers of the Earth, the separate and equal Station to which the Laws of Nature and of Nature's God entitle them, a decent Respect to the Opinions of Mankind requires that they should declare the causes which impel them to the Separation.

We hold these truths to be self-evident, that all Men are created equal, that they are endowed by their Creator with certain unalienable Rights, that among these are Life, Liberty and the Pursuit of Happiness—That to secure these Rights, Governments are instituted among Men, deriving their just Powers from the Consent of the Governed, that whenever any Form of Government becomes destructive of these Ends, it is the Right of the People to alter or to abolish it, and to institute new Government, laying its Foundation on such Principles, and organizing its Powers in such Form, as to them shall seem most likely to effect their Safety and Happiness. Prudence, indeed, will dictate that Governments long established should not be changed for light and transient Causes; and accordingly all Experience hath shewn, that Mankind are more disposed to suffer, while Evils are sufferable, than to right themselves by abolishing the Forms to which they are accustomed. But when a long Train of Abuses and Usurpations, pursuing invariably the same Object, evinces a Design to reduce them under absolute Despotism, it is their Right, it is their Duty, to throw off such Government, and to provide new Guards for their future Security. Such has been the patient Sufferance of these Colonies; and such is now the Necessity which constrains them to alter their former Systems of Government. The History of the present King of Great-Britain is a History of repeated Injuries and Usurpations, all having in direct Object the Establishment of an absolute Tyranny over these States. To prove this, let Facts be submitted to a candid World.

He has refused his Assent to Laws, the most wholesome and necessary for the public Good.

He has forbidden his Governors to pass Laws of immediate and pressing Importance, unless suspended in their Operation till his Assent should be obtained; and when so suspended, he has utterly neglected to attend to them.

He has refused to pass other Laws for the Accommodation of large Districts of People, unless those People would relinquish the Right of Representation in the Legislature, a Right inestimable to them, and formidable to Tyrants only.

He has called together Legislative Bodies at Places unusual, uncomfortable, and distant from the Depository of their public Records, for the sole Purpose of fatiguing them into Compliance with his Measures.

He has dissolved Representative Houses repeatedly, for opposing with manly Firmness his Invasions on the Rights of the People.

He has refused for a long Time, after such Dissolutions, to cause others to be elected; whereby the Legislative Powers, incapable of Annihilation, have returned to the People at large for their exercise; the State remaining in the mean time exposed to all the Dangers of Invasion from without, and Convulsions within.

He has endeavoured to prevent the Population of these States; for that Purpose obstructing the Laws for Naturalization of Foreigners; refusing to pass others to encourage their Migrations hither, and raising the Conditions of new Appropriations of Lands.

He has obstructed the Administration of Justice, by refusing his Assent to Laws for establishing Judiciary Powers.

He has made Judges dependent on his Will alone, for the Tenure of their Offices, and the Amount and Payment of their Salaries.

He has erected a Multitude of new Offices, and sent hither Swarms of Officers to harrass our People, and eat out their Substance.

He has kept among us, in Times of Peace, Standing Armies, without the consent of our Legislatures.

He has affected to render the Military independent of and superior to the Civil Power.

He has combined with others to subject us to a Jurisdiction foreign to our Constitution, and unacknowledged by our Laws; giving his Assent to their Acts of pretended Legislation:

For quartering large Bodies of Armed Troops among us:

For protecting them, by a mock Trial, from Punishment for any Murders which they should commit on the Inhabitants of these States:

For cutting off our Trade with all Parts of the world:

For imposing Taxes on us without our Consent:

For depriving us, in many Cases, of the Benefits of Trial by Jury:

For transporting us beyond Seas to be tried for pretended Offences

For abolishing the free System of English Laws in a neighbouring Province, establishing therein an arbitrary Government, and enlarging its Boundaries, so as to render it at once an Example and fit Instrument for introducing the same absolute Rule into these Colonies:

For taking away our Charters, abolishing our most valuable Laws, and altering fundamentally the Forms of our Governments:

For suspending our own Legislatures, and declaring themselves invested with Power to legislate for us in all Cases whatsoever.

He has abdicated Government here, by declaring us out of his Protection and waging War against us.

He has plundered our Seas, ravaged our Coasts, burnt our Towns, and destroyed the Lives of our People.

He is, at this Time, transporting large Armies of foreign Mercenaries to compleat the Works of Death, Desolation, and Tyranny, already begun with circumstances of Cruelty and Perfidy, scarcely paralleled in the most barbarous Ages, and totally unworthy the Head of a civilized Nation.

He has constrained our fellow Citizens taken Captive on the high Seas to bear Arms against their Country, to become the Executioners of their Friends and Brethren, or to fall themselves by their Hands.

He has excited domestic Insurrections amongst us, and has endeavoured to bring on the Inhabitants of our Frontiers, the merciless Indian Savages, whose known Rule of Warfare, is an undistinguished Destruction, of all Ages, Sexes and Conditions.

In every stage of these Oppressions we have Petitioned for Redress in the most humble Terms: Our repeated Petitions have been answered only by repeated Injury. A Prince, whose Character is thus marked by every act which may define a Tyrant, is unfit to be the Ruler of a free People.

Nor have We been wanting in Attentions to our British Brethren. We have warned them from Time to Time of attempts by their Legislature to extend an unwarrantable Jurisdiction over us. We have reminded them of the Circumstances of our Emigration and Settlement here. We have appealed to their native Justice and Magnanimity, and we have conjured them by the Ties of our common Kindred to disavow these Usurpations, which, would inevitably interrupt our Connections and Correspondence. They too have been deaf to the Voice of

Justice and of Consanguinity. We must, therefore, acquiesce in the Necessity, which denounces our Separation, and hold them, as we hold the rest of Mankind, Enemies in War, in Peace, Friends.

We, therefore, the Representatives of the UNITED STATES OF AMERICA, in General Congress, Assembled, appealing to the Supreme Judge of the World for the Rectitude of our Intentions, do, in the Name, and by Authority of the good People of these Colonies, solemnly Publish and Declare, That these United Colonies are, and of Right ought to be, FREE AND INDEPENDENT STATES; that they are absolved from all Allegiance to the British Crown, and that all political Connection between them and the State of Great Britain, is and ought to be totally dissolved; and that as FREE AND INDEPENDENT STATES, they have full Power to levy War, conclude Peace, contract Alliances, establish Commerce, and to do all other Acts and Things which INDEPENDENT STATES may of right do. And for the support of this Declaration, with a firm Reliance on the Protection of divine Providence, we mutually pledge to each other our Lives, our Fortunes, and our sacred Honor.

The 56 signatures on the Declaration appear in the positions indicated:

John Hancock, President

Georgia:
Button Gwinnett
Lyman Hall
George Walton

North Carolina:
William Hooper
Joseph Hewes
John Penn

South Carolina:
Edward Rutledge
Thomas Heyward, Jr.
Thomas Lynch, Jr.
Arthur Middleton

Massachusetts–Bay:
Samuel Adams
John Adams
Robert Treat Paine
Elbridge Gerry

Maryland:
Samuel Chase
William Paca
Thomas Stone
Charles Carroll of Carrollton

Virginia:
George Wythe
Richard Henry Lee
Thomas Jefferson
Benjamin Harrison
Thomas Nelson, Jr.
Francis Lightfoot Lee
Carter Braxton

Pennsylvania:
Robert Morris
Benjamin Rush
Benjamin Franklin
John Morton
George Clymer
James Smith
George Taylor
James Wilson
George Ross

Delaware:
Caesar Rodney
George Read
Thomas McKean

New York:
William Floyd
Philip Livingston
Francis Lewis
Lewis Morris

New Jersey:
Richard Stockton
John Witherspoon
Francis Hopkinson
John Hart
Abraham Clark

New Hampshire:
Josiah Bartlett
William Whipple

Rhode Island:
Stephen Hopkins
William Ellery

Connecticut:
Roger Sherman
Samuel Huntington
William Williams
Oliver Wolcott

New Hampshire:
Matthew Thornton

United States of America

UNITED STATES OF AMERICA

Washington
Montana
North Dakota
Minnesota
Vermont   Maine
Oregon
Idaho
South Dakota
Wisconsin
New Hampshire
New York   Massachusetts
Wyoming
Michigan
Rhode Island
Nevada
Iowa
Pennsylvania   Connecticut
New Jersey
Nebraska
Illinois   Indiana   Ohio   Delaware
Utah
Maryland
Washington, D.C.
California
Colorado
Kansas   Missouri
Virginia   West Virginia
Kentucky
Arizona
Oklahoma   Arkansas
Tennessee
North Carolina
New Mexico
South Carolina
Mississippi   Alabama   Georgia
Texas   West Florida
Louisiana   East Florida
Hawaii
Florida

Alaska

LEGEND
- Boundary
- Original Thirteen Colonies
- Lousiana (Annexed in 1803)
- Oregon Country (Claimed by USA, England, Spain, and Russia)
- Land Reserved for Native Americans by Proclamation of 1763
- English Possessions
- Spanish Possessions

Glossary *

Acquit/Acquittal – A not-guilty verdict in a criminal case

Act – A statute

Act of Commission – An act that is an element of a crime

Act of Omission – The failure to perform a legally required act that causes harm and results in a crime

Adjourn – To recess or end a meeting

Adjudicate/Adjudication – The resolution of a dispute by a court

Admissible Evidence – Information that may be presented in court to prove or disprove a fact related to a legal dispute; admissible evidence must be relevant and may not be either privileged or hearsay unless it qualifies as a hearsay exception

Adversarial System – The American litigation system in which opposing parties present disputed legal issues to a court to be decided by a judge or jury

Affidavit – A statement made under oath

Affirm – An appellate or supreme court ruling that upholds a lower court ruling

Alien – A foreign-born citizen of a nation other than the United States

Allegation – A factual claim

Amicus Curiae – A non-party to a lawsuit who is allowed to file a brief in order to provide advice to a court on a disputed matter

Amnesty – An act of forgiveness by a President or Governor that eliminates the punishment for an illegal act that a person has not yet been convicted of committing

Answer – A pleading that is filed in response to a complaint in which a defendant admits or denies a plaintiff's allegations, asserts defenses against the allegations, and asserts counterclaims against the plaintiff

Ante – A Latin word meaning "before" that is used in judicial opinions to refer to a prior section of the opinion

Anti Federalists – An early American political party that favored strong state governments rather than a strong federal government

Appeal – A higher court proceeding that determines the accuracy of a lower court ruling

Appellate Court – An intermediate court that reviews the rulings of a trial court

Appellate Jurisdiction – The authority of a higher court to review a lower court decision

Appellant – The party who appeals a lower court decision; see also *Petitioner*

Appellee – The party against whom an appeal is taken and whose role is to defend the lower court decision; see also *Respondent*

Apportion/Apportionment – The determination of the number of Representatives each state can elect to the House of Representatives based on each state's population

Arraignment Hearing – A criminal proceeding conducted in a court during which the prosecutor states the charges against the defendant and the defendant enters a plea of guilty or not guilty to the charges

Arrest Warrant – A judicial order authorizing the arrest of a specific person for a specific criminal offense

Article I – The article of the Constitution that creates the legislative branch of the federal government

Article II – The article of the Constitution that creates the executive branch of the federal government

Article III – The article of the Constitution that creates the judicial branch of the federal government

Articles of Confederation – America's first national government plan established by the 13 states after the Revolutionary War

Assistance of Counsel – The Sixth Amendment guaranty to criminal defendants to be represented by a licensed attorney

Associate Justices – The eight Supreme Court Justices other than the Chief Justice

Attainted/Attainder – An Old English term that literally means "stained" or "dead in the eyes of the law," which, as used in the Constitution, means "convicted"

Attorney-Client Privilege – The right of clients to prevent the disclosure of confidential communications between themselves and their attorneys

Attorney General – The head of the Justice Department and the chief law enforcement officer of the federal government

Bail – Money paid to a court for the release of a criminal defendant as a guarantee of that person's appearance at trial; if the person appears at trial the bail is returned; if the person fails to appear at trial the bail is forfeited

---

* Words listed in the glossary are defined as they are used in this book.

245

Bail Hearing – A public hearing before a judge within 48 hours of a person's arrest to determine if the person qualifies to be released on bail

Ballots – Papers or computer forms on which voters cast their votes for political candidates

Bankrupt – A person or business that seeks judicial relief due to the inability to pay debts owed to others

Bankruptcy Laws – Federal laws that grant relief to bankrupt persons or entities from some or all of the debt owed to others while allowing creditors to receive repayment of some of the money owed to them

Bar Associations – Non-governmental organizations within each state operated by lawyers to regulate professional legal standards and conduct

Bar Exam – A test developed by a state bar association to determine if a law school graduate is qualified to practice law within a specific state

Beyond a Reasonable Doubt – The evidentiary standard of proof a government prosecutor must satisfy in a trial in order to convict a defendant of a crime

Bill – A proposed law developed by either chamber of Congress

Bill of Attainder – A provision in Article I Section 9 of the Constitution bans Bills of Attainder that allow a person to be punished for a crime without a trial

Bill of Impeachment – Official charges by the House of Representatives that accuse a government official of "treason, bribery, and other high crimes and misdemeanors"; if a Bill of Impeachment is approved by the House, the Senate conducts the trial of the official who, if convicted of any of the impeachment charges, is removed from office

Bill of Rights – The first 10 amendments to the Constitution that limit the federal government from violating the rights and liberties of the people and the powers of the states

Branches of Government – The legislative, executive, and judicial units of the federal government among which governing authority is shared and distributed

Breach – Violation of a legal duty

Bribery – Exchanging something of value for an illegal benefit

Brief – A lawyer's written arguments on behalf of a client; a case summary; see also *Case Brief*

Burden of Proof – The evidentiary standard that a party must satisfy to prove disputed facts in order to win a lawsuit; see also *Clear and Convincing Evidence, Preponderance of Evidence, Proof Beyond a Reasonable Doubt*

Cabinet – Advisors to the President who are heads of the executive departments

Call-Up – The authority of a state Governor or the President to order a National Guard unit into service

Capital Punishment – A criminal death sentence

Caption – The section of a judicial opinion that contains the names of the parties

Case Brief – A summary of a judicial opinion that includes the caption, citation, facts, legal analyses, and ruling

Case or Controversy – An Article III provision that limits federal court jurisdiction to legal disputes that have already occurred, rather than potential disputes that have not yet occurred

Case Reporters – Books that contain court opinions

Census – A federal program that counts all of the people residing in every state of the United States every ten years

Central Intelligence Agency/CIA – A federal intelligence agency that investigates international issues related to national security

Cert. Petition – An appellate petition to the United States Supreme Court; see also *Writ of Certiori*

Cf. – A reference in a judicial opinion to another case that decided a different legal issue that was sufficiently similar to the issue before the court to support its ruling

Chambers – The two divisions of the federal Congress that consist of the Senate and the House of Representatives

Check – The power of one branch of government to restrain or counter-balance another branch; see also *Checks and Balances Doctrine*

Checks and Balances Doctrine – The constitutional power of each branch of the federal government to restrain or counter-balance the actions of the other branches so that no single branch can control the entire government

Chief Justice – The presiding Justice of the United States Supreme Court

Circuit Courts of Appeals – Federal appellate courts

Citation – The volume and page number in which a judicial opinion is published in a legal reporter

Civil Cases – Lawsuits brought by and against individual persons, entities, or the government

Civil Rights Act of 1964 – A federal statute based on the commerce clause that made it illegal for businesses engaged in interstate commerce to deny people the use of their facilities because of their race, color, religion, or national origin

Civil Rights Movement – Political dissension and activities in the mid-20th Century that challenged racial discrimination against black Americans

Civil War – A war fought in the United States from 1861 to 1865 between the northern and southern states over the legality of slavery and the rights of southern states to withdraw from the nation

Classified Information – Secret government information that is not subject to disclosure without government permission

Clear and Convincing Evidence – The standard of evidence that allows a civil case to prevail if the evidentiary facts presented at trial are highly probable and substantially convincing

Closing Arguments – A lawyer's final speech that presents his or her client's case to a judge or jury

Cognizable Claim – A legal dispute that qualifies to be ruled on by a court

Colonies –Territorial settlements that are governed by another nation; the British colonies that formed the original 13 states were New Hampshire, Massachusetts, Rhode Island, Connecticut, New York, New Jersey, Pennsylvania, Delaware, Maryland, Virginia, North Carolina, South Carolina, and Georgia

Commander in Chief – The President's title under Article II, Section 2, Clause I of the Constitution as the leader of the nation's military

Commerce Clause – An Article I provision of the Constitution that authorizes Congress to regulate commerce among the states, with American Indian tribes, and with foreign nations

Commutation – The reduction of a criminal sentence or other punishment by a President or Governor

Complaint – The initial document in a civil lawsuit that contains the plaintiff's allegations against the defendant, damages, and requests for relief

Concurrent Jurisdiction – The shared authority of the federal and state court systems to preside over cases involving each other's laws

Concurring Opinion – An appellate or supreme court opinion that agrees with the decision of the court but disagrees with some of the reasons expressed in the majority opinion

Concurring and Dissenting Opinion – An appellate or Supreme Court opinion that agrees with some, but not all, of the majority opinion

Conference Committee – A committee that includes members of both chambers of Congress for the purpose of reaching agreement on a bill

Confirmation Process – The process by which the Senate investigates and approves or disapproves of a person nominated by the President to hold a high level executive branch office, or to serve as a judge or Justice in the judicial branch

Confrontation Clause/Confrontation – A constitutional provision of the Sixth Amendment that guarantees a criminal defendant the right to be present in the courtroom during his or her trial in order to hear and cross-examine adverse witnesses

Congress – The legislative branch of the federal government created under Article I Section 1 of the Constitution

Congressional Districts – Geographically divided sections of a state that are created in proportion to population and from which one member of the House of Representatives is elected

Congressional Record – The published record of daily proceedings of the Senate and House of Representatives

Congressional Term – The two year period during which Congress meets that begins January 3rd of every odd-numbered year

Constituents – Voters

Constitution of the United States of America – The foundational and supreme law of the United States that establishes the structure of the American government, the nature and extent of its powers, and the rights of the American people

Constitutional Convention – A conference in the summer of 1787 during which delegates from 12 of the 13 colonies met to create a federal government plan and draft the Constitution

Contempt of Court – Conduct that disobeys a court order that is punishable by a fine or imprisonment

Continental Army – The colonial military force that was organized and led by General George Washington to defend America against the British during the Revolutionary War

Construe/Construction – Interpretation of the meaning of a law or a judicial opinion

Convene – To assemble or begin, as in "convene a committee"

Convict – A determination by a judge or jury that a person is guilty of a crime; a person who has been found guilty of a crime

Copyright – The legal right to protect the publication, production, sale, or distribution granted to an author, composer, or publisher

Counterclaim – Allegations against a plaintiff set forth in a defendant's answer to a civil complaint

Court Record – The official report of the proceedings of a court case that includes the filed documents, transcript, and evidentiary exhibits

Court Reporter – The person who records and prepares the verbatim record of judicial proceedings in a courtroom

Covert Operative – An intelligence agency spy

Credibility – Accuracy, truthfulness, and believability of a witness's testimony

Criminal Act – An element of a crime by which a defendant does or refuses to do something required by law

Criminal Defendant – The person accused of committing a crime in a criminal proceeding

Cross-Examination – A method of questioning by which the lawyer for the opposing party attempts to discredit a witness at a trial before the judge or jury

Cruel and Unusual Punishment – A provision in the Eighth Amendment that prohibits a criminal sentence that is disproportionately severe to the convicted offense and has been rejected by a significant number of states

Custody – Police detention

Deadlock – The failure of a jury to reach a verdict

Declaration of Independence – The American colonists' formal proclamation of their independence from England on July 4, 1776

Declaratory Judgment Action – A judicial proceeding to declare the rights and obligations of parties when a legal dispute has arisen but injuries have not yet occurred

Defendant – The person sued in either a civil or criminal case

Defenses – A defendant's arguments in opposition to a plaintiff's or prosecutor's case

Delegates – State representatives who participated in the two conventions in Philadelphia, Pennsylvania to create a federal government

Deliberate/Deliberations – The process by which a jury analyzes evidence and reaches a verdict; see also *Jury Deliberations*

Denial – Judicial rejection

Deposition – The oral questioning of a party or witness in the discovery stage of a lawsuit

Detention/Detain – Military imprisonment without due process

Direct Examination – The questioning of a witness at a trial by the attorney for the party who called the witness to testify

Discover/Discovery Stage – The investigative stage of a lawsuit

Dismiss/Dismissal – The voluntary termination of a case by the plaintiff or all of the parties, or a court ruling that terminates the case

Dissenting Opinion – A judicial opinion by an appellate or supreme court judge who disagrees with the decision reached in the majority opinion

District Courts – The trial courts of the federal judicial system

Diversity Jurisdiction – A case that qualifies to be presided over by a federal court because the adverse parties are citizens of different states, the dispute is based on state law, and the amount in controversy exceeds the statutory minimum, which is currently $75,000

Doctrine of Official Immunity – A legal principle that protects a government official from being sued or prosecuted for official conduct that is lawful but disagreed with by others

Double Jeopardy – A Fifth Amendment provision that prohibits governments from prosecuting a person more than once for the same crime

Draft – A preliminary version of a legal document, judicial opinion, or law before the final version is completed

Due Process – A provision in the Fifth and Fourteenth Amendments that requires governments to provide legal procedures by which people can defend themselves against coercive government action against their life, liberty, and property

Eighteenth Amendment – An amendment passed in 1919 that prohibited the manufacture, sale, and transportation of intoxicating liquors anywhere within the United States

Eighth Amendment – A provision of the Bill of Rights that prohibits the government from imposing on criminal defendants excessive bails, fines, and cruel and unusual punishments

Election Boards – The panel of appointed persons who supervise elections and voting procedures

Electoral College – The electors from each state who directly vote for presidential and vice presidential candidates

Elector – A member of the Electoral College who directly votes for a presidential and vice presidential candidate; see also *Electoral College*

Element of a Crime – The components of a crime that require specific acts and a specific state of mind which a prosecutor must prove beyond a reasonable doubt in order to convict a criminal defendant of the charged offense

Eleventh Amendment – Enacted in 1795, this amendment prohibits federal courts from presiding over cases in which a state is sued by a person from another state or country

Enemy Combatant – A person who engages in armed warfare on behalf of a religious ideology rather than a nation and, therefore, may not be entitled to the protections specified in the Geneva War Conventions

Enumerate/Enumerated Power – A power that the Constitution expressly grants to Congress

Equal Protection Clause – The Fourteenth Amendment provision that requires states to treat people equally under the law

Evidence – Information, such as witness testimony, documents, and tangible objects that is admissible to prove or disprove disputed facts in a trial

Exclusionary Rule – An evidentiary rule that bars illegally obtained evidence from being admissible at a trial

Exclusive Jurisdiction – One judicial system's sole authority to preside over a specific type of case to the exclusion of all other judicial systems

Executive Branch – The branch of the federal government, led by the President of the United States, that controls the administration and enforcement of federal laws and the military

Executive Detention – President George W. Bush's theory that presidential power authorizes the President, as Commander in Chief of the military, to order the indefinite detention of enemy combatants without judicial proceedings

Executive Privilege – A rule of evidence that prevents the disclosure of certain communications between a President and presidential advisors

Ex Post Facto Law – Laws that are banned by Article I Section 9 of the Constitution because they criminalizes conduct that was not illegal when committed

Faction – A political group that is primarily committed to its own issues and values

Federal – National

Federal Question Jurisdiction – A category of cases that qualify to be presided over by a federal court because they are based on a violation of the federal Constitution, a federal statute, or a treaty; under **Concurrent Jurisdiction** many of these cases can also be presided over by state courts

Federalism – The American system of government that distributes powers throughout the federal government and among the 50 state governments

Federalists – An early American political party that favored a strong federal government and weak state governments

Federal Marshal – A federal law enforcement officer

Felonies – Serious crimes that are punishable by imprisonment for more than one year or capital punishment

Fifteenth Amendment – A post Civil War amendment that granted black males the right to vote regardless of race, color, or prior conditions of slavery

Fifth Amendment – A provision of the Bill of Rights that grants people the rights to be (1) indicted by a grand jury; (2) due process of law; (3) just compensation for government takings of private property; and (4) protection from double jeopardy and self-incrimination

File/Filing – The submission of a document to a court in a judicial proceeding

Fine – A financial penalty

First Amendment – A provision of the Bill of Rights that limits government restraints on the rights to freedom of speech, religion, press, assembly, and petitioning of the government

Floor – The central meeting areas in each chamber of Congress where members have seats, make speeches, and vote

Foreman/Forewoman – The juror who is selected by the jury to lead its deliberations

Forum – A court

Founding Fathers – The men who played leading roles in establishing the United States and drafting the Constitution

Fourteenth Amendment – A post Civil War amendment that applies most of the Bill of Rights amendments to the states and which also prohibits states from denying people due process, equal protection, and the privileges and immunities of the laws

Fourth Amendment – A provision of the Bill of rights that prohibits a government from conducting unreasonable searches and seizures of people or places without a warrant or probable cause to believe that a crime has been committed or is in progress

Free Speech Clause – A provision of the First Amendment that bars a government from placing restrictions on speech

Fruits of the Poisonous Tree Doctrine – An evidentiary rule that prohibits the admission of evidence at a trial that was acquired by unconstitutional methods; see also **Exclusionary Rule**

Full Faith and Credit Clause – A provision of Article IV of the Constitution that requires the state governments to recognize and give effect to the legislative acts, public records, and judicial decisions of the other states

General – A high-level Military Officer

Geneva Conventions – A treaty on international warfare to which the United States is a participant and which grants certain categories of war prisoners certain protections

Governor – The executive leader of a state

Grand Jury – A panel of independent citizens who determine if there is sufficient evidence to indict a person for a crime

Grand Jury Indictment – A decision by a group of citizens that a prosecutor has sufficient evidence to arrest a person for a crime

Grounds – The legal basis for accusations in civil or criminal cases

Guilty Plea – A criminal defendant's admission of guilt to a crime in exchange for a more lenient sentence than would be imposed if convicted at a trial

Hearsay – Testimony of one person that repeats what he or she was told by another person; under the rules of evidence hearsay is generally inadmissible in a legal proceeding because the original speaker is not present in the courtroom to be cross-examined

High Crime – An historical term that referred to political misconduct by a governmental official; a basis for impeachment of a federal government official under Article II Section 4 of the Constitution

Holding – A court's specific ruling based on the facts of the case

House of Representatives – The chamber of Congress for which membership is based on the population of each state

Ibid. – A Latin term meaning "in the same place," which is used in legal documents to refer to the immediately preceding citation

Id. – A reference used in legal documents that refers to the immediately preceding citation

Impartial Jury – A Sixth Amendment provision that requires neutral citizens from the community in which a criminal trial is conducted to decide the guilt or innocence of the defendant

Impeach a Witness – Discrediting the credibility and reliability of a witness's testimony

Impeachment/Impeach – The first stage of a congressional procedure to remove a federal official from office by which the House of Representatives creates and then votes on a Bill of Impeachment that charges the official with conduct that amounts in "treason, bribery, or other high crimes and misdemeanors"; removal of the impeached official then requires conviction of the impeachment charges at a trial conducted by the Senate

Implied Power – The federal government's authority to exercise a power that is not expressly granted to it by the Constitution but which is necessary to carry out a power that is expressly granted by the Constitution

Inadmissible Evidence – Information that does not meet the legal standards required by the rules of evidence

Inalienable Rights – A political philosophy that people are born with certain natural rights that cannot be denied or restrained by a government without the people's consent

Inauguration Ceremony – A formal ceremony during which a newly elected President takes the Presidential Oath of Office

In Camera Inspection – A confidential inspection of evidence by a judge to determine if such evidence should be provided to parties in a lawsuit

Indictment/Indict – Criminal charges

In Forma Pauperis Petition – A request by a poor person to file a lawsuit without paying court costs

Infraction – A minor violation of a local rule that is usually punishable by payment of a fine

Injunction/Injunctive Relief/Enjoin – A court order requiring a party to do or stop doing a specific act

Insurgents/Insurgencies – Participants in armed warfare against a nation who are not acting on behalf of another nation and are not members of another nation's military

Integration – A legal principle that requires persons of all races to be treated equally under the law

Intellectual Property Laws – Legal protections for patents, trademarks, and copyrights

Intelligence Agencies – Federal agencies responsible for collecting, analyzing, and using information to support law enforcement, national security, military operations, and foreign policies

Interrogatory – Written questions asked among parties during the discovery stage in a civil lawsuit

Interstate Commerce – Commercial transactions that cross state boundaries and commercial activities that affect commerce in more than one state

Issue (an opinion) – The publication of a judicial opinion

Jim Crow Laws – Historical state laws that promoted segregation of the races and which are now deemed illegal under the anti-segregation laws

Joint Committees – Legislative committees composed of members of both chambers of Congress that oversee and research matters of continuing concern such as taxation, economic, and environmental matters

Joint Chiefs of Staff – Military advisors to the Secretary of Defense who are representatives of the Army, Navy, Air Force, and Marines

Judge – The presiding officer of a courtroom who has the authority to decide disputed legal issues in lawsuits

Judgment – A final decision of a court

Judicial Branch – The federal court system branch of government created by Article III of the Constitution

Judicial Chambers – A judge's office

Judicial Review – The authority of the judicial branch to review and determine the legal validity of the actions of the other two branches of the federal government

Judicial System – Court system

Judiciary – Court system

Judiciary Act of 1789 – The first law passed by the first Congress that established the federal system of courts

Jurisdiction – The authority of a court to preside over certain kinds of cases and persons

Juris Doctor Degree/J.D. – A law degree

Jury – A group of citizens who are selected to evaluate the evidence presented during a trial in order to determine which party prevails

Jury Box – The area of the courtroom where the jurors sit together throughout a trial

Jury Deliberations – Discussions among jurors to determine the outcome of a criminal or civil case

Jury Instructions – Instructions given by a judge to a jury that explain how to appropriately apply the correct law to the disputed facts of the case

Jury Pool – A group of potential jurors

Jury Room – The room adjacent to a trial court where the jury deliberates

Justices – Judges of appellate or supreme courts

Law Clerk – A recent law school graduate who is selected to assist a judge by doing legal research and drafting legal memoranda

Lawyer – A professional who is licensed to represent people in legal proceedings

Leaked Information – Secret or classified information that is disclosed to the press

Legal Briefs – A written summary of a judicial opinion; a document prepared by an attorney that sets forth the legal and factual arguments of the client

Legal Issue – A disputed question of law addressed in legal briefs and judicial opinions

Legal Rulings – Judicial decisions

Legal Secretary – A judge's secretary

Legislative Branch/Legislature – The lawmaking branch of the federal government created under Article I of the Constitution

Legislative Immunity – A provision of Article I Section 6 of the Constitution that provides legal protection from criminal prosecutions and civil lawsuits to members of Congress while performing legislative duties

Legislative Process – The process by which Congress makes laws

Legislature – The lawmaking unit of government

Liable/ Liability – A judicial finding of responsibility for harm done by one party to another party

Liberty – The powers to act, think, make choices, and express oneself without government control or restraint

Life Tenure – According to Article III Section 1 of the Constitution, federal judges are appointed to hold their offices "during good behavior," which means that they are appointed for life or until they resign or are removed from office. The purpose of life tenure is to provide judicial

independence by protecting judges from retaliation or political pressure

Line-Up – An investigative procedure that takes place at a police station in a room divided by one-way glass where the victim stands on one side of the glass to view people on the other side of the glass in order to identify the suspect

Litigant – A party to a lawsuit

Litigation Process – The process by which lawsuits are prepared and presented at trial

Living Constitutionalism/Living Constitutionalists – A theory that the Constitution should be interpreted to reflect contemporary changes in America while also adhering to its fundamental principles

Majority Opinion – An appellate or supreme court opinion that receives a majority of votes

Mandamus – A Latin term referring to an order issued by a higher court to compel a lower court to do or refrain from doing a specific act

Mens Rea – A Latin term meaning "guilty mind" that refers to the state of mind element of a crime that a prosecutor must prove to convict a defendant

Military brigs – Military prisons

Militia – State armed forces

Minute Clerk – A judicial staff member who prepares a judge's orders and maintains the judge's schedule of cases

Miranda Warnings – Under Miranda v. Arizona, 384 U.S. 436 (1966), before commencing an interrogation, the police must inform a criminal suspect of the constitutional rights under the Fifth and Sixth Amendments to (1) remain silent, (2) receive the assistance of counsel, (3) and that any statements the suspect makes to the police can be used in court as a basis for conviction

Misdemeanor – A crime that is less serious than a felony and is usually punishable by a fine or confinement in a local jail for less than one year

Mistrial – An invalid trial caused by a serious error or the inability of the jury to reach a verdict; a mistrial can result in retrial of the case

Monetary Damages – Financial compensation that a court orders to be paid by the party who loses a lawsuit to the party who wins the lawsuit

Motion – A procedural request to a court to address a legal issue

Motion to Dismiss – A request by a civil defendant that the court terminate the case at the pleading stage of the lawsuit

National Guard – State militias

Naturalization/Naturalization Laws – The federal legal process by which a citizen of another nation becomes a citizen of the United States

Necessary and Proper Clause – A provision in Article I of the Constitution that grants Congress the implied power to carry out its expressed powers

Negligence – The breach of a duty of care that causes injury to another party

Nineteenth Amendment – A constitutional amendment ratified in 1920 that granted women the right to vote

Ninth Amendment – A provision of the Bill of Rights which states that the rights specifically listed in the Constitution are not to be regarded as the exclusive rights retained by the people

Not Guilty Plea – A criminal defendant's formal denial of a criminal charge

Notice – Legal notification to a civil or criminal defendant that informs him or her of the duty to appear in court and defend against the lawsuit

Oath – A promise to tell the truth

Opening Statements – Speeches made by lawyers at the beginning of a trial to the judge or jury that explain the case and the evidence they will present on behalf of their clients

Opinion – A written explanation of a court's ruling that includes the court's analysis of the disputed facts, legal arguments, applicable laws, and its decision

Oral Arguments – Verbal presentations to a court by which lawyers for the parties present their legal positions and are questioned by judges

Originalism/Originalists – A theory that the Constitution should be interpreted according to the original intent of the Founding Fathers

Original Jurisdiction – A court's authority to be the first court to preside over a case

Oval Office – The official White House office of the President

Override (a veto) – If a President refuses to sign a bill into law, the bill can still be enacted into law if two-thirds of both Congressional chambers vote to pass it

Panel – The group of appellate judges who sit in judgment of a case

Pardon/Pardon Power – The authority of a President or Governor to eliminate or reduce the criminal punishment of a convicted person

Parole Board – The people who periodically review a prisoner's criminal conviction and behavior while in prison to determine if the prisoner should be released from prison before serving the entire sentence

Parties – Participants in a lawsuit

Patent – A federal grant to the creator of an invention to the exclusive use and control of the invention for a specified period of time

Pentagon – The Department of Defense's main office building, located in Virginia

Per Curiam Opinion – A Latin phrase referring to a decision "by the court" that does not identity the judge who wrote the opinion; many per curiam opinions are unanimous but some also include dissents

Perjury – A false statement made under oath

Petitioner – The party who appeals a lower court decision; see also **Appellant**

Plaintiff – The party who files a civil law suit against a defendant

Plantation – A southern tobacco or cotton farm

Plea – A criminal defendant's formal response of "guilty" or "not guilty" to a criminal charge

Plea Bargain – The negotiating process between a prosecutor and a defense attorney that allows a defendant to plead guilty to a less serious crime in exchange for a less severe sentence

Pleading Stage/Pleadings – The first stage of a lawsuit during which the parties submit documents to the court that set forth their allegations against each other, denials of the allegations, defenses, injuries, and requests for relief

Plurality Opinion – An appellate or supreme court opinion that receives less than a majority of votes

Political Speech – Expression about political issues that receives the highest level of First Amendment protection

Poll the Jury – After a jury announces its verdict, the judge may ask each juror if he or she agrees with the verdict in order to verify that no juror was coerced into agreeing with the other jurors

Precedent – Judicial opinions of appellate and supreme courts that create rules of law that lower courts must obey

Preliminary Hearing – A state court criminal proceeding during which the judge determines if there is sufficient evidence to prosecute the accused person of a specific crime

Preponderance of Evidence – The evidentiary standard that applies in most civil cases which requires that the facts necessary to win the case are more likely to be true than false

President – The chief executive officer of the United States under Article II of the Constitution

Presidential Oath of Office – During the presidential inauguration the President makes the following promise: *"I do solemnly swear (or affirm) that I will faithfully execute the Office of President of the United States, and will to the best of my Ability, preserve, protect and defend the Constitution of the United States"*

President Pro Tempore – A Latin phrase meaning "for the time being" that originally referred to a senator who would preside over the Senate when the Vice President was unavailable, but which now refers to the leader of the Senate

Presumption of Innocence – An evidentiary rule of criminal law that assumes the innocence of a defendant whose guilt the government must prove beyond a reasonable doubt

Prior Restraint – Government censorship of speech

Privilege – A rule of evidence that prevents the disclosure of relevant and truthful communications between persons in legally protected relationships from being admitted into evidence in a judicial proceeding; see **Attorney-Client Privilege/Executive Privilege**

Probable Cause – A provision in the Fourth Amendment that requires police to have a reasonable basis for believing that a suspected person has committed or is committing a crime, or that a location contains specific items connected to a crime, before conducting a search of either the person or the place

Probation – A criminal sentence that allows a convicted defendant to be free from imprisonment subject to specific conditions which, if violated, will result in the defendant's imprisonment

Probation Officer – A government officer who prepares a pre-sentence investigative report of a convicted criminal defendant for a judge and who, after the defendant has been released from prison and placed on probation, supervises the defendant for a specified period of time

Proof Beyond a Reasonable Doubt – The evidentiary standard used in criminal cases that requires the prosecutor to disprove the defendant's presumption of innocence by proving facts that leave no reasonable doubt as to the defendant's guilt

Pro Se – To act as one's own lawyer

Public Trial – A Sixth Amendment provision that allows the public and media to attend a criminal trial in order to prevent a government from conducting a secret trial

Quorum – The minimum number of persons who must be present before a meeting can take place

Range of Years Sentence – A criminal sentence, such as 5 to 10 years, that specifies a period of years a convicted defendant must be imprisoned based on the circumstances of the crime, the defendant's criminal background, behavior, and attitude

Ratify/Ratification – Official authorization by Congress of constitutional amendments and international treaties

Rational Basis Test – A constitutional due process and equal protection standard that requires courts to uphold statutes that are rationally related to legitimate government purpose

Recess Appointment – A presidential appointment made while Congress is not in session

Recognition – One nation's acknowledgment of the sovereignty of another nation

Reconcile/Reconciliation (of a bill) – The process by which both chambers of Congress meet to negotiate agreement on a bill

Redirect Examination – Re-questioning of a witness about matters raised during cross-examination

Relevant – A rule of evidence that requires information used in civil and criminal cases to be accurate, true, and logically related to other disputed facts in the case

Relief – The compensation sought as a remedy for the injuries alleged in a lawsuit

Remand – To return; when an appellate or supreme court reverses a lower court's holding, it may return the case to the lower court with instructions to make specified corrections

Reporter's Privilege – State laws that prevent reporters from being compelled to reveal the identity of their confidential sources in government investigations and legal proceedings

Reprieve – The postponement of a criminal sentence by a President or Governor

Respondent – The party against whom an appeal is filed; see also **Appellee**

Rest – The conclusion of a party's case at trial

Revenue Bills – Laws that propose the raising or lowering of taxes that must originate in the House of Representatives

Reverse/Reversal – A judicial decision by a higher court that rejects the decision of a lower court

Revolutionary War – The American colonists' war of independence against England fought from 1775–1783

Rights – Conduct, beliefs, and status of individuals that must be recognized and protected under the law

Right of Confrontation – A Sixth Amendment provision granting a criminal defendant the authority to confront and cross-examine adverse witnesses during a trial

Rule of Finality – A final, unappealable, and binding ruling by a court

Rules of Evidence – Rules that determine the type of information that can and cannot be presented at trial

Rules of Procedure – Rules for conducting a lawsuit

Rules of Professional Conduct – Rules of ethics and professionalism that control and define acceptable behavior by lawyers

Ruling – A judicial decision

Sanction – Lawsuit penalties

School Board – Local people who are elected or appointed to manage local schools

Search and Seizure – The investigation of people and places by the police

Search Warrant – A judicial order allowing police to conduct a search

Second Amendment – A Bill of Rights provision that guarantees people the right to own guns and other weapons

Secretaries – Leaders of executive departments

Segregation/Segregationist – A political philosophy asserting that the races, especially the black and white races, should be legally separated

Select Committees – A temporary congressional committee that is convened to investigate a specific matter

Self-Incrimination – Testifying to one's own involvement in a crime

Senate – The chamber of Congress that consists of 100 members, two from each state, who are elected to six-year terms of office

Sentence – A type of criminal punishment that imprisons a convicted defendant for a pre-determined period of time

Separation of Powers – The constitutional separation of the federal government into the legislative, executive, and judicial branches so that no one branch has the authority to preside over the entire government

Sequester – Isolation of an endangered jury during a trial or deliberations

Session – One year of a two year congressional term

Settle/Settlement – The private agreement among parties to resolve and end a lawsuit

Seventeenth Amendment – Enacted in 1913, the Seventeenth Amendment modified Article I Section 3 of the Constitution by granting citizens, rather than state legislatures, the authority to elect Senators. Originally, Article I Section 3 did not allow citizens to elect Senators because the Founding Fathers believed they were too ill-informed and self-interested

Seventh Amendment – A Bill of Rights provision that guarantees the right to a jury trial in federal civil cases when the amount in controversy exceeds $20

Sixth Amendment – A provision of the Bill of Rights that grants criminal defendants the rights to receive notice of arrest charges, a speedy, public trial by jury at which they can confront adverse witnesses, compel the attendance of favorable witnesses, and be assisted by legal counsel

Social Security Programs – Federal government pension programs for retired persons

Sovereign Power – The authority of a state or nation to govern itself; the power of a state to govern matters occurring within its boundaries, such as crimes, family relations, and commercial transactions

Speaker of the House – The presiding officer of the House of Representatives

Special Counsel/Prosecutor – An attorney who is appointed by the legislative or executive branches to investigate government misconduct

Speech or Debate Clause – An Article I provision of the Constitution that protects members of Congress from arrest or prosecution for statements made while performing legislative functions in either the House or the Senate; see also *Legislative Immunity*

Speedy Trial – A Sixth Amendment constitutional provision that guarantees a criminal defendant the right to a quick trial which, under the Speedy Trial Act, must take place within 100 days of arrest, unless both the defense and prosecution request an extension of time; the purpose of this provision is to prevent the government from indefinitely detaining a criminal suspect

Standing Committees – Permanent congressional committees that specialize in specific matters

State of the Union Address – An annual speech made in January by the President to Congress, Supreme Court Justices, Cabinet Secretaries, and the public that reports the President's plans and concerns for the coming year

Statute – A law

Stay – Postpone

Strict Constructionism/Strict Constructionists – A theory that the Constitution should be interpreted according to its literal wording

Strike – When employees stop working in order to obtain more benefits from their employers

Subpoena – An order issued by a court, Congress, or a grand jury that commands the presence of people and evidence to appear in a legal proceeding

Subpoena duces tecum – A court order commanding a person or entity to produce documents or evidence in a court proceeding

Summary Judgment – A judicial proceeding that rules on the outcome of a case before trial based on the judge's ruling that the relevant facts are not in dispute

Summons – A court order that instructs a person to appear in a courtroom on a specified date and time to defend and answer claims in a civil lawsuit or give testimony about facts relevant to a lawsuit

Supra – A Latin word meaning "above" that is used in legal documents to refer to a prior case citation

Supremacy Clause – A provision of Article VI that federal laws, treaties, and the Constitution are the "supreme law of the land" that are superior to any conflicting state constitutions or laws

Supreme Court – The highest level court to which a case can be appealed

Suspension Clause – A provision of Article I Section 9 of the Constitution that limits Congress's power to temporarily eliminate a prisoner's right to file a Writ of Habeas Corpus

Symbolic Speech – A type of non-verbal expression that is protected by the First Amendment free speech clause

Table (a bill) – A legislative act that delays or eliminates voting on a bill

Tenth Amendment – A provision of the Bill of Rights that any constitutional powers not specifically granted to the federal government or prohibited to the states are reserved for the states or the people

Testify/Testimony – Statements made in a judicial proceeding under oath by a party or witness

Third Amendment – A provision of the Bill of Rights that prohibits the federal government from housing soldiers in private homes without the owner's consent

Third Party – A political party that is independent from the Republican and Democratic parties

Thirteenth Amendment – The post Civil War amendment that made slavery illegal throughout the United States

Tie – Evenly divided votes for and against a bill that prevent the bill from passing because it fails to receive a majority of votes

Tories – American colonists who remained loyal to King George III and opposed the Revolutionary War

Trademark/Trademark Laws – Intellectual property laws that allow products and services to be identified by words, name, symbols, or phrases that cannot be used by other products or services

Transcript/Transcribe – The official, verbatim (word by word) record of courtroom proceedings

Treason – The betrayal of one's nation

Treaty – An agreement between nations

Trial – A judicial proceeding where evidence and legal arguments are presented to determine the legal rights and liabilities of the parties

Trial Court – The first level court in the American judicial systems in which parties present evidence and legal arguments at a trial to resolve their legal disputes

Twentieth Amendment – Passed in 1933, this amendment to the Constitution modified the method by which the Vice President becomes the President if the current President dies or is removed from office

Twenty-Fifth Amendment – Passed in 1967, this amendment to the Constitution specifies the government officials who determine if a President is incapable of continuing in office

Twenty-First Amendment – Passed in 1933, this amendment to the Constitution repealed the Eighteenth Amendment in order to again allow the manufacture, sale, and transportation of liquor within the United States

Twenty-Second Amendment – Passed in 1950, this amendment to the Constitution limits a President to two four-year terms in office

Twenty-Sixth Amendment – Passed in 1971, this amendment to the Constitution lowered the voting age from 21 years of age to 18 years of age

Twelfth Amendment – Passed in 1804, this amendment to the Constitution requires each elector to cast separate votes for the presidential and vice presidential candidates.

United States Supreme Court – The highest court in the federal judicial system

Unreasonable Searches and Seizures – A Fourth Amendment provision to the Constitution that protects criminal suspects by requiring police to obtain a search warrant and/or have probable cause before searching a person or a place; see also *Probable Cause* and *Search Warrant*

Verdict – The decision of a jury or judge that determines the outcome of a case

Veto – A Latin phrase meaning "I forbid" that refers to the power of a President to refuse to sign a congressional bill into law

Vice President – The Article II executive official who becomes the President if the President dies, becomes incapacitated, resigns, or is removed from office

Voir Dire – A French term meaning "to speak the truth" that refers to the process by which potential jurors are questioned to determine their qualifications to serve on a jury

Waive – To relinquish or forfeit a claim or right

Warrant – A court order authorizing the arrest of a person or the search of a place

Witness – A person who gives testimony at a trial or legal proceeding

Witness Stand – The place in a courtroom where a witness sits while giving testimony

Writ of Certiorari/Cert. Petition – A Latin phrase meaning "to be more formally prepared," which refers to a party's petition to the United States Supreme Court requesting it to accept the appeal of a case

Writ of Habeas Corpus – A Latin phrase meaning "produce the body" that refers to a judicial order to the custodian of a prison to bring a person held in custody before a court for the purpose of determining the legality of the person's detention

Bibliography

Books

Bernstein, Carl, and Bob Woodward. *All the President's Men.* New York: Simon and Schuster, 1974.

Bernstein, Richard B. "Introduction." In *The Constitution of the United States of America: with the Declaration of Independence and the Articles of Confederation.* New York: Barnes & Noble Books, 2002.

Bickel, Alexander M. *The Least Dangerous Branch: The Supreme Court at the Bar of Politics.* Indianapolis: Bobbs-Merrill Co., 1962.

Chemerinsky, Erwin. *Constitutional Law: Principles and Policies.* 2nd ed. New York: Aspen Publishers, 1997.

Clayton, Andrew R.L., Elisabeth Israels Perry, Linda Reed, and Allan M. Winkler, *American Pathways to the Present.* Needham: Prentice Hall, 2000.

Emerson, Thomas I. *The System of Freedom of Expression.* New York: Random House, 1970.

Feinman, Jay M. *Law 101: Everything You Need to Know About the American Legal System.* Oxford: Oxford University Press, 2000.

Fineman, Howard. *The Thirteen American Arguments: Enduring Debates That Define and Inspire Our Country.* New York: Random House, 2008.

Fletcher, George P., and Steve Sheppard. *American Law in a Global Context the Basics.* Oxford: Oxford University Press, 2005.

Gove, Philip Babcock. *Webster's New International Dictionary.* Springfield, Mass.: Merriam-Webster, 2000.

Hall, Kermit L., ed. *The Oxford Companion to American Law.* New York: Oxford University Press, 2002.

Hamilton, Alexander. "Federalist No. 78." In *The Federalist Papers.* New York: Penguin Classics, 1987.

Hamilton, Alexander, John Jay, and James Madison. *The Federalist Papers.* New York: Penguin Classics 1987.

Harris, Leslie J., and Lee E. Teitelbaum. *Children, Parents, and the Law: Public and Private Authority in the Home, Schools, and Juvenile Courts.* New York: Aspen Law & Business, 2002.

Hill, Gerald N., Kathleen Hill, and Nolo Editors. *Nolo's Plain-English Law Dictionary.* Berkeley: Nolo, 2009.

Huntington, Samuel P. *American Politics: The Promise of Disharmony.* Cambridge, Mass.: Belknap Press, 1983.

Janda, Kenneth, Jeffrey M. Berry, and Jerry Goldman. The Challenge of Democracy: Government in America. 8th ed. Boston: Houghton Mifflin, 2005.

Lineberry, Robert L. *Government in America: People, Politics, and Policy.* Boston: Little, Brown, 1980.

McAlinn, Gerald Paul, Daniel Allan Rosen, and John P. Stern. *An Introduction to American Law.* Durham, NC: Carolina Academic Press, 2005.

McClellan, Scott. *What Happened: Inside the Bush White House and Washington's Culture of Deception.* New York: Public Affairs, 2008.

McClenaghan, William A., and Frank Abbott Magruder. *Magruder's American Government.* Needham, Mass.: Prentice Hall, 2000.

Meador, Daniel John, and Gregory Mitchell. "Chapter 5: Dramatis Personae." In *American Courts.* St. Paul: West Group, 2000.

Mill, John Stuart. *On Liberty.* Charleston: Nabu Press, 2010 (1859).

Milton, John. *Areopagitica.* Cambridge: Cambridge University Press, 1907 (1644).

Nowak, John E., and Ronald D. Rotunda. *Constitutional Law.* 7th ed. St. Paul: Thomson/West, 2004.

Obama, Barack H. The Audacity of Hope: Thoughts on Reclaiming the American Dream. New York: Crown Publishers, 2006.

Sullivan, Kathleen M., and Gerald Gunther. *Constitutional Law.* 15th ed. Westbury, N.Y.: Foundation Press, 2004.

Surrency, Erwin C. *History of the Federal Courts.* New York: Oceana Publications, 1987.

The Columbia Encyclopedia. 5th ed. Barbara A. Chernow & George A. Vallasi eds. New York: Columbia University Press, 1993.

News Articles

"A Victory for the Rule of Law." *N.Y. Times,* June 6, 2006. Accessed March 4, 2015. http://www.nytimes.com/2006/06/30/opinion/30fri1.html?_r = 2&th = &emc th&pa...6/30/2006.

Lithwick, Dahlia. "When Reason Meets Rifles." *Newsweek,* March 24, 2008.

Will, George F. "About Those Categories..." *Newsweek,* January 29, 2006, 68.

Speeches

O'Connor, Sandra Day. "Remarks to the American Academy of Appellate Lawyers." Speech, November 7, 2005.

Souter, David H. "Harvard Commencement Remarks." Lecture, Harvard University's Commencement from Harvard University, Cambridge, May 27, 2010, *available at* http://news.harvard.edu/gazette/story/2010/text-of-justice-david-souters-speech/.

Internet Sites

"23 Legal Medical Marijuana States and DC Laws, Fees, and Possession Limits." ProCon.org. January 8, 2015. http://medicalmarijuana.procon.org/view.resource.php?resourceID = 000881 (accessed March 2, 2015).

"37 States with Legal Gay Marriage and 13 States with Same-Sex Marriage Bans." ProCon.org. March 2, 2015. http://gaymarriage.procon.org/view.resource.php?resourceID = 004857 (accessed March 2, 2015).

"Affidavit." Oxford Dictionaries. http://www.oxforddictionaries.com/us/definition/american_english/affidavit (accessed March 2, 2015).

"Amendment XI Suits Against States." National Constitution Center. http://constitutioncenter.org/constitution/the-amendments/amendment-11-judicial-limits (accessed March 2, 2015).

"Article Three of the United States Constitution." Wikipedia the Free Encyclopedia. http://en.wikipedia.org/wiki/Article_Three_of_the_United_States_Constitution (accessed March 2, 2015).

Bailey, Holly. "Where Everybody Knows Your Name." *Newsweek*. April 25, 2009. http://www.newsweek.com/id/195086 (accessed March 4, 2015).

Barker, Robert S. "Government Accountability and Its Limits." *Issues of Democracy, Accountability in Government* 5, no. 2 (August 2000): 21. http://usa.usembassy.de/etexts/gov/ijde0800.pdf (accessed March 4, 2015).

Bartlett, John, comp. "Benjamin Franklin. (1706-1790)." John Bartlett (1820–1905)." Familiar Quotations, 10th ed., rev. and enl. by Nathan Haskell Dole. Boston: Little, Brown, 1919; Bartleby.com, 2000. http://www.bartleby.com/100/245.html (accessed March 2, 2015).

Bodenhamer, David J., "Federalism and Democracy." *Democracy Papers*. November 28, 2007. Available at http://iipdigital.usembassy.gov/st/english/article/2007/11/20071128094357abretnuh0.8318903.html#axzz3TSkMyXBs (accessed April 26, 2010).

"C-SPAN Congressional Glossary." C-SPAN.org. http://legacy.c-span.org/guide/congress/glossary/alphalist.htm (accessed March 4, 2015).

Christopher, Maura, Anne Cusack, Michael Cusack, Fredric A. Emmert, David Goddy, Holly Hughes, Norman Lunger et al., "Ch. 4 - A Responsive Government, Separation of Powers and the Democratic Process." *Portrait of the USA*. September 1997. Edited by Clack, George, Rosalie Targonski, and Dennis Drabbelle. http://webharvest.gov/peth04/20041107233109/http://usinfo.state.gov/usa/infousa/facts/factover/ch4.htm (accessed March 9, 2015).

"Corruption of Blood and Forfeiture." Justia. http://law.justia.com/constitution/us/article-3/44-corruption-of-blood.html (accessed March 2, 2015).

"Ex post facto." The Free Dictionary. thefreedictionary.com/ex+post+facto (accessed March 4, 2015).

Forte, David F. "Vice President." The Heritage Foundation. http://www.heritage.org/constitution#!/articles/2/essays/78/vice-president (accessed March 2, 2015).

Gideon, Clarence Earl. "Petition for a Writ of Certiorari from Clarence Gideon to the Supreme Court of the United States, 01/05/1962." U.S. National Archives and Records Administration. January 5, 1962. http://research.archives.gov/description/597554 (accessed March 9, 2015).

Goldstein, Amy and Leonnig, Carol D. "Ex-Time Reporter Testifies in Libby Trial." Washington Post. February 1, 2007. http://www.washingtonpost.com/wp-dyn/content/article/2007/01/31/AR2007013100900.html (accessed March 2, 2015).

Goldstein, Amy and Leonnig, Carol D. "Reporter's Account Hurts Libby Defense." Washington Post. January 31, 2007. http://www.washingtonpost.com/wp-dyn/content/article/2007/01/30/AR2007013000178.html (accessed March 2, 2015).

Hamilton, Alexander. The "Federalist No. 78." In *The Federalist Papers*. New York: McLean, 1788. http://thomas.loc.gov/home/histdox/fed_78.html (accessed March 4, 2015).

"High Crimes and Misdemeanors." Constitutional Rights Foundation." http://www.crf-usa.org/impeachment/high-crimes-and-misdemeanors.html (accessed March 5, 2015).

Holland, Max. "Beyond Deep Throat: The Hidden Watergate Sources That Helped Topple a

President." Newsweek. October 9, 2014. http://
www.newsweek.com/2014/10/17/many-sources-
behind-woodward-and-bernsteins-deep-throat-
276291.html (accessed March 2, 2015).

"Illinois Congressional Districts, 113th Congress
(January 2013-January 2015)." National Atlas of
the United States of America. http://
nationalmap.gov/small_scale/printable/images/
pdf/congdist/pagecgd113_il.pdf (accessed
March 5, 2015).

Issues of Democracy, Accountability in Government
5, no. 2 (2000). Accessed March 4, 2015. http://
usa.usembassy.de/etexts/gov/ijde0800.pdf.

Kimberling, William C. "The Electoral College."
Dave Leip's Atlas of U.S. Presidential Elections.
http://uselectionatlas.org/INFORMATION/
INFORMATION/electcollege_history.php
(accessed March 5, 2015).

"Korean War." HISTORY.com. www.history.com/
topics/korean-war (accessed March 2, 2015).

"Korean War." Wikipedia, the Free
Encyclopedia.en.wikipedia.org/wiki/
Korean_War (accessed March 2, 2015).

"List of Justices of the Supreme Court of the United
States." Wikipedia, the Free Encyclopedia. http://
en.wikipedia.org/wiki/List_of_Justices_of_
the_Supreme_Court_of_the_United_States
(accessed March 2, 2015).

"Map of Territorial Growth 1775." Wikipedia, the
Free Encyclopedia. http://en.wikipedia.org/wiki/
File:Map_of_territorial_growth_1775.svg
(accessed March 5, 2015).

"Marbury v. Madison, 5 U.S. 137 (1803)." FindLaw.
February 1803. http://caselaw.lp.findlaw.com/
scripts/getcase.pl?court = US&vol = 5&invol
= 137 (accessed March 4, 2015).

Mazzetti, Mark, and Kate Zernike. "White House
Says Terror Detainees Hold Basic Rights." *N.Y.
Times.* July 12, 2006. http://www.nytimes.com/
2006/07/12/washington/12gitmo.html?th&emc t
(accessed March 4, 2015).

"McCulloch v. Maryland, 17 U.S. 316 (1819)." Oyez
Project.1819. http://oyez.org/cases/1792-1850/
1819/1819_0 (accessed March 4, 2015).

"McCulloch v. Maryland (1819): State Taxes, National
Supremacy." Street Law, Inc. & The Supreme
Court Historical Society. http://www.streetlaw
.org/en/Case.2.aspx (accessed March 5, 2015).

McKinley, Mike. "The Cruise of the Great White
Fleet." Naval History and Heritage Command.
http://www.history.navy.mil/research/library/
online-reading-room/title-list-alphabetically/c/
cruise-great-white-fleet-mckinley.html
(accessed March 2, 2015).

"Medical Marijuana States—Compassionate Health
Options." Green215. www.green215.com/medical-
marijuana-states (accessed March 2, 2015).

Miller, Judith. "My Four Hours Testifying in the
Federal Grand Jury Room." *N.Y. Times*, October
16, 2005. http://www.nytimes.com/2005/10/16/
national/16miller.html?pagewanted = all
(accessed March 4, 2015).

Newport, Frank. "Presidential Job Approval: Bill
Clinton's High Ratings in the Midst of Crisis,
1998." Gallup. June 4, 1999. http://
www.gallup.com/poll/4609/presidential-job-
approval-bill-clintons-high-ratings-midst.aspx
(accessed March 2, 2015).

"Official Declarations of War by Congress."
United States Senate. https://www.senate.gov/
pagelayout/history/h_multi_sections_and_
teasers/WarDeclarationsbyCongress.htm
(accessed March 2, 2015).

"Overview of the 1992 Election." President Elect, The
Unofficial Home of the Electoral College. http://
presidentelect.org/e1992.html (accessed
September 3, 2014).

Petteway, Steve. "Collection of the Supreme Court of
the United States." Roberts Court (2010-). Oyez
Project. http://www.oyez.org/courts/robt6
(accessed March 2, 2015).

Pious, Richard M. The Powers of the Presidency,
United States Department of State. November
28, 2007. http://iipdigital.usembassy.gov/st/
english/article/2007/11/20071128181124
akllennoccm0.148617.html#axzz3TaHuoAgV
(accessed March 5, 2015).

"Place of Trial—Jury of the Vicinage." Justia. http://
law.justia.com/constitution/us/amendment-06/
08-jury-of-the-vicinage.html (accessed March 2,
2015).

"Plame affair." Wikipedia, the Free Encyclopedia.
en.wikipedia.org/wiki/Plame_affair (accessed
March 2, 2015).

"Rational Basis Test." Cornell University Law School
Search Cornell LII. www.law.cornell.edu/wex/
rational_basis_test (accessed March 2, 2015).

"Stand in the Schoolhouse Door." Wikipedia, the
Free Encyclopedia. http://en.wikipedia.org/wiki/
Stand_in_the_Schoolhouse_Door (accessed
March 5, 2015).

"The Emancipation Proclamation." Featured
Documents. National Archives & Records
Administration. January 1, 1863. http://www
.archives.gov/exhibits/featured_documents/
emancipation_proclamation/transcript.html
(accessed March 2, 2015).

"The Great White Fleet." Oregon Maritime
Museum. http://www.oregonmaritimemuseum
.org/veWebsite/vex4/images/A27E1251-B949-
4175-9C2F-853205274350.jpg (accessed
March 2, 2015).

"Theodore Roosevelt." Sheppard Software. http://
www.sheppardsoftware.com/History/

presidents/Presidents_26_Roosevelt.htm (accessed March 2, 2015).

"United States House of Representatives Elections, 2012." Wikipedia, the Free Encyclopedia. http://en.wikipedia.org/wiki/United_States_House_of_Representatives_elections,_2012 (accessed March 2, 2015).

"Vice President of the United States (President of the Senate)." United States Senate. https://www.senate.gov/artandhistory/history/common/briefing/Vice_President.htm (accessed March 2, 2015).

"Watergate: A Chronology." FindLaw. http://news.findlaw.com/hdocs/docs/watergate/watergate_chron.html (accessed March 5, 2015).

"Which Vice Presidents Ran for President and Lost?" Answers.com. http://wiki.answers.com/Q/Which_vice_presidents_ran_for_president_and_lost (accessed June 11, 2014)

"Which Vice Presidents Ran for President and Lost?" Answers.com. http://wiki.answers.com/Q/Which_vice_presidents_ran_for_president_and_lost (accessed June 11, 2014).

"Who Gets Social Security?" National Academy of Social Security. http://www.nasi.org/learn/socialsecurity/who-gets (accessed March 2, 2015).

Woodward, Bob. "How Mark Felt Became 'Deep Throat'." *Washington Post*. June 20, 2005. http://www.washingtonpost.com/politics/how-mark-felt-became-deep-throat/2012/06/04/gJQAlpARIV_story.html (accessed March 5, 2015).

Appendix

The Constitution "The Constitution." The U.S. National Archives & Records Administration. http://www.archives.gov/exhibits/charters/constitution_transcript.html (accessed March 4, 2015).

The Declaration of Independence "The Declaration of Independence." The U.S. National Archives & Records Administration. http://www.archives.gov/exhibits/charters/declaration_transcript.html (accessed March 4, 2015).

Map of the United States "US Map Series 1." Cardhouse.com. October 17, 2005. Public Domain. http://cardhouse.com/design/free/usa.htm (accessed March 4, 2015).
1) "General Reference." Nationalatlas.gov. http://nationalmap.gov/small_scale/printable/images/pdf/reference/genref.pdf (accessed March 4, 2015).

Photos

A 19th Century Painting Entitled "Gentlemen of the Jury," by John Morgan Morgan, John.

"Gentlemen of the Jury." Wikipedia, the Free Encyclopedia. 1861. Public Domain. http://en.wikipedia.org/wiki/File:The_Jury_by_John_Morgan.jpg (accessed March 3, 2015).

"Al Gore, Former Vice President of the United States." Wikipedia, the Free Encyclopedia. Public Domain. http://commons.wikimedia.org/wiki/File:Al_Gore,_Vice_President_of_the_United_States,_official_portrait_1994.jpg (accessed March 10, 2015).

Amish Family "Free Photo: Amish, People, Persons, Religion - Free Image on Pixabay - 51171" Pixabay. September 2009. http://pixabay.com/en/amish-people-persons-religion-51171/ (accessed June 2, 2015).

BONG HITS 4 JESUS Photo "Original banner now hanging in the Newseum in Washington, DC." Wikipedia, the Free Encyclopedia. http://en.wikipedia.org/w/index.php?title=File:Bong_Hits_for_Jesus.jpg (accessed March 3, 2015).

Brown v. Board of Education Newspaper Headlines Delinder, Jean Van. "Brown v. Board of Education of Topeka A Landmark Case Unresolved Fifty Years Later, Part 2." U.S. National Archives and Records Administration. Spring 2004. http://www.archives.gov/publications/prologue/2004/spring/brown-v-board-2.html (accessed March 3, 2015).

Bush v. Gore: United States Presidential Election, November 7, 2000 "United States Presidential Election, 2000." Wikipedia, the Free Encyclopedia. http://en.wikipedia.org/wiki/2000_Presidential_Election (accessed March 3, 2015).

CC-BY-SA-3.0/Matt H. Wade at Wikipedia. "West Face of the United States Supreme Court Building in Washington, D.C." May 2008. Wikipedia, the Free Encyclopedia. http://en.wikipedia.org/wiki/File:USSupremeCourtWestFacade.JPG (accessed March 9, 2015).

Chairman Mao Zedong and President Richard M. Nixon meet in China, February 29, 1972 "1972 Nixon visit to China." Wikipedia, the Free Encyclopedia. http://en.wikipedia.org/wiki/1972_Nixon_visit_to_China (accessed March 3, 2015).

Chief Justice John Marshall Inman, Henry. "John Marshall." Wikipedia, the Free Encyclopedia. 1832. Public Domain. http://commons.wikimedia.org/wiki/File:John_Marshall_by_Henry_Inman,_1832.jpg (accessed March 9, 2015).

Christoper Simmon's Mug Shot Wachtel, Maximillian. "The Death Penalty Is Cruel and Unusual Punishment for Juveniles: Roper v. Simmons (2005)." PsychLaw Journal. http://www.psychlawjournal.com/2013/04/the-death-penalty-is-cruel-and-unusual.html (accessed March 9, 2015).

Christy, Howard Chandler. "Scene at the Signing of the Constitution of the United States." Public Domain Clip Art Photos and Images. September 17, 2008. Public Domain. http://publicdomainclip-art.blogspot.com/2008/09/scene-at-signing-of-constitution-of.html (accessed March 2, 2015).

Clarence Earl Gideon "Gideon at 50: This Aug. 6, 1963, file photo shows Clarence Earl Gideon, 52, the mechanic who changed the course of legal history, after his release from a Panama City, Florida, jail. Gideon was wrongly charged in 1961 with burglary and sentenced to five years in prison." AP Images.

Clarence Earl Gideon's In Forma Pauperis Petition Gideon, Clarence Earl. "Petition for a Writ of Certiorari from Clarence Gideon to the Supreme Court of the United States, 01/05/1962." U.S. National Archives and Records Administration. January 5, 1962. , http://research.archives.gov/description/597554 (accessed March 9, 2015).

"Colored Waiting Room" at bus station during Jim Crow Era Delano, Jack. "At the Bus Station in Durham, North Caroline." Wikipedia, the Free Encyclopedia. May 1940. Public Domain. http://en.wikipedia.org/wiki/File:JimCrowInDurhamNC.jpg (accessed March 3, 2015).

Donald Rumsfeld "Portrait of Donald Rumsfeld, United States Secretary of Defense." Wikipedia, the Free Encyclopedia. Public Domain. http://en.wikipedia.org/wiki/File:Donald_Rumsfeld_Defenselink.jpg (accessed March 3, 2015).

Dr. Daniel Ellsberg "Circa 1975: American political activist Daniel Ellsberg speaks in front of microphones." Hulton Archive / Getty Images.

Draper, Eric. "George W. Bush Official Photo." Wikipedia, the Free Encyclopedia. January 20, 2001. Public Domain. http://commons.wikimedia.org/wiki/File:GeorgeWBush.jpg (accessed March 10, 2015).

Draper. Eric. "President Bush Welcomes President-Elect Obama, Former President Clinton, Former President Bush and Former President Carter to the White House." The White House: President George W. Bush. January 7, 2009. http://georgewbush-whitehouse.archives.gov/news/releases/2009/01/images/20090107-3_x0h6544-515h.html (accessed March 3, 2015).

Duplessis, Joseph-Siffrein. "Portrait of Benjamin Franklin." Wikipedia, the Free Encyclopedia. 1785. Public Domain. http://commons.wikimedia.org/wiki/File:BenFranklinDuplessis.jpg (accessed March 2, 2015).

Five Living Presidents Draper, Eric. "Five Presidents Oval Office." Wikipedia, the Free Encyclopedia. January 7, 2009. Public Domain. http://en.wikipedia.org/wiki/File:Five_Presidents_Oval_Office.jpg (accessed March 3, 2015).

General George Washington Peale, Rembrandt. "George Washington." Wikipedia, the Free Encyclopedia. 1850. Public Domain. http://en.wikipedia.org/wiki/File:Portrait_of_George_Washington.jpeg (accessed March 4, 2015).

Governor George Wallace and General Henry Graham "Wallace Integration: Alabama Gov. George C. Wallace stands in the "school house door" confronting National Guard Brig. Gen. Henry Graham at the University of Alabama in Tuscaloosa June 11, 1963 in a symbolic effort to block integration of the institution." AP Photo.

Governor George Wallace, Guarded by Members of the National Guard Leffler, Warren K. "Wallace at University of Alabama." Wikipedia, the Free Encyclopedia. June 11, 1963. Public Domain. http://commons.wikimedia.org/wiki/File:Wallace_at_University_of_Alabama_edit2.jpg (accessed March 3, 2015).

Hammond, Ken. "The Pentagon US Department of Defense Building." Wikipedia, the Free Encyclopedia. April 1998. Public Domain. http://en.wikipedia.org/wiki/File:The_Pentagon_US_Department_of_Defense_building.jpg (accessed March 9, 2015).

Holman, Francis. "Battle of Cape St Vincent." Wikipedia, the Free Encyclopedia. January 16, 1780. Public Domain. http://commons.wikimedia.org/wiki/File:Holman,_Cape_St_Vincent.jpg (accessed March 4, 2015).

"Homer Plessy." Glogster.com. Public Domain.http://www.glogster.com/media/2/3/73/28/3732885.jpg (accessed March 3, 2015).

Illustration of British Soldiers at the Battle of Bunker Hill, by Howard Pyle "A Collage of American Revolutionary War Public Domain Images." Wikipedia, the Free Encyclopedia. Public Domain. http://en.wikipedia.org/wiki/File:Rev_collage.png (accessed March 4, 2015).

Lee, Russell, "Negro drinking at "Colored" water cooler in streetcar terminal, Oklahoma City, Oklahoma." Wikipedia, the Free Encyclopedia. July 1939. Public Domain. ttp://commons.wikimedia.org/wiki/File:%22Colored%22_drinking_fountain_from_mid-20th_century_with_african-american_drinking.jpg (accessed March 3, 2015).

Map of Arizona's 9 Congressional Districts. United States Department of the Interior. Wikipedia, the Free Encyclopedia. Public Domain. http://commons.wikimedia.org/wiki/File:Arizona_US_Congressional_District_9_%28since_2013%29.tif (accessed March 3, 2015).

Map of Every State's Total Number of Representatives as of 2014. United States Census 2010. "United States Congressional Apportionment 2012-2022." Wikipedia, the Free Encyclopedia. Public Domain. http://commons.wikimedia.org/wiki/File:2010_census_reapportionment.jpg (accessed March 3, 2015).

Map of Illinois' 18 Congressional Districts United States Department of the Interior. Map of Illinois' 18 Congressional Districts. Wikipedia, the Free Encyclopedia. Public Domain. http://commons.wikimedia.org/wiki/File:Illinois_Congressional_Districts,_113th_Congress.tif (accessed March 3, 2015).

Map of the Thirteen Federal Circuit Courts of Appeal "Geographic Boundaries of the United States Courts of Appeals and United States District Courts." USCourts.gov. http://www.uscourts.gov/uscourts/images/CircuitMap.pdf (accessed March 3, 2015).

Map of Wyoming's 1 Congressional District "List of United States Congressional Districts." Wikipedia, the Free Encyclopedia. http://en.wikipedia.org/wiki/List_of_United_States_congressional_districts (accessed March 3, 2015).

Mark Felt "Mark Felt a.k.a. alleged 'Deep Throat'." Wikipedia, the Free Encyclopedia. Public Domain. http://commons.wikimedia.org/wiki/File:MarkFelt.jpg (accessed March 3, 2015).

McSmith, Andy. "The Chilcot Inquiry: September 11 and the Road to the Iraq War." *The Independent.* January 23, 2015. http://www.independent.co.uk/news/world/middle-east/the-chilcot-inquiry-september-11-and-the-road-to-the-iraq-war-9999788.html (accessed March 3, 2015).

Nixon Resignation Letter Nixon, Richard M. "Richard M. Nixon's Resignation Letter, 08/09/1974." U.S. National Archives and Records Administration. August 9, 1974. Public Domain. http://research.archives.gov/description/302035 (accessed March 3, 2015).

Nixon, Richard M. Wikipedia, the Free Encyclopedia. August 9, 1974. Public Domain. http://en.wikipedia.org/wiki/File:Letter_of_Resignation_of_Richard_M._Nixon,_1974.jpg (accessed March 3, 2015).

Petteway, Steve. Collection of the Supreme Court of the United States --"Roberts Court (2010-)." Oyez Project. http://www.oyez.org/courts/robt6 (accessed March 2, 2015).

Petteway, Steve. Supreme Court US 2010. Wikipedia, the Free Encyclopedia. October 8, 2010. Public Domain. http://en.wikipedia.org/wiki/File:Supreme_Court_US_2010.jpg (accessed March 3, 2015).

Photo of Destroyed World Trade Center "9/11 Anniversary in Pictures: The Attack on the World Trade Center in New York." *The Telegraph.* http://www.telegraph.co.uk/news/picturegalleries/worldnews/8739384/911-anniversary-in-pictures-the-attack-on-the-World-Trade-Center-in-New-York.html?image =35 (accessed March 3, 2015).

"Photograph of the Capital Building." Wikipedia, the Free Encyclopedia. April 3, 2007. Public Domain. http://en.wikipedia.org/wiki/File:Capitol_Building_Full_View.jpg (accessed March 2, 2015).

"Photograph of Watergate Complex." Wikipedia, the Free EncyclopediaPublic Domain. http://commons.wikimedia.org/wiki/File:Watergate FromAir.JPG (accessed March 2, 2015).

"Photograph of Watergate Complex." Wikipedia, the Free Encyclopedia. Public Domain. http://commons.wikimedia.org/wiki/File:Watergate FromAir.JPG (accessed March 2, 2015).

President Barack Obama Signs the American Recovery and Reinvestment Act of 2009 Souza, Pete. "United States President Barack Obama Signs into Law the American Recovery and Reinvestment Act of 2009 as Vice President Joe Biden Looks On." Wikipedia, the Free Encyclopedia. February 18, 2009. Public Domain. http://commons.wikimedia.org/wiki/File: Barack_Obama_signs_American_Recovery_and_Reinvestment_Act_of_2009_on_February_17.jpg (accessed March 3, 2015).

"President Nixon meets with China's Communist Party Leader, Mao Tse- Tung, 02/29/1972." U.S. National Archives and Records Administration. February 29, 1972. http://research.archives.gov/description/194759 (accessed March 3, 2015).

President Obama Taking the Oath of Office Ricardo, Cecilio. "US President Barack Obama taking his Oath of Office – 2009 Jan 20." Wikipedia, the Free Encyclopedia. January 20, 2009. Public Domain. http://commons.wikimedia.org/wiki/File:US_President_Barack_Obama_taking_his_Oath_of_Office_-_2009Jan20.jpg (accessed March 3, 2015).

Pyle, Howard. "Battle of Bunker Hill." Wikipedia, the Free Encyclopedia. 1897. Public Domain. http://commons.wikimedia.org/wiki/File:Bunker_Hill_by_Pyle.jpg (accessed March 4, 2015).

Ranney, William Tylee. "Battle of Cowpens." Wikipedia, the Free Encyclopedia. 1845. Public Domain. http://commons.wikimedia.org/wiki/File:Cowpens.jpg (accessed March 4, 2015).

Separate Drinking Fountains for White and Black people during Jim Crow Era Lee, Russell, "Negro drinking at "Colored" water cooler in streetcar terminal, Oklahoma City, Oklahoma." Library of Congress. July 1939. http://www.loc.gov/pictures/item/fsa1997026728/PP/ (accessed March 3, 2015).

Soldiers escorting black students into an all-white high school in Little Rock, Arkansas US Army. "101st Airborne at Little Rock Central High." Wikipedia, the Free Encyclopedia. Public Domain. http://en.wikipedia.org/wiki/File:101st_Airborne_at_Little_Rock_Central_High.jpg (accessed March 3, 2015).

Student entering the University of Alabama Leffler, Warren K. "Vivian Malone Entering Foster Auditorium to Register for Classes at the University of Alabama." Library of Congress. June 11, 1963. Public Domain. http://www.loc.gov/pictures/item/2004666305/ (accessed March 9, 2015).

The 13 American Colonies "Eastern North America in 1775." Wikipedia, the Free Encyclopedia. Public Domain. http://en.wikipedia.org/wiki/File:Map_of_territorial_growth_1775.svg (accessed March 4, 2015).

The Pentagon Hammond, Ken. "The Pentagon, Headquarters of the Department of Defense." U.S. Department of Defense. Public Domain. http://www.defense.gov/photos/newsphoto.aspx?newsphotoid = 1309 (accessed March 9, 2015).

The White House Yoshida, Teddy. "South View of the White House." Public Domain Clip Art. June 30, 2004. Public Domain. http://publicdomainclip-art.blogspot.com/2007/09/white-house.html (accessed March 3, 2015).

Trumbull, John. "Oil on Canvas Portrait of Alexander Hamilton." Wikipedia, the Free Encyclopedia. 1806. Public Domain. http://commons.wikimedia.org/wiki/File:Alexander_Hamilton_portrait_by_John_Trumbull_1806.jpg (accessed March 9, 2015).

Trumbull, John. "The Death of General Montgomery in the Attack on Quebec, December 31, 1775." Wikipedia, the Free Encyclopedia. 1786. Public Domain. http://commons.wikimedia.org/wiki/File:Death_of_Montgomery.jpg (accessed March 4, 2015).

United States Department of the Interior. Arizona Congressional Districts, 113th Congress. National Atlas of the United States. Public Domain. http://nationalmap.gov/small_scale/printable/images/pdf/congdist/pagecgd113_az.pdf (accessed March 3, 2015).

United States Department of the Interior. Illinois Congressional Districts, 113th Congress. National Atlas of the United States. Public Domain. http://nationalmap.gov/small_scale/printable/images/pdf/congdist/pagecgd113_il.pdf.view terms (accessed March 3, 2015).

United States Department of the Interior. Wyoming Congressional Districts, 113th Congress. National Atlas of the United States. Public Domain. http://nationalmap.gov/small_scale/printable/images/pdf/congdist/pagecgd113_wy.pdf (accessed March 3, 2015).

Vanderlyn, John. "James Madison." White House Historical Association. 1816. Public Domain. http://www.whitehouseresearch.org/assetbank-whha/action/viewAsset?id = 156&index = 0& total = 2&view = viewSearchItem (accessed March 9, 2015).

"Vivian Malone Entering Foster Auditorium to Register for Classes at the University of Alabama." Wikipedia, the Free Encyclopedia. June 11, 1963. Public Domain. http://en.wikipedia.org/wiki/File:Vivian_Malone_registering.jpg (accessed March 9, 2015).

Watergate complex "Watergate Complex." Wikipedia, the Free Encyclopedia. en.wikipedia.org/wiki/Watergate_complex (accessed March 3, 2015).

World Trade Center Photo Radford, Benjamin. "Did Nostradamus Really Predict the 9/11 Terrorist Attacks?" *Live Science*. September 11, 2011. http://www.livescience.com/16001-nostradamus-predict-9-11-world-trade-center.html (accessed March 9, 2015).

Yasser Esam Hamdi Eklund, Shawn P. "Yaser Esam Hamdi Kneels Down Thursday During One of Five Prayer Services Performed by Detainees in Camp X-ray, Guantanamo Bay Detention Camp, Guantánamo Bay, Cuba." Wikipedia, the Free Encyclopedia. April 4, 2002. Public Domain. http://commons.wikimedia.org/wiki/File:Yaser_Esam_Hamdi_in_Camp_X-ray,_Guant%C3%A1namo_Bay,_Cuba_-_20020404.jpg (accessed March 9, 2015).

Table of Cases

Index